SO LATE.

SO SOON *a memoir*

D'ARCY FALLON

HAWTHORNE BOOKS & LITERARY ARTS | Portland, Oregon

Hawthorne Books
& Literary Arts

P.O. Box 579
Portland, Oregon 97207
hawthornebooks.com

Editorial:
Michelle Piranio,
Portland, Oregon

Form:
Pinch, Portland, Oregon

Printed in China
through Print Vision, Inc.

Set in DTL Albertina.

9
8
7
6
5
4
3
2
1

Library of Congress
Cataloging-in-
Publication Data

Fallon, D'Arcy.
So late, so soon: a memoir
/ by D'Arcy Fallon.
p. cm.
ISBN 0-9716915-3-3
I. Fallon, D'Arcy.
2. Lighthouse Ranch –
Biography.
3. Christian biography –
United States.
I. Title.

BR1725.F28 A3 2003
248.8'33 – dc21

2002152854

I AM INDEBTED TO MANY PEOPLE FOR HELPING MIDWIFE THIS memoir, which has been a long time abornin'. Thanks to my writer friends for reading various drafts with devotion and keen insight: Joanna Bean, Virginia Carlson, Barbara Cotter, Mary Ellen Davis, Katie Flemate, Ruth Karch, Sara Kirschenbaum, Brenda Paik Sunoo, Cate Terwilliger, and the Present Tense Writer's Group at the University of Colorado – Colorado Springs. Blessings on my old Bay High friend Cynthia Franz, who magically reappeared in my life with the gift of long-lost poetry. Thanks also to my siblings, Mary, Brian, Chris, and Michael Fallon, who read early drafts of the book and told me to go for it, family warts and all. I needed encouragement to write the unvarnished truth and you gave it to me with both hands. I could not have finished this book without the guidance and wisdom of my editor, Kate Hengerer, of Hawthorne Books & Literary Arts. To my husband, Rudy Bahr, and my son, Joel, thank you for believing in the importance of this story, and graciously giving me the space to tell it.

For my parents, Joel Fallon and Carolyn Raine Fallon, who gave me laughter, books, and solitude.

A Note to the Reader

THIS IS A WORK OF NONFICTION. ALL OF THE PEOPLE IN THIS memoir who were (or still are) involved in Gospel Outreach are real, though I have changed their names for reasons of privacy (with the exception of Jim and Dacie Durkin, who were public figures, and Forrest Prince, who asked to be named). I did not seek anyone's permission in the writing of this memoir; if I had, it would have been a drastically different book.

"If we refuse to do the work of creating this personal version of the past, someone else will do it for us. That is the scary political fact," Patricia Hampl writes in her book *I Could Tell You Stories: Sojourns in the Land of Memory.* I wrote so I wouldn't forget this formative period in my life as an impressionable teenager living in a remote spiritual commune. I wrote to bear witness to the truth of my experience. I wrote to explain the seductiveness of getting swept up in religious fervor. I wrote to describe how easy it was to give away personal power and how hard it was ultimately to reclaim it.

I needed a lot of distance to write *So Late, So Soon.* It percolated inside me for nearly three decades before I could love the person I had once been and begin to see my brethren with appreciation, humor, and compassion. By the time I started writing, I wasn't angry but oddly… curious about us all, as if my life at the Lighthouse Ranch had happened to someone else. I had become a character in a narrative, someone trying to come to grips with contradictory messages about femininity, creativity, and spirituality.

"Memory is always more true to the present mind than to the past, always more true to itself than to anything else," Robert Olmstead writes in *Stay Here with Me: A Memoir.* Olmstead is right; although the story I'm writing about happened in the distant past, it is only now, after prolonged reflection on and immersion in the narrative, that I have finally begun to perceive its meaning.

D'ARCY FALLON
February 2003
Colorado Springs, Colorado

SO LATE, SO SOON

Some beings go from dark to dark;
Some beings go from dark to light;
Some beings go from light to dark;
May you go from light to light.

NAGARJUNA, *Buddhist philosopher and mystic*

Prologue: Flax at Dawn

MY MOTHER USED TO HAVE A POSTER HANGING IN HER KITCHEN of a wild-haired woman gripping a broom. Underneath her was the caption: "Fuck Housework." It summed up my mother's and a lot of other women's attitudes in the early '70s. Rebellion was in the air, fueled by the feminist movement, and a Zeitgeist that urged self-expression and fulfillment at any cost, whether that meant living in a lesbian vegetarian commune in Vermont or throwing pots in the backyard. But my mother was hardly a barefoot Isadora Duncan experimenting with new forms of dance. And for whom would she dance? My dad? Us five kids? She worked a series of thankless office jobs, did endless loads of ripe teenage laundry, took our Irish setter, Timothy Leary, to the vet. She got dinner on the table every night. My mother was tired, and, I suspect, a little depressed. So she put up a poster, drew the line at ironing, and jokingly called herself the Queen of Perma Press. If we needed clean clothes, we checked the dryer first.

Around the time my mother put up her "Fuck Housework" poster, Marabel Morgan's book *The Total Woman* became a best seller. Morgan, an antifeminist Christian, urged women to graciously submit to their husbands—or there could be serious consequences. She cited research into early morning airplane crashes by test pilots, which found that when pilots left home upset and tense, their judgment was severely impaired. Morgan also advised women to spice up their marriages by greeting their husband at the front door wearing only Saran Wrap or by seducing him under the dining room table with sex positions from the *Kama Sutra*. When Morgan's book found its way into the library of the Lighthouse Ranch, an isolated fundamentalist Christian commune where I lived with 130 other committed souls, I read with furtive interest.

The chances of me greeting my new husband at the front steps of the commune like a package of Oscar Mayer wieners would be nothing short of miraculous. A good sex life requires time and privacy, and we had neither. The problem, as I saw it, was that we were supposed to be in love with Him, while the two of us struggled for intimacy in our little shoebox of a room. It felt a little like a three-way. Jesus was supposed to be in charge of the marriage, my husband was supposed to be in charge of me, and, well,

I was supposed to let him. The blueprint for marital authority had been clearly spelled out in the Bible: God, husband, wife. Because of the critical, independent part of myself that I had inherited from my mother, this was a hard sell. All around me, women were storming the barricades of manly careers and muscling out the men to work on oil rigs, race sled dogs, run big-time ad agencies. Meanwhile, back at the ranch, I folded the brothers' clothes, swabbed out the communal bathroom, and baked carrot bread. I tried to Keep My Eyes On Jesus, ignoring Satan's whisperings that these jobs were oppressive and sexist. All the while, the ghost of my mother fluttered outside our mildewed bedroom window, rapping smartly on the glass, reminding me that housework was vastly overrated.

She wasn't happy that I was living at the Lighthouse Ranch, a former Coast Guard station perched on a windblown bluff in Northern California. The ranch was located in Loleta, a little dairy town miles from anywhere. There was plenty of housework to do at the ranch, only very little of it pertained to me in a personal sense. Our "house" was a single room, ten quick paces back and forth past a rickety double bed, a chest of drawers, a redwood burl table that had washed up on the beach, and two metal folding chairs. The front door to our room was right across the hall from the communal bathroom and kitchen. In the morning, we were serenaded by squeaking faucets, mumbled hallelujahs, and shower oratorios. The ranch's namesake, a lighthouse, towered over an ambitious garden of red-veined Swiss chard, stringy rhubarb, mottled pumpkins, and revved-up zucchini. A plot of land at the edge of the world, a garden where seeds took root and flourished in a coma of fog and rain – this was where I was supposed to thrive and find fulfillment as a young Christian and brand-new bride.

All of us women at the ranch had memorized Proverbs 31:10–31. These verses praise the wife of noble character, the Virtuous Woman, a woman whose price is "far above rubies." She's generous, outspoken, and a spiritual spitfire. She sews. Sometimes – probably suffering from menopausal insomnia – she's up at the crack of dawn. Maybe her hormones are in overdrive, but she's never weepy. She does long division in her head and doesn't take any guff from her kids, who call her "blessed," at least to her face. Most of all, her husband loves her. I rated myself against Mrs. Proverbs 31, as if I were taking a how-good-is-your-marriage quiz in *Woman's Day*. I wanted to reap my husband's admiration. I wanted his name to be "praised in the gates." But at the same time, I yearned for some honeymoon romancing too, a little Marabel Morgan nooky and spice. I wasn't ready yet to move from radiant newlywed to Old Testament wife, fingering the flax at dawn. If Marabel could get it on under the dining room table to save her marriage, Praise His Holy Name, why shouldn't I?

Caught between these images – my independent mother, the submissive yet sexually adventurous wife, and the granite-armed Überfrau – I tried to please God, my husband, my peers. It never occurred to me that I could be anything I wanted, and didn't require "fixing." When I came to the ranch in 1972, at the age of eighteen, I didn't know that this particular landscape would haunt me, move me, engage my imagination for years to come. I had no way of knowing that the weather-beaten buildings – which are now mostly empty and reclaimed by the wind and sea air – would become the psychic backdrop for my life, measured against all places past and present.

I.

But We Know

I NEVER SCREAMED IN DELIVERANCE TEMPLE THE TWO YEARS
I spent worshiping there, but toward the end, every time I settled back in
my seat to listen to Papa Jim preach, I feared I would. There always seemed
to be a dangerous undercurrent in that church, as if the modest building
on California Street straddled buried power cables. This unseen electrical
presence was most intense when we prayed in tongues. Then there was a
charge in the air, a burr, a buzz. Words, the ecstasy of words. A tapestry of
vowels and consonants, murmurs and glottal stops, punctuated by sighs.
There was nothing wrong with shouting, if it was Holy Ghost–inspired. I
formed my words in secret, mindful that they weren't prompted by God.
I wanted to yell out that I'd spent my free time reading ungodly books at
the Eureka Public Library, that I'd spent whole days dreaming in the stacks,
thumbing through back issues of *National Geographic* and *Ladies' Home
Journal*, gorging on photos of China and cheesecake. As Papa Jim urged
us to make a joyful noise unto the Lord, I wanted to yell: "Henry Miller!
Rod McKuen! *Cosmo* magazine! Betty Crocker!"

I wanted to tell the saints–those upright men and women I lived with–
that I wanted to go to Egypt, wade into the Nile with kohl-rimmed eyes,
drift on the current like baby Moses in my own homemade basket of sturdy
reeds. I wanted to tell them that anywhere was better than here. I needed
to confess that I wasn't the Virtuous Woman Papa Jim always invoked at
weddings.

The chasm between who I really was and the face I presented to the
brethren seemed too wide to bridge. Honesty was out of the question. I
wanted to confess every shameful thing about myself (and where would
I start?), the most shameful of which was that I had no faith, that I was a
fraud. In the Book of James, Jesus says it's not enough to have faith, we
must do good works too. I had the whole works–I did things, labored,
helped out–but I lacked real faith. Not truly repentant, not really saved, I
was a Christian changeling, a dilettante toying with damnation. My newly
minted marriage was a sham, filled with deceit and violence. I was supposed to be an older sister, a leader, but sometimes my husband and I fought
in our room, which was barely a shoebox with a cardboard lid. When we

came to blows I expected one of my fists to come flying through the wall like Wonder Woman's. *Pow!*

Now Papa Jim mopped his face with a yellowed handkerchief. More than a hundred of us sat in plain unvarnished pews, facing the stocky preacher. Legs planted squarely on the ground, he stood before us with a microphone in hand, sweat running down his fleshy cheeks. He told stories about himself – about the times he resisted the Lord, felt low, even left his wife and the church he was in. There was a time of aimless drifting, "like a vagabond," with no place to call home. I didn't know what being a vagabond entailed, but in my mind, being separated from his wife played out in a surreal and cinematic way, with him falling for some redheaded cashier from Ukiah in tight black Capri pants and a filmy midriff blouse. As he testified, I imagined Jim holed up in a rotting cabin with mushy floorboards in the redwoods near Garberville, lonely and broken-hearted. I imagined Jesus and Jim having a long heart-to-heart. And oh, Satan hates that. Satan must've pulled out all the stops, using every trick up his sleeve to keep this Man of God's heart from softening. Satan loves the hardened heart.

Jim talked about the danger of applying one's own limited human understanding to God's word. Although we have a very human tendency to rationalize and equivocate, to think we already know and understand what God is telling us, it's important to take God's word at face value.

"One day I was praying out there," he continued. "I asked God, 'Why do you say in your book we shall have life, and live more abundantly? What is this thing about joy unspeakable and full of glory? I don't have it, and I don't know anyone who does.'" My heart went out to him because I knew how much he loved Jesus. And I could relate to the feeling that salvation wasn't all it was cracked up to be. He continued, "It was a time of contending with the Lord, although I never yelled at God or challenged Him with things like, 'Where is it?' or 'I know you exist, Jesus, but you're not real to me.' It was, rather, a sincere searching of my soul."

"And then God spoke to me. 'Behind everything in my word,' He said, 'you've added three of your own. That is, "But we know." Henceforth, I want you to do my word. Even if you don't understand it, do it. And in the doing of it, you'll come to know what it means.'"

I glanced over at Jim's wife, Dacie, the plump, shy woman who was his ordained helpmeet. She looked at Jim with her bottomless eyes, eyes that saw everything. Dacie, who had the gift of prophecy, didn't blink.

Jim's sermon about the word of God was the foundation of his ministry: Don't equivocate, don't rationalize, don't intellectualize, just believe it, confess it, and do it.

"Jesus," he whispered into the microphone, spearing our eyes with his own and jingling the change in his pocket like a carnival barker on the midway. "Jesus … set … me … free. Hallelujah! Can you say Hallelujah with me?"

We could.

We did.

A five-o'clock shadow shaded Papa Jim's fleshy cheeks as Brother Leo, in his Can't Bust 'Em overalls, started to play the piano in the corner, knuckling the keys just a little in a bluesy riff. Papa Jim, the small-town realtor who believed he was called to be God's apostle, began pumping his arms as he marched in place. The big man closed his eyes and shivered. I half-expected him to levitate.

"Well, bless the Lord, oh, my soul!" he shouted suddenly, his palms stretched wide open so the dove, the Holy Spirit, could alight on a finger. It was a sign. Everybody stood up, sisters and brothers, eyes closed, arms raised, breathing in and out in oceanic oneness. We were marching, marching, marching to Zion.

Two years earlier, in the Bay Area suburb where I'd gone to high school, I'd smoked fat joints rolled in yellow Zig-Zag papers and tippled wine. Buzzed, I'd whirl around my bedroom in my underwear, snapping my fingers and scatting along to Van Morrison's fantabulous "Moondance." Now, in my embroidered corduroy jumper, long underwear, and scuffed oversized hiking boots, I clapped my hands and weaved from side to side like Herman Munster looped on a bottle of Blue Nun. At church, far from cynical classmates, I danced and sang, "Jesus Loves the Little Children." Washed in the blood of the Lamb, saved and sanctified by grace, that's who I was, as serious and sober as any foot-washing Baptist. If my old high school friends could have seen me – eyes squeezed tight in prayer, braids wrapped around my head in a crown like a hippie Heidi – they'd have howled in disbelief.

Dacie, sitting in a pew adjacent to me, dabbed her eyes. A sob escaped her throat. She shuddered. As I stared at her, I heard the tinkling bells from the ice cream truck idling on the street, chiming "It's a Small World, After All" and it was, it was. Mute we sat, reeking of wood smoke and chamomile, motor oil and newsprint. Entranced, floating, I felt the room tilt. A saffron light greased the windows of Deliverance Temple. And Dacie, in her simple cotton dress, cocked her head like a schoolgirl listening to playground gossip. Her thinning gray hair was pinned up in a raggedy bun that accentuated the puffiness of her pale face. Still clutching her purse, she began nodding. *Uh-huh. Uh-huh. You don't say.* Nodding. *I hear you, Jesus.*

And then she began muttering in tongues: "*Sha-na. Sha-na-na-na. Condola. Gondola. Shondola agondola.*" I repeated the words to myself, spinning out new phrases: *Shonda. Gonda.* Was I really speaking in tongues? Go with it. Let it flow. *Shonda. Gonda. I've got a Honda!* Stop it!

Dacie's eyelids fluttered. What did she see behind those trembling shutters of skin? Her head shook up and down, conferring. *Yes, Lord. Yes, Lord.* Dacie, the dutiful daughter of Zion, smiled. I could feel it coming; it was close; at any moment she was going to give us the Word of the Lord.

Sweat ran down my neck, pooled in the runnels of my ears, in my bra, between my legs, in the pale bud of my navel.

Dacie's voice quavered. "You who have hardened your heart must repent or I will cast you out, yea, I will turn from you as you have turned from me, you know who you are, you must –"

Take a breath.

"–step forward and repent of your secret sins. You are bound up in lies. Everyone thinks you are good but I see into your heart." Dacie paused.

God's word was true, and yet I felt like a fraud. I had been saved, yet I felt lost. Her husband's words rang in my ears: *But we know.* Instead of relying on what I thought I knew and what I felt, I should claim His promises. These opposite ideas bickered within me.

Dacie tucked a strand of hair behind her ear and stood waiting. A moment later she sat down meekly. I watched and fought the urge to scream. What if I shouted during an altar call, when we all held our breath and prayed for the lost ones? What if I shouted during the laying on of hands, when we prayed for the sick ones? I imagined the tight-lipped married men, so thin and anxious, so spiritual they never made love to their wives anymore, I saw them reaching for me, shaking me the way a dog shakes a sock. Scowling with concentration, punching the word "Jesus," I imagined them spraying spit, commanding: "Come out of her! I command you in the *name of Jesus!*"

I imagined their hands – men's hands – on my head, a babble of voices, fingers squeezing the wings of my shoulder blades. And the women – my sisters – staring at me with pity, murmuring, "Thank you, Jesus," as they balanced their bright-eyed babies on cocked hips before turning away. *But we know.*

I knew I wanted to be separate from "them," but they were also part of me, closer than kin, spiritual siblings in the Lord. I opened my mouth to sing along with the saints, and felt the warm rush of air in that humid room. Around me, people's mouths were moving, but I couldn't hear them. It was as if we were in a vacuum. I could see Dacie's lips opening and closing, felt Leo pounding those keys. The sun hid behind a cloud. Birds chattered on telephone wires as the ice cream truck's bells chimed and tinkled. Trees shuddered. The wind rose and I fluttered with it, a Chagall bride, no longer earthbound but floating high above the pews. *Shonda. Gonda. Help me, Rhonda!* Drifting, I skirted above the drab tract houses and lighted Victorian mansions of Eureka, above Pete's Suprette and the Northwood Chevrolet car lot, above the cold stone jetty and the tidal wetlands and the beach of spun gray sugar. Accelerating higher and higher, above the vibrating landscape, I looked down and saw all of us muddled together, swaying, praying. And I saw my own frightened self, sweating, frowning, shuffling in place, trying so hard to be careful, to be good, to be blameless. There was something else, too, mixed in with the desire and the dread. I was caught up in the grip of raw longing; it was as real as the thick wedding ring that squeezed my left finger, the scratchy stubble on my legs, the yeasty bread dough beneath my nails. But what was I longing for? Three little words. *But we know*. But we know what? Help me, Lord. Find, know, love.

The Table of the Lord

JESUS SAID, "THE KINGDOM OF GOD IS WITHIN YOU." IN THE kingdom where I lived, demons danced in the air and angels flew unseen beside me. The simplest decision was fraught with peril. Should you take a vacation to Disneyland? Fast and pray. Is that cough Satan's way of keeping you home from church? Rebuke it in the name of Jesus! The van won't start? Sister, that's no dead battery, but the Lord saying your soul needs jumper cables. The idea was to be in the spirit at all times, mindful of God even in the little things.

"Every job should be done as unto the Lord," instructed Amber Joy, handing me a sponge and a toilet brush. In any family, there were chores to do, and when I first arrived at the ranch as a free-spirited hitchhiker, my chores included swabbing out the communal bathroom next to the dining hall. Amber Joy was one of the single sisters who'd been at the ranch the longest. The night I was saved, Amber Joy had cried. She'd hugged me.

"Thank you, Jesus!" she'd kept saying. "Praise you, Lord!" That night she had felt like a soul sister, but our apparent closeness soon evaporated. Amber Joy, I was to learn, did not share her heart, at least not with a little sister in the Lord. Eternal salvation was one thing, sisterly bonds quite another. Amber wasn't mean, she just had her own friends.

"Remember that Jesus is watching you," Amber Joy said. "Think of yourself as His handmaiden."

"OK, fine," I told her, "but do you think we could get the brothers to put the toilet seat down when they're done? I mean, this is really gross."

"As unto the Lord," she said, sucking in her stomach as she caught sight of herself in the mirror. I swiped at the bowl. Holy apple butter! What would it take to remind these men that women used the bathroom too? Amber Joy tripped off in her hiking boots, singing, "I come to the garden alone."

A woman in Tijuana once claimed she'd seen Our Lord's beloved face in a flour tortilla, the wisps of his beard lacy as a scorched mantilla. "Hay-zeus, He is everywhere!" she told the crowd of believers gathered in front of her church. I scanned the bowl, looking for a sign. Pubic hairs and yellow crud. Nesting on the communal commode was not for the faint of heart. As I scrubbed, George Harrison's song "My Sweet Lord" reverberated in my head. "I really want to see you, Lord! I really want to feel you, Lord!"

When he started chanting "Hare Krishna, Krishna Hare," I rinsed out the bowl with bleach, put the lid down, and flushed.

WHEN I ARRIVED AT THE LIGHTHOUSE RANCH A FEW WEEKS earlier, I was just one of many people who wandered through the dusty parking lot, sauntered up the concrete steps to the dining hall and into the heart of this close-knit Christian community. For me, like so many new-comers, coming to the ranch was an accident, although some saints will disagree. They believe it was all part of God's magnificent play, and willing or not, we were His actors. Whether we chose to speak the Director's preordained lines or to step out of character, that was up to us, but Jesus cast us.

The summer after I graduated from high school with a GED, I spent weeks at a stretch hitchhiking up and down the California coast. I did what seemed normal and comfortable, what I'd been doing my whole life as a peripatetic Army brat: I wandered. Sometimes I hitchhiked with friends, but more often I was alone. One balmy day in June, I stood near the on-ramp to Highway 101, just south of the Oregon state line. It had been a time of desultory travel, camping in the redwoods, visiting hot springs; now I was slowly drifting back to my parents' home, although precisely why, I couldn't say. On the road, I'd met Josh, a lit major headed back to UC Berkeley. We passed the time waiting for rides by swapping travel stories: how to tell if the driver who stopped was safe or squirrelly, what to do if someone made a pass. Short and compact, Josh wore his frizzy brown hair in a page-boy, like Prince Valiant with a bad perm. The bottoms of his faded Levis were rolled up around his Earth shoes. Josh had an intense way of jabbing the air with a finger for emphasis when he got carried away talking about Beat poets. He wanted to be a writer, and when he grew restive waiting for a ride, he recited Lawrence Ferlinghetti poems as the cars zoomed by.

"'Don't let that horse eat that violin, cried Chagall's mother,'" Josh shouted, waving his arms. A Chevy Suburban filled with Boy Scouts chugged by, leaving behind a noxious tail of fumes. The boys pointed at us and made faces. One of them flipped us the bird.

"You'll never make Eagle Scout that way, dickhead," I yelled. When I coughed, Josh handed me his canteen. Should we have taken the bus? What was with these people anyway? Or were we the ones who looked dangerous? Josh began reciting another favorite Ferlinghetti poem, repeating a line that seemed to have personal resonance: *Fortune has its cookies to give out*. And then fortune did appear on the horizon, not as a flesh-colored cookie but as a dusty gray Datsun pickup. Fate was a wheezing vehicle that sounded like somebody's grandfather trying to cough up a wad of phlegm. *Hack-hack-hack-hack-hack!*

The back of the truck was filled with bales of hay, greasy tools, and bags of groceries; in the cab, a man sat hunched over the wheel. He was lean and earnest-looking, with a big Adam's apple and a sunburned face. His blue eyes burned in his head. Fine thinning hair lay across his forehead like spun gold. Grimy mechanic's fingers gripped the steering wheel.

"You want a ride?" he bawled from the window. I stared at him, trying to pick up any signs of weirdness on my internal radar. The frequency was jammed. I glanced at Josh. He shrugged. Guy seems OK. It was two against one.

"Would you like some dinner?" he called. "I'm going as far as Loleta."

"Lolita? Like the novel?" I said.

"No, like the town. It's near Eureka."

Josh nodded his head and clambered into the back of the truck; now I eased into the passenger seat.

"Isaac," the man said, proffering a callused paw. "Where you from?"

"San Francisco," I said.

"Ah, yes, the City," said Isaac. There was an edge of dismissal in his voice, as if recalling an old girlfriend who'd dumped him. Isaac drummed his cracked fingertips on the dashboard, then put the truck in gear and gunned it.

"I know 'Frisco well," he said. "It's been years since I've been any farther south than Ukiah." He cranked open the window and his words flew away with the cool rushing air. "No reason ... anymore ... to go down there."

The miles clicked by. Bait shops. An ice cream parlor. Dunkin' Donuts. In Trinidad, we paused at a stoplight. A woman in a yellow sundress stood over a hedge of white rhododendrons, wielding her pruning shears like a divining rod. At her feet, a Pekinese barked ferociously at the passing traffic. A house loomed behind her, lilac and cream, a confectioner's Gothic dream. The light turned green. Isaac put the truck in first and we lurched forward. *Hack-hack-hack-hack-hack!*

As we passed her, I thought, as I had thought so many times before when a house beckoned: I could live here. I could be that woman in the yellow sundress. Let me try on your life. It was so easy to imagine being someone else, to imprint on a stranger, to be anybody but who I was.

The towns spun by, a jumble of gas stations and convenience stores, sagging houses with snaggle-toothed picket fences. I leaned against the back of my seat and closed my eyes, lulled by the truck's engine. The air grew pungent, spiced with salt and fish and brackish water. In the grassy marshes next to the highway, long-legged herons walked slowly through the mud flats. Then Isaac veered off the highway and headed west. I opened my eyes in time to see an exit sign: Hookton Road.

The late summer sun struck the cracked windshield and flashed on the dusty road like a strobe light. Off in the distance, weeping willows glowed from within, lit like green sparklers. I caught my breath; the sky was porous, close, topsy-turvy.

I glanced at my watch. Six. My three younger brothers were probably home by now, horsing around in the living room, watching TV. Maybe Brian, sixteen, was getting high in the tree house out back, smoking a joint and fingering the keys of the battered saxophone he bought at Goodwill. My mother might be home too, tired and maybe a little pissed off. She worked in an insurance office and disliked her job. After work, I imagined her opening the fridge and taking out the package of ground beef that had defrosted, grating the cheese, rinsing off the lettuce. Closing my eyes, I heard the clank of knives and slotted spoons in the sink, the hiss of hot water, the squeak of the liquor cabinet above the boxes of Cheerios and Shredded Wheat. I saw her reaching for the bottle of Early Times bourbon, holding it up to the light, noting that it was watery, pale as jasmine tea. Someone had been drinking it and replacing the missing booze with water. And I imagined my mother, crisp with anger, folding her arms across her chest, staring out the window over the sink, wondering how her children had become so wild. She would see the apple trees in the backyard, note the rotting fruit on the ground. So much waste.

"Exactly where is it you said we're going?" I asked Isaac.

The Adam's apple bobbed. "Have you ever heard of the Lighthouse Ranch?"

"You live on a ranch? You're kidding, right?"

Isaac glanced at me. "Nope."

"Far out."

"Yes," he said, with hooded eyes. "Very far out." I felt a chill.

"So what do you do on this ranch?"

Isaac pressed his lips together. An enigmatic smile. "All things in the fullness of time," he said. What was that supposed to mean? Had Josh and I miscalculated? This spacey man in overalls, who'd seemed as goofy and harmless as the Scarecrow from The Wizard of Oz, was he really a serial killer? Slowly, I placed my right hand on the door handle; metal burned in my palm.

The road curled. We passed a few farmhouses set against the hills, framed by blackberry bushes, Queen Anne's lace, cottonwoods, and grazing cows. The muddy fields, waddling ducks, rusty weather vanes atop dilapidated barns all seemed straight out of a Grandma Moses painting.

Isaac turned and smiled. "Welcome to metropolitan Loleta, land of a thousand cows."

"This is Loleta?"

"Moo."

As we drove into the sun, the air grew cooler, the light more luminous.

Coming over the crest of a hill, I could see the beach, and beyond it, the ocean. At long last, near a stand of wind-sculpted cypresses, we turned onto a rubble road. A crudely lettered sign hammered to the fence rail read: "Everyone who loves has been born of God and knows God." Isaac started humming as we pulled into the parking lot, next to a dozen dented cars and rusting trucks. Next to the parking lot was a weather-beaten concrete building. This was a ranch? It looked more like a spare fort, a lonely outpost.

"We're here," Isaac announced, pulling hard on the hand brake. "Follow me into the kitchen and the sisters will show you where to stash your gear." In a flash, he was out of the truck. "The sisters?" I called after him.

The ranch's dining hall was cavernous and quiet. Long wooden tables with benches filled the room. It reminded me of an empty swimming pool at dusk: hollowed out, waiting, with the damp residue of the day still clinging to its sides. The beige walls conjured up memories of crowded hospital waiting rooms on Army posts, rooms filled with feverish kids too sick to cry. Narrow vertical windows stood sentry to the road. Above an old piano hung a crude painting of a man with shoulder-length hair. One eye was looking slightly inward, as if it had been painted by Picasso. Rays of light streamed from behind the man's head. Suddenly it dawned on me: Isaac's blissed-out evasive answers, the wooden sign about loving God, this painting. Holy shit! Jesus freaks! Josh looked at me and raised an eyebrow. I rolled my eyes. Oh, swell. Just our luck. But for now, at least, we were stuck at the edge of the world.

"Praise the Lord," Josh said with a snicker.

"Amen, brother," I replied.

We sat on the concrete steps outside the dining hall. Nearby was a small garden with a bench filled with herbs and flowers surrounded by a picket fence. A child's upended plastic bucket lay next to a clump of daisies. A handful of buildings were scattered across the land, including a small bungalow and a duplex. Window curtains, flower boxes, and spider plants in macramé hangers couldn't dispel the institutional aura that clung to these dowdy structures. The corrosive salt air had done its damage to all of them; they cried out for sanding and fresh paint. Josh and I strolled through a large, neatly tended vegetable garden. Leaves of Swiss chard moved in the breeze like the ears of alert baby elephants. A rickety one-room cabin perched near the edge of the bluff looked like it could go tumbling over in a strong wind. When I saw the lighthouse building I realized this property must've once belonged to the government. We stood at the edge. The burning sun tongued the ocean. Below was the beach. Josh took a step back and pulled me with him.

"Careful," he said

A bell rang. We walked back toward the dining hall. Suddenly the yard out front was swarming, alive with wall-to-wall people: apple-cheeked toddlers, women in long baggy patchwork skirts and peasant blouses, bearded men with hoes and rakes who purposefully hiked up their jeans as they walked. They came from every corner, headed for a patch of grass in front of the dining hall. Josh and I watched in awkward silence as the men and women milled around, talking and laughing. They seemed to be members of a private clan, conversing in a regional dialect I couldn't place. Every third word was "blessing," "hallelujah!" or "Jesus!" It was one thing to be happy, but these folks seemed stoned on some holy roller, high-octane juice that made them wet-eyed and huggy. I'd seen the Billy Graham revivals on TV and these people were nothing like the Christians you saw coming forward for prayer in their pantyhose and cotton shirt-waists. These folks clasped hands and formed a wide circle.

"Oh, what the hell," Josh mumbled, grabbing my hand and pulling me toward the circle.

"Thank you, Jesus, for this day," prayed a woman in a straw hat and loose wraparound dress.

"And thank you for our guests," added Isaac, materializing beside me.

"Bless the godly women who labored over dinner in the kitchen, Lord," said a lanky young man, his blond hair gathered in an enormous Vaselined forelock like Li'l Abner's. It was so stiff you could've surfed on it. "Bless"– the man's voice cracked–"bless the godly, saintly, virtuous, wonderful sisters who–"

"He gets your drift, Lance," the woman in the hat said. Somebody giggled.

"And they all said …" Isaac shouted.

"Amen!" everybody answered.

In the dining hall, conversations swirled around Josh and me as we found places together at a long trestle table.

"Did you finally get the transmission fixed on the Dodge?"

"The Lord is really putting me through trials these days."

"Thank you, Jesus! This cornbread is great!"

"… So then we prayed about it and now I don't know, I feel … a peace about it, you know?"

"Well, I'm *not* doing the dishes again. I did them last night and my back is still sore."

"That's just your flesh talking …"

Josh kept his eyes on his bowl of barley soup. Perhaps he feared that eye contact with his hosts would automatically lead to conversation. Studiously, he dipped a hunk of cornbread into the bowl, and, with half-closed eyes, chewed meditatively. Lance, sitting across from Josh, watched him with an air of agitated restraint, a retriever on point. The forelock quivered.

Josh set his spoon down and belched softly. "Excuse me," he said, reddening.

"Hallelujah," said Lance, as a kind of preamble. "Thank you, Jesus!"

I glanced at Josh.

"Could you pass the bread?" he mumbled.

Lance ignored his request. Leaning forward, he said, "Do you know the Lord? Have you met Jesus?"

"Look," said Josh, blushing. "I'm Jewish."

"'Jesus has been found worthy of greater honor than Moses, just as the builder of a house has greater honor than the house itself.'" Lance grinned. "Hebrews 3:3."

"Oh, boy," Josh said, rubbing his temples.

"You're in God's hands now, brother. Verily I say unto you …"

"Sir, I appreciate the dinner and all, but–"

"The Lord brought you here, friend."

"Well, we're leaving tomorrow."

"Lord willing," Lance said.

Miss Clavel Turns Out the Light

"HOME" IS A SLIPPERY WORD. LIKE A SET OF RUSSIAN NESTING dolls, you open it up and there's another meaning, and another, and another. Like all military families, ours was on the move. I learned to keep my eye on the horizon, not the hearth. My character was defined by moving frequently. Even now, at forty-nine, I'm geographically reckless. Sometimes I think about moving somewhere I've never been. I have a weakness for real estate catalogues and travel brochures. It's a fever in the blood, and I don't expect to outgrow it. Sometimes outward, sometimes inward, home is a moving target. This is a fact of life, something that can't be changed. It's handed to you, like a childhood nickname that ends up sticking.

BACK IN 1964, PEOPLE DANCED THE FRUG, THE WATUSI, THE Monkey, and the Funky Chicken. I didn't know how to dance – I was only ten and too uncoordinated even for the Twist – but that didn't stop Teddy from sliding a note under the door of our apartment in Frankfurt, Germany. Just like Maynard G. Krebs in the TV sitcom *The Many Loves of Dobie Gillis*, Teddy thought he was the world's coolest beatnik. In his jeans and gray sweatshirt, Teddy said Maynardish things like "You rang?" and "Let's make like a banana and split." Slapping the top of his metal desk in our fourth-grade class on post, sometimes he'd pretend to play bongo drums. Other times he'd stroke an invisible goatee and say, "Dig it, man." My father – who worked as a code breaker in Army Intelligence – picked the note up off the floor in our hallway, slowly unfolded it, scanned its contents. His brow furrowed. The note said: "Dear D'Arcy, I think you're cool in the face. Teddy." Blue eyes alight, my father tried to suppress a belly laugh. "Cool in the face, eh?" he said, over and over, wiping his eyes. Teddy's note made my father get, as Maynard might say, like, all misty. That's how it happens in families. I became known as Cool-in-the-Face, while my older sister, Mary, was "a real brain." My parents observed that child number three, Brian, was artistic and intense, and most resembled our father. Chris, next in line, loved to laugh and exuded an animal magnetism over dogs and cats, who always followed him home. Michael, the youngest, was a bruiser; as young as fifteen months he rearranged the living room furniture, pushing aside chairs like a miniature icebreaker. These are vague, misleading labels; I'm sure we all had complex inner lives that defied neat categorization, but at the time we were young and there were five of us, and any differentiation in a pack of kids is a plus. Of course, each one of my siblings will recount a different version of our collective childhood, but this one is mine. What we can all agree on is that we spent an excessive amount of time on the move: California, Maryland, Arizona, the Philippines, California, Germany, Florida, Alabama, Virginia, back again to California, completing the loop. The year of Teddy's note, I was elected president of my fourth-grade class in a landslide victory after campaigning on a platform of extra field trips. (I reneged on this promise, although my heart was in the right place; I'd certainly hoped we would get more trips to the zoo.) It was the first and only time I felt successful and popular in school.

My parents gave us plenty of room to roam, not on the streets but in books. They were the kind of enraptured, myopic readers who read all the time, and they passed the habit on to us. My mother read us the *Narnia* series by C. S. Lewis, all of the Oz books. My favorites, though, were Ludwig Bemelmans's illustrated stories about Madeline, a wayward redhead who lived in a convent school in Paris. It was run by Miss Clavel, a tall, skinny nun in a dark blue habit. She had a sixth sense about her girls getting into trouble. I liked the orderliness of Madeline's life, how she and the other girls, in two straight lines, "broke their bread, brushed their teeth and went to bed." This symmetry extended to their emotional lives as well, where goodness elicited smiles, bad behavior was rewarded with a frown, and sadness was as uncomplicated and pure as a tear.

Drinking in the illustrations, I studied the tidy beds in the dormitory, the toothbrushes all in a line, the modest nightgowns the girls wore. Everything had its place.

The idea of living in a vine-covered Parisian house that ran like clockwork was very appealing to me. Sometimes I wanted to be the angular, all-knowing Miss Clavel, herding a flock of girls in wide-brimmed yellow hats through the Louvre; sometimes I wanted to be spunky Madeline herself, testing the limits of Miss Clavel's patience, but ultimately always safe in her unwavering love.

My life wasn't like that. Two of my three younger brothers were brawlers, wild and irreligious. They would sword fight with their First Holy Communion candles. They tossed stink bombs down the apartment stairwell and squeezed off armpit farts during Mass. They belched the "Star-Spangled Banner." Mary and I weren't convent school material either. We had imaginary boyfriends – hers was big buff Clint Walker from the TV cowboy series *Cheyenne* and mine was Elvis Presley, partly because the King and I shared the same birthday but mostly because he was sex incarnate, something I recognized even at the age of seven. Compared to Madeline's cloistered dorm, our room usually looked like a land mine had been detonated, a war zone filled with the grubby detritus of two sisters deep in books and play. When we had to clean it up, we pretended to be maids, providing a running commentary about the occupants as we fished for old underwear flung under our twin beds.

"Who lives here anyway?" Mary sputtered, wrinkling her nose. Her curls shook. There was a Three Musketeers candy wrapper stuck to her elbow. "This is horrifying!"

"Ee – ow," I echoed, scooping up gum wrappers, plastic Barbie shoes, broken barrettes, a dusty copy of *The Black Stallion*. "These people are disgusting."

My sister snatched the book from the pile. A member of the Walter Farley Book Club, she was so crazy about horses she insisted on wearing saddle shoes and sometimes made neighing noises, slapping her thighs and yelling "giddyup" when we rode brooms down the narrow apartment hall.

"Pigs," my sister said with a sorrowful shake of her head, putting the book on a shelf. "Filth. I just don't understand it."

After Germany, we moved to St. Petersburg, Florida, where my mother taught at St. Raphael's, the parochial school we attended. My parents bought a white two-story house with a red door and black shutters in a new subdivision. My mother bought a sleek lemon of a car, a red secondhand Jaguar that spent more time in the garage than on the road. My brothers sailed a little dinghy in the canal behind our house. My sister played flute in the school band and much to my envy acquired a beau. I joined the swim team, practiced every day after school, and grew comfortable in my own sturdy skin.

Two years later, at Cloverdale Junior High School in Montgomery, Alabama, I learned about the contours of shame. Like the body it enfolds, shame covers soft spots, surprising edges, stubborn tufts of tenderness. Shame always gives you away, even if you try to camouflage it under lip gloss, deodorant, or bravado. The girls in my seventh-grade class, noting the homemade cotton skirt I wore, said, "Did your mother make that?" I was mortally embarrassed, although I hoped it didn't show beneath my mask of studied uncaring.

"You're a Yankee, aren't you?" drawled Missy, one of the girls on the cheerleading team. She was as languid as Greta Garbo, tan from lying out by her parents' pool, supple and firm from years of gymnastics classes and cotillion dances. She wore expensive paisley Villager dresses, and sandals, and carried a little straw purse with leather handles. I couldn't compete. Where do girls learn to be cool? I lack that gene. Can a lip really curl? Hers did.

"You're not from around here," Missy said, tossing back her hair. She wrinkled her nose. Did I smell bad? "You're a Yankee," she declared again.

"Yeah," I snapped, "but we won the war." Did I really say this? In memory, that's how I answered her, but I probably made some fumbling reply. Rebel, Yankee. Who cared a rip about a war fought one hundred years ago? It was 1967, and I was surrounded by dozens of Missys, Mandys, Susans, stuck-up girls who learned early to note differences in accent, clothing, carriage, pedigree. I was only thirteen but I already knew that sitting on a front porch sipping lemonade with a sweet-faced local boy was a quaint fiction, like the town of Mayberry on *The Andy Griffith Show*. Friendship was a country I could not enter; I would be turned back at the border, lacking the necessary papers.

One night, filled with self-loathing, I borrowed a can of my father's Burma Shave and his razor. Behind the locked door, I ran the bath water and slowly drew the blade against my shin. Crrrh, crrrh. I imagined the virginal hairs shouting and quivering in protest, pleading for another chance before being guillotined. Undaunted, I ran the blade down my leg.

Tiny brown hairs floated on the surface of the water. Stroking my smooth legs, I felt proud, a member of a special club. I had crossed over into sleekness, but not without a price. To keep those hairs from sprouting again, I would have to keep shaving for the rest of my life.

IN THE SINGLE SISTERS' DORM AT THE LIGHTHOUSE RANCH, I stashed my backpack in the sitting room. In the bathroom, a dozen toothbrushes hung next to the mirror. A bottle of Dr. Bronner's Castile Liquid Soap perched on the edge of the porcelain, claw-footed tub. Long, high-necked flannel nightgowns dangled from hooks on the door. I was struck by those nightgowns; they seemed imbued with innocence, old-fashioned hope. Wandering through the sleeping quarters, I paused at the beds, each hidden behind a privacy curtain. Lifting a curtain, one bed was covered with a patchwork quilt. On a small shelf rested a reading lamp and a stuffed elephant. I wanted to lie in that bed, nestle under the quilt, become as small as Madeline and her sisters in that old house in Paris. A simple existence with simple emotions: smile at the good, frown at the bad. Miss Clavel, softly patrolling the room, could turn out the light. I lifted the pillow to my face and breathed it in. Corn starch, musk, chamomile, vinegar douche. The long day receded.

The next morning I found Josh pacing in the front of the dining hall. "I don't care if we have to walk ten miles to Highway 101, we're out of here," he said, pointing to the road. "These people are nuts! I mean, they're a bunch of Jesus-y robots!"

"Well," I said, and cleared my throat.

"Grab your backpack," Josh barked. He stopped pacing and looked at me. "Well, what?"

"I'm going to stay a little longer," I said, embarrassed.

Josh whistled softly. "Shit, they got you. You're brainwashed, aren't you?"

"I'm not," I sputtered, "I just want to stay awhile."

Josh caught a ride back to the highway that morning. I never saw him again.

Fortune has its cookies to give out.

Ruint

I'D WANTED TO EXPLAIN TO JOSH THAT SOMETHING ENORMOUS
had happened to me, something momentous: When I prayed, God respond-
ed. God listened! God was real! But Josh's incredulity withered any words.

The night before, I sat on the bluff next to a large, rough-hewn wooden
cross, listening to the waves crash on the beach below. The sky was the
falling-through-space navy blue of a newborn's eyes; there was just no
end to it. For the second time that day, it was hard to tell which end was
up. Down on the beach, lights flickered; people danced with flashlights
and candles. Muffled cheers floated up from sand dunes. "Praise the Lord!"
someone shouted. *Ahhhh, ahhhhh, ahhhh,* the ocean sighed and exhaled as
the waves reached land. A line from a song I had heard people singing
after dinner floated into my head: "It is well with my soul." I didn't know
precisely what that meant – for one's soul to be well – but I liked the sound
of the words. And my soul needed to be well, to be healed.

A few months earlier, I'd been standing by an on-ramp to Interstate
80 near Chicago with my boyfriend. Four o'clock on a windy afternoon
in March and we'd been waiting for a ride all day. We'd already eaten all the
beef jerky, studied the road map half a dozen times, and consulted Alan's
I Ching by casting three pennies on the frozen asphalt. According to that
ancient system of Chinese divination, we were in for a dramatic reversal
of fortune. "The further you go, the less you know." At least that was how
Alan interpreted the hexagram fate had given us. And now we fought.

Alan and I had been sniping at each other since we'd left Berkeley the
week before. We fought mostly about things like who'd forgotten to fill
up the canteen (me) or whether we should try our luck hitching a ride at
a truck stop (Alan). We argued about other things too, but on that cold
day we were fighting over whether we should head south, to Summertown,
Tennessee, where a twinkly guru named Stephen Gaskin had recently
started a hippie commune in the state's poorest county. Alan and I, we
liked to think we were on a spiritual path. I had seen a photograph of Gaskin in the newspaper; he looked the way I imagined Huckleberry Finn
would look as a grown up. Gaskin grinned from the pages, a mischievous
seer. Alan was no Huck Finn. He wore his long black hair in two sproingy

braids, just like Pippi Longstocking. Alan was what my mother would call full of himself. I'd met Alan a few months earlier in Berkeley when my high school friend Cyndi, playing matchmaker, said I should meet her smart, owlish friend who was visiting from the Midwest. I was in awe of Cyndi. She was tall, fit, and fun, with an amazing pair of knockers. Once we got drunk on rum and Coke and gave ourselves haircuts. When we were done, Cyndi looked like Scout from *To Kill a Mockingbird* and I bore a scary resemblance to Alfred E. Newman – all teeth and ears. We belted out Rodgers and Hammerstein show tunes from *South Pacific*; sometimes we were Bloody Mary, the island souvenir dealer, sometimes Nellie Forbush, the irrepressible Navy nurse. We sang "Happy Talk," "Bali Ha'i," "Honey Bun," and "A Cockeyed Optimist."

"Alan is sensitive," Cyndi told me in a serious tone. "He's a free spirit. I think you two will get on." Back then we were earnest about everything – song lyrics, Ayn Rand, red dye no. 3, Richard Brautigan poetry, Cambodia, wheat germ, and Ravi Shankar's sitar ragas. The world just wasn't big enough to contain all of our *feelings*.

"You're right about your friend," I reported back to her after meeting Alan at the Orange Julius on the corner of University and Telegraph Avenue. "He is sensitive. Does he have a girlfriend back home? Does he ever shut up?"

Sentences spooled out of him in an endless stream. Alan had an opinion about everything, he *knew* things, he felt them deeply, and he was always right. When I first met him I was charmed by his pronouncements and beliefs. Nixon was the devil; AT&T was ripping us off; we should pull out of Vietnam immediately, no questions asked. The universe was neatly ordered to him; planets revolved around the sun of his certainty. I was too young to discern the difference between self-centeredness and romantic mystery; I believed cool, emotionally withholding people signaled a deeper, more profound self. Looking back, I can see how things fit together – my attraction to Alan, the aimless hitchhiking, feeling unmoored in the world – but at the time, everything seemed separate and happened of its own accord.

Dipping into Alan's stash of Turkish coffee, we got wired on caffeine and the idea of traveling together. America's crossroads beckoned and we would sally forth on a joyous journey. The omens looked good. Spring was right around the corner and, well, we had nothing better to do. Alan had applied to Swarthmore, and been wait-listed. In the meantime, he was hitchhiking around the country, phoning his mother from time to time with a stolen credit card number to see if there was any word.

"You have strong hands." We were in Orange Julius again. Alan cradled my hand in his. My hand seemed bigger. In comparison to his hand, it looked like a catcher's mitt. My fingers were short and thick. "Good hands." He patted them. "Good for baking bread." He stroked my thumb. "This is a special hand."

"If you say so."

"What's the matter? Can't you take a compliment?"

I took my hand back and looked at it. It just looked like my hand.

He ran his fingers along the side of my face. "I'm glad I met you. Things happen for a reason."

I'd just graduated from high school. Bay High was a newly established "free" school started by independent-minded teachers fed up with the public school system. The school was located in an old warehouse in the industrial area of Berkeley where the air smelled like burnt coffee. In addition to extracurricular activities such as nude sunbathing on the banks of the Russian River and primal screaming (there was a room set aside for such important venting), it offered classes in creative writing, utopia, flute-making, yoga, and existentialism. The Political Action Collective, committed to ending the war, was committed to visiting with other "tribes" and collectives in the area to foment social change. One student, Rusty, described Bay High this way in a promotional brochure about the school: "Bay High is people connected by umbilical cords to a center core of energy and light." We rapped and ranted, gooed our hands with clay, built cabinets, talked revolution, did street theater, star-gazed, and made 16mm movies like Fellini wannabes.

I took the hour long bus ride to Bay High from my parents' suburban house in Contra Costa County. Commuting to an alternative school was expensive and inconvenient for my parents, but they were worried about me dropping out and figured even an unaccredited one was better than nothing. Those of us at Bay High who felt ready to matriculate took a high school equivalency test. I took the test just days after I turned eighteen, and to my immense surprise, I passed.

A month later, I moved out of my parents' house and into a three-bedroom house in Oakland with Cyndi and two other Bay High grads. The house was situated behind a modest Baptist church. The congregants were black, including my landlady, Mrs. Dunn, whose house was in front of ours. She was a tall, dignified woman who looked like Dionne Warwick on an off day, a day she spent lazing around in a loose flowered house dress and slippers. Like Alan, Mrs. Dunn felt things strongly, righteously, and she became deeply incensed when others didn't see things her way. Maybe that's why she had a Doberman – as an enforcer to keep us all in line. But it didn't work. I often saw Mrs. Dunn peering out her window at our house, her pink foam curlers framed in the gleaming glass. Nostrils flaring, she'd shake her head, then pull the curtains shut, as if the thought of partying, pot-smoking teenage tenants was too much to bear.

We lived from hand to mouth, cobbling together rent money through menial jobs. I had a part-time job housecleaning; my regular clients included a pair of black psychologists in Oakland who were amused that I, a white, middle-class kid, was their "girl." I didn't care. Money was money, and there was precious little of it. Across the street from our house was a big grocery store. Sometimes I'd steal gigantic Cadbury Fruit 'N Nut Bars from it, which was very bad karma, but I rationalized that the grocery chain had been ripping off its customers for years through price gouging. A candy bar or two wouldn't hurt. Once I stole a filet mignon, put it in the waistband of my drawstring pants, and went through the checkout lane with a bag of carrots. When the man behind me, a bland-looking character in mirrored sunglasses buying a pack of gum, turned out to be an undercover security officer, I was hustled into the store's office upstairs and grilled.

"Where are your parents?" the security officer demanded. He popped a piece of Wrigley's in his mouth.

"They're dead," I lied.

"Sure they are." He looked at me. I was scum, lower than the yellow grime I cleaned off my clients' toilet seats. "Let's see some ID."

"I left it at home."

"Where do you live?"

"Uh, New York?"

"Yeah, right. New York my ass." I saw a pale, washed out version of myself reflected in his sunglasses. The marbled steak lay between us on his desk, getting warmer by the minute. I shifted in my seat and realized with a jolt I had a bag of M&Ms in my bra. I crossed my arms and hoped the bag wouldn't crackle.

"I'm so ashamed," I blubbered. "I don't know what came over me."

"Oh for god's sake," the man said, standing up and opening the door. He gestured toward the street. "Get the hell out of here and don't ever come back."

I crossed the street quickly. Mrs. Dunn was sitting on the front porch in her house slippers, reading the *Oakland Tribune*. She nodded at me as I walked stiffly toward the house in back, the candies rattling with each step. I'd almost reached the front door when she called, "Come to church sometime."

The truth was, I wanted to go to church, but not for the preaching. The music floating from the windows made me pace back and forth in my room. It stirred something deep and pleasurable in me, something more satisfying than stolen steak. On Friday nights, when the organist struck deep, rib-rocking chords and congregants began to sing in response, clapping and stomping and raising their arms, I wanted to sing along too. Sometimes when they really got going, it seemed like the shingles would fly off the church roof. I'd stare at my poster of Cat Stevens on my wall, light a stick of incense, and read Kahlil Gibran's *The Prophet* to calm down.

A steel pedal electric guitar pierced the air. The waa-waa of the organ, the pondering beat of the drums, the sliver-hiss of the cymbals: God's people making God's music. "Amen!" someone would shout. "Praise you, Lord!" The congregants would sing about standing on the promises of God. My heart was a balloon on a string. "Glory!" someone would shout. Glore-ree. The word expanded and opened up like a peony. It was sweet and dense, butterscotch on the tongue. I felt it kick in my womb. The balloon tugged and sailed free, over the top of the church.

I didn't confess these feelings to Alan. Alan didn't steal steak and he didn't do windows. When I thought about it – and I was thinking about it seriously that day as we stood fighting near the outskirts of Chicago – we had very little in common. I balled up my frozen hands, hands good for baking bread, and stuffed them into my pockets.

"Let me see the map for a second," Alan said. I had stashed the map in my backpack for safekeeping. When he snapped his fingers I wanted to yank his braids off his head.

"Just a minute," I said, bending over to get it. I can still hear that girl's impatient voice, fretful, angry. It was cold by the side of the freeway. The wind was blowing in from the north. It had rained earlier in the day. Now the sky was iron gray and it felt like snow.

I unfolded the map and peered at a constellation of highways, towns, and rivers. I couldn't get a fix on where we were. The map snapped and fluttered in the wind. Alan grabbed it out of my hands.

"You didn't have to snatch it, Alan," I said, hurt.

"I didn't snatch it, I, ah, relieved you of it," Alan said. "I was afraid it was going to blow away."

A big eighteen-wheeler roared by, sending puddles of water over the tops of our hiking boots. "Thanks, asshole," Alan yelled after the truck driver. Sputtering in the blinding spray, he flipped the trucker the bird. The trucker blew his air horn in response. It made a long blaaating fart that trembled along the asphalt, traveled up through the soles of my soggy feet, and rattled in my skull.

"Well," Alan said after studying the map for a few minutes. He folded it up and put it in his back pocket. "I think we should head east."

"East?" I said. "Alan, I thought we'd talked about going to Tennessee. Tennessee, my friend, is south."

"Aw, let's forget about Tennessee." He put his arm around me. "Let's go to Chicago. My friend Brad lives there. We can stay with him for a few days."

"I don't want to go to Chicago, Alan. I thought we were going to visit the Farm. We were going to talk to Stephen Gaskin, remember?"

"Aw, those guys down there are a bunch of crackers."

"That's not what you said a few days ago."

"I don't want to go," Alan said, a pout in his voice. "You can go without me."

"I don't believe this."

"Remember what the *I Ching* said? 'The further you go, the less you know.'"

"That's your interpretation," I shot back.

Alan shrugged. "Hey, I'm not going to go against thousands of years of metaphysical insight."

"You're a real friend, Alan, you know that? You're aces."

"Thank you" – Alan bowed – "and fuck you very much."

"Fuck you too." I grabbed my backpack and headed for the freeway overpass, where I-80 splintered off and veered west, in the opposite direction. It was starting to snow. Off in the distance, across the white fields of stubble, I could see silos and barns and lighted farmhouses. I'd never thought about the phrase "darkness falls" before, but it was falling so fast now I expected to hear a thud. Darkness falls by degrees and it happens all at once. One minute it's twilight, the next, you can't see at all.

A minute later Alan hollered after me, "Will you just calm down?" I heard footsteps behind me and quickened my pace.

All the grievances I held against Alan hardened and lodged in my aching throat. Tears clotted my lashes. I kept walking down the on-ramp to where it almost merged with the freeway. Alan ran after me. I turned my back on him and stuck out my thumb. A big rig toting Ford Pintos slowed down. Brakes hissed. A man wearing overalls stuck his head out the window. From thirty yards away his face was smooth and blank as a hard-boiled egg. As I drew closer, I noticed the puckered seams and wrinkles around his eyes, set off by a nest of black curls. He looked like a sleepy farmer instead of a truck driver. Reflexively I thought of the TV show *Hee-Haw*.

"You alone?" the man drawled. He looked at me, then glanced in his rearview mirror. I turned around. Alan was running hard toward the truck, his backpack bouncing off his shoulders. "Or are there two of you?"

"It's just me," I said, panting in the wind. I squinted up at him. "Where are you headed?"

"Los Angeles. Want a lift?"

"Thanks." I hauled myself up into the warm cab and tried to catch my breath. "Man, it's cold out there." I shuddered a little in the warmth and rubbed my hands together.

"Who's that little twerp by the door?" the man said sharply.

I peered out the window at Alan. He was making frantic gestures to step out of the truck.

"Nobody."

Alan was pointing to the map. It jerked in his hands like a kite. "You win," he shouted. "We'll go to Tennessee, OK?"

"Well, which way is it, Miss?" the man said, lifting an eyebrow. "Tennessee or L.A.?"

I turned away from Alan. "I'm headed west."

"You sure?"

I looked at Alan again. His mouth was open but I couldn't make out his words. He waved his arms. His long black hair had unbraided itself; it blew about his face like an electrified mane. I knew he would lecture me if I stepped out of the truck and I was sick of his lectures. I turned back to the truck driver.

"Whenever you're ready," I said. We roared off. The heater kicked hot air in my face. Shutting my eyes, I tried to extinguish the image of Alan standing by the side of the road.

"Thanks for stopping," I said, cutting my eyes to the driver. He was huge. His stomach strained the denim stitching of his jeans; his thighs were the size of Easter hams, and his meaty arms were covered with tattoos of red dragons.

"No worry," he said. "I'm Jim."

"Nice to meet you," I said, glancing around the cab. On the dashboard was a photo of three blond teenage boys in cut-offs standing stiffly in front of a swimming pool. Their hands were cupped over their genitals, as if they were cold. Another photo – this one attached to the sun visor – showed a large woman wearing red Bermuda shorts and a halter top. The expression on her face looked pained, but maybe it was just the angle of the sun as she faced the camera.

"That feller back there," Jim said after we'd driven a few miles, "was he with you? Was he your boyfriend?"

"*Was* is right," I said. "He's not any more."

"What happened? Do you mind me asking?"

"Oh, I don't know," I said. "Nothing, I guess."

"Didn't look like nothin' to me."

We rode on in white silence, away from Chicago. The road was icy and snow was starting to come down hard. The light was gone, save for a faint line of gray along the horizon. I thought of Alan back on the interstate and wondered if he'd gotten a ride. I was sorry we'd separated like that.

"Where you from?" Jim said.

"California."

"You're a long way from home, young lady," he said. There was a formality in the way he said that. "A very long way."

"Don't I know it."

"How old are you?"

"Eighteen."

He looked relieved. "Your parents know where you are?"

I shrugged.

"Exactly where in California are you headed?" Jim said.

"San Francisco," I said, staring at the road, trying to calculate the distance we'd come since leaving Alan behind. "But L.A.'s fine for now."

Jim looked at me. I noticed that his ear lobes were unusually large, flesh-colored, like the skin of a ripe yellow pear. He smiled.

"Where are you from?" I said. "I mean, originally."

"I live in Georgia. Me and the missus and the boys. Three teenage boys and lord if they don't give me fits."

"Wow. Three sons. Just like the TV show!"

Jim smiled and gave me a sideways glance. It was hard to read him. "You must miss them," I said. "Do you ever take them on the road with you?"

"Now why would I want to do a thing like that? The reason I drive a truck is to get away from all that blessed racket back at the home." The snow was really coming down now.

"Do you think you'll drive straight through tonight?" I asked.

"Well now, that depends," Jim said, glancing at me. "Tell me about your boyfriend. What's his name? What happened back there on the road between y'all?"

"Alan," I said. "There's really nothing to tell. We had an argument, that's all."

"An ar-gu-ment. Well, what'd you have an ar-gu-ment about?"

"I don't know. We'd been getting on each other's nerves for a while."

"You engaged to him? He give you a ring?"

"God, no. It wasn't like that. I don't ever want to get married."

"Were you, did you, ah, were you intimate with him? Did he have relations with you?"

"Why do you ask?" I said. "What difference does it make?"

"You're in my truck and I have a right to know what kind of person's riding with me. Did you do it with him?" His teeth flashed.

Staring straight ahead, I nodded.

Jim rubbed his right palm across the steering wheel, as if it itched.

"I thought so," he said. "Well now, so you ain't no virgin anymore, are you? You're ruint. Once you've done it, you can never go back to the way you were before."

"He was the first man I ever loved," I said, hearing the panic in my voice. "He was my first."

"Don't matter if he was your first or your fiftieth, ma'am," Jim said flatly. "You're ruint." We climbed a hill. He shifted into a lower gear.

"Tell you what I'm proposing," Jim said. "How 'bout we get a room for the night, and you give me a little of what you gave your boyfriend. And I'll take you to California. What do you say to that?"

"No thanks, Jim."

"Look," he said. "You put out for him, you can put out for me."

"I don't even know you," I said. "I ... I don't love you."

"Love's got nothin' to do with it."

"It does to me."

We drove past a Shell station. The sign on the highway said: Next Gas 38 Miles.

"If you don't, then you're walking to California," he said with a half smile. "If you don't, I'm pulling over right now." He put on his turn signal and swerved into the right lane.

"I can't. I just can't."

He pulled over on the shoulder of the highway.

"It's cold out there," he warned.

I looked at the photo of his wife and felt sad.

"I'm sure it is," I said.

"Get out and walk then, you little slut. And take your cooties with you."

I grabbed my backpack and opened the door. Snow swirled into the cab, heat seeped out into the dark. It was a long step down.

"Hurry up, bitch," Jim said. "You're letting the cold in."

I threw my backpack into the snow and slithered down.

Jim reached over for the door handle. "See you in California!" he yelled, then shut the door and roared away.

I stood in the snow for a long minute and watched the rig's taillights recede. It was cold. "You're all right," I said aloud, and laughed a little. "You're fine." I walked. It was freezing. As cars raced past me, the air shuddered hard. I walked. All the way through my thick leather boots, my toes stung. How did I come to be walking along the freeway on a snowy spring night? Only a few hours ago I had been with a man I'd trusted, a fellow traveler in the wide world. But this was my life too. Alan, that pious asshole, would say of this night: Things happen for a reason. I walked on and on, thinking about my parents back in their house and how sometimes I told people they lived far away, in a state far from California, when all along they were less than fifty miles away. I thought about all the things I was ashamed of: stealing and lying, getting high and sleeping around. Everything *didn't* just happen for a reason. I thought of the way I had poured my life out on the side of the road, carelessly emptying it like canteen water on concrete, not calculating that I might need it later. I was sorry, but mainly I was freezing. I walked. I thought of Mrs. Dunn's church and the sound of glory and how far I was from it now. I thought of the people singing and clapping their hands. I couldn't feel mine. I stopped and stuck out my thumb. A few minutes later a man driving a boxy sedan pulled over and unrolled his window. He said he was a high school principal coming home from a basketball game and he just couldn't believe a girl would be stupid enough to hitchhike by herself on a night like this. Did I want a ride? I did. As he scolded me, his voice rose with indignation and in it I heard the well-worn cadence of my own parents: furious, exasperated, hectoring.

"For Pete's sake, get in out of the cold, young lady," he said, and I knew I was home free.

I got in the car, put on my seatbelt, sucked down the warm air. Deep heaving sobs punched their way through my chest. The man looked over at me with alarm. "Are you OK? Are you hurt? Did something happen to you?" I shook my head. Snow pinged against the windows. Still I cried. I was far from home and a truck driver who didn't know me had pronounced me "ruint" because I wasn't a virgin, because a membrane hidden inside me had been torn and could never be mended. I didn't realize then that innocence was deeper than skin, that deflowering, like darkness, happened by degrees.

The Beds of Spices

THAT NIGHT SEEMED FAR AWAY AS I SAT ON THE BLUFF WATCHing the waves. Carole, a woman who'd befriended me in the sisters' dorm a few hours ago, told me Jesus loved me. It was a story I'd heard many times before, not only through my Catholic upbringing but also from some of my old high school friends who had become Bible thumpers. But as Sister Carole sang from the Song of Songs, the familiar sin-and-salvation story took on a new twist.

"Draw me, Oh Lord, draw me, I pray, and I will run after thee," she sang, rocking back and forth on the bluff. I gazed down at the waves. Her voice, ringing out sweet and clear and high, made my skin pucker. Carole recited:

"My lover has gone down to his garden,
to the beds of spices,
to browse in the gardens
and to gather lilies.
I am my lover's and my lover is mine;
he browses among the lilies." (Song of Songs 6:2–3)

It was hot stuff.

Christians believe the Song of Songs tells the story of Christ's marriage to the church, Carole explained earnestly.

"Wow," I said. I immediately felt foolish.

"Jesus is my lover," Carole said matter-of-factly.

I swallowed hard. Josh, I mentally telegraphed, where are you? It was hard to view Jesus as a lusty, flower-browsing shepherd.

"God's love is intense," Carole said. "God loves you very much." She idly strummed a few chords as she gazed at me. "Do you know that? Do you know how much you're loved? God has brought you to this place. It's no accident that you're here."

"It's all karma, Carole, right?"

"No, you've done nothing to earn this, not in this life or another. This is about grace, not about being good enough. Jesus wants *to be one with you.* All you have to do is ask Him into your heart. Will you do that? Will you pray with me?"

Jesus. Sexy savior. Heavenly husband. Rescuing Romeo. A weird mix of Billy Graham and Harlequin romance. I suppressed the urge to giggle. Carole clasped her hands together and prayed, "Jesus, I know you're right here, Lord. I know you love this woman. Please show her that you're real."

"Uh, I —"

"God has brought you to this place. It's no accident that you're here."

"You know ..."

"Let's pray." Carole took my hand.

I watched Carole, flooded with simultaneous thoughts: I'm so tired. This is weird. What if it's true? Is Jesus really the way? God's my boyfriend! Oh, please. People will laugh. I can't take this seriously. I want to believe. I don't care what people think. Shit, I'm exhausted. Give it a whirl. Am I a sinner? Did God really bring me to this point?

Carole cradled my hands like they were Fabergé eggs and invoked the name of Jesus. I closed my eyes and imagined a man with sexy bedroom eyes and long brown hair, wearing sandals and a white toga. I saw him striding down the sidewalk, purposefully headed up my walkway. *Brriiiiinnng!* The buzzer rang. The door to my heart, glossy as a red satin Valentine, swung open. Jesus stood at the doorway, an aureole of light behind his head. (Could a single prayer redeem a life?)

"Come on in," I said, and began apologizing. "The house is a mess ..."

Jesus looked grave and beautiful as he held out his hands to me. There were holes in his callused palms; I felt them as I drew him across the threshold. Jesus took me in his arms and kissed me on the lips. He knew everything about me. He knew about French-kissing. Jesus was so sweet! I noticed he had long lashes and a little mole under his left eye. We started slow-dancing. Jesus led. I put my head on his shoulder–it felt like home – and inhaled the odor of his windblown hair. Apples and cinnamon, rainwater and sage. The weight of my own life fell away. (Why was I crying?) After an eternity of dancing, we sat on a sea-green velvet loveseat, held hands, gazed into each other's eyes.

"I'm sorry, Jesus," I said, although no words were spoken. "Will you forgive me?"

He caressed my cheek. "I've always loved you, honey," he said with a catch in his throat. A tear slid down the side of my face. I needed to blow my nose. The Man from Galilee whisked a Kleenex out of his sleeve. This was our first date. I was safe, far from the desperate night on the snowy freeway. My ride had come. This was it. I took a deep breath. A curious sweetness enveloped me; I felt like I was floating in a bubble.

Jesus the man looked at me and saw into the deepest part of myself, past sin, past appearances, past comprehension, past personality, past all the things I held dear about myself. His look seared me. I was *seen* and I was *loved*.

Carole gave my hands a final squeeze and stopped praying. "Amen," she said, as if my life was settled. She smiled. We didn't know each other, not even a little. "Welcome to the family," she said.

Training Your Soul

THE LIGHTHOUSE RANCH, LIKE ANY SMALL COMMUNITY fortified against outsiders, was a world unto itself. We were a gated community without the gate, a collective with our own unwritten rules about culture, language, clothing, and, of course, what it meant to be *spiritual*. Women were called *sisters*, men *brothers*; difficult situations or people were considered *trials*. Trials could also be considered *blessings*.

A stranger first coming to the ranch would see only happy chaos amidst warm communal belonging. He or she would notice the women in their long dresses, the men in sandals and overalls, the excited children in their bandannas and braids. The visitor might note the archaic formality between the sexes, as well as a certain "look": no artifice but an intensity of gaze, and a sameness in speech, the way people reflexively said, "Praise the Lord" or "Thank you, Jesus." These were surface observations. It would take several months of living at the ranch to sort out who was who, who held power, and who wanted it. And it could take a year or more to decipher the shadings of such seemingly neutral words as "soul," "family," and "witness."

I was unaware of these nuances when I first came to the ranch. What I found was a place so strange and intense, filled with people who seemed to burn with a genuine love for the Lord. Of course, the fact that the Lighthouse Ranch was miles from anywhere, perched on a windswept bluff, added to its romantic cachet. It's one thing to get religion at a strip mall in Fresno and quite another at the edge of the world. The ranch members didn't belong to the Rotary Club or sell appliances at Montgomery Ward; they toiled in the garden, milked cows, made yogurt, believed in natural childbirth. To a baby bohemian who was also new in Christ, the ranch seemed hip to me. It fit my craving for high drama and a back-to-the-land experience –without the drugs and premarital sex. It seemed, literally, out of this world. And although I couldn't articulate it at the time, the ranch was a powerful draw because living there meant postponing initiation into adulthood. I was only too happy to forestall answering the big, unsettling, what-are-you-doing-with-your-life questions. At the center of my life was Jesus, who had saved me from wandering America's highways. I was trying to get to know Him.

During those first weeks at the Lighthouse Ranch, I sometimes got up at dawn and hiked down to the beach. It was good to be alone. Waves clawed the shore. Sea gulls sailed over the water on spanking breezes, their shrill cries barely audible over the crashing surf. Tiny sandpipers sped across the wet beach on toothpick legs, their frantic beaks pecking at the sand. As I stared up at the shimmering sky, it seemed as if only the sheerest membrane was keeping me from falling straight into God. Sun, clouds, waves. The sky swiveled. The Bible promises believers that we will be reborn, and on those mornings, sandblasted by the elements, I felt ecstatic, holy, and strong.

I raised my voice with praise for God. Everything was a prayer to God for God was everywhere: in the roaring ocean, the pristine sand dunes, the great blue herons and snowy egrets, marshes and mudflats. I stared up at the weathered lighthouse perched at the edge of Table Bluff, a promontory of land that rose 165 feet above me. It, too, was a prayer, a spire to the sky. You live here now, I told myself. Watching the waves, counting them as they pulsed in, one-two-three-four, a memory rolled up like a piece of driftwood spit from the churning surf. Big Sur. Camping with my younger cousin Sharon. We are eight and ten years old, two fidgety girls up way past our bedtime. My tomboy cousin is endlessly entertaining. She is fearless and tough. There has never been a horse she couldn't ride and she will say anything for a laugh. My mom and my aunt – Sharon's mom – sit at a nearby picnic table, laughing and talking with their heads together. They're sipping Gallo Rosé out of coffee mugs and smoking cigarettes. The fire crackles. Sharon and I lie on our backs, staring up at the redwoods. The branches seem entwined with the sky, which has been swept clean by a steady wind off the Santa Lucias. Sharon stirs. The plastic barrettes that keep her long blonde hair free from her face glow like the bones of phosphorescent fish. She sighs, folding her hands across her flat chest. In five years she'll be a busty knockout in a bikini, but now she's all edges and angles.

"You know," she says, "sometimes I wish I were a sleeping bag so people could sleep in me and zip me up." I had no idea what she meant that night, although I've never forgotten the words. Perhaps they were a kind of prophecy. She died at a young age, killed (and killing someone else) as she drove drunk on Interstate 5. Sharon, forever young, would sleep zipped up in the cool earth. But as I stood on the beach that summer in Loleta, my spirited cousin was very much alive, still a teenager, and her fanciful idea that one's body could be an inhabitable container made sense to me. The Holy Spirit – the comforter – was dwelling in me; He had moved in and zipped me up, tight and snug. Walking slowly back up the road to the Lighthouse Ranch, I was filled up with God.

Papa Jim often preached about the principle of confessing God's truth, even if the facts presented another picture. "This is the day the Lord has made; let us rejoice and be glad in it," he would say, quoting from Psalm 118:24. But what if the day started badly, with an argument or menstrual cramps or a leaky roof? Confess the truth! Proclaim the Word! Glorify God's holy name! Make a bold confession about what it says in the Bible, rather than how you feel. This was a revolutionary idea. Believe what it says in the Bible, confess it, and act on it. And so we did. A husband nursing a secret grievance against his wife might say, "You are a virtuous woman of God." A sister in the dorm given to depression and anxiety might profess, "I have the mind of Christ." A brother who had strep throat might proclaim, "By His stripes, I am healed." These confessions of faith, Jim preached, were important, even if the facts seemed contrary to God's word. "Facts shift and change, but God's truth remains constant," he said. "The Lord has arranged the circumstances you will face. He is carefully setting up difficult situations and unusual circumstances so that you can learn to apply your faith in Him."

Jim talked about "training the soul," whipping it into shape, making it fall in line with God's word, as if it were a cranky toddler. The soul needed chastisement, not coddling. The soul was rebellious and sneaky. When you didn't want to get out of bed at five in the morning and pray for an hour or read The Word after dinner, that was your soul talking. You had to be firm with your soul. Talk to it, instruct it, and if it was still being stubborn, then send it to bed without any dessert.

The elders called the commune a "discipleship training group," a "spiritual bootcamp for young Christians." It was a bootcamp, all right. There were dorms for single people, with rules and schedules. No drugs, no radios, no cigarettes, no premarital sex, no pets, no alcohol.

I tried to practice what Jim preached. "I can do everything through

Him who gives me strength," I told myself as I began making vegetarian lasagna for one hundred people in the cluttered ranch kitchen. Everything was industrial-sized: ovens, sinks, pantry, refrigerator, cooking utensils. We tried to warm the room up with patchwork curtains and scriptures posted on the walls, but nothing softened its utilitarian spirit. This was a place where massive meals were cooked assembly-line style and dishes were washed in a low, punishing sink, only to be used again in a few hours for another round of meals.

The ranch attracted people at a crossroads in their lives, struggling with addiction, or looking for a tailor-made "family" without all the baggage and history that come with real-life families. Some, like Brother Joel, who was separated from his wife, came to the ranch and soon took a job as a baker in the ministry's bakery. Wearing a paper hat and floury apron, he maintained a stoic, wounded silence as he pummeled loaves of rye and whole wheat for the ovens. When he reconciled with Peggy several months later, they moved into the married quarters. With her makeup case, nail polish, and hot electric curler set, Peggy made some of the wives nervous, especially since she insisted on wearing tight jeans and clingy sweaters. "Joel likes me this way," said Peggy, who never left their room without mascara, blush, and come-hitherish eyeliner that made her eyes look like Sophia Loren's. "I'm doing this for him."

Well.

What could the women say to *that*? Peggy's dress code, praise God, was a matter of scriptural compliance. She was pleasing her man, just like it says in the Bible.

Brother Calvin had been a hard-core drunk in Eureka before coming to the ranch. He rose at dawn and walked across the land, ringing a brass gong. "Arise and shine, for the light has come and the Glory of God has risen up in thee," he shouted. Sometimes he fell off the wagon and disappeared for weeks at a time, only to return from town shaky, grateful, and sober anew.

Mike, a disaffected Vietnam vet who was single, dragged his anger around like a broken wing. At breakfast, he sat over his oatmeal, eating in stony silence. He seldom made eye contact with anybody. In contrast,

Lance, who had witnessed so doggedly to Josh and me when we first arrived, was as sweet and guileless as the calves he tended, although sometimes he chewed his eggs with an irritating, lip-smacking gusto.

The broken, the mentally ill, the lost, and the found – that's who we were, all trying to work out our salvation together. Most of us weren't "normal" in the conventional sense: there were very few bank tellers or accountants bunking in the ranch dorms or spooning up steamed vegetables next to the toothless homeless guy with the DTs. But we had something mainstream Christians didn't have: We believed we were "called" by God to a life of hard-core discipleship and utter submission to His will. That religious fervor lent a thrill to our lives. Yielding to the siren call of the Holy Spirit, we were locked in a larger-than-life drama that required tolerance and faith, even if it meant serving Jesus with a bunch of people we would've considered losers in the outside world.

People wandered in as sinners and graduated as fired-up baby Christians. Some returned home to their church communities and families, others went back to school or a different Christian ministry, but many of us stayed among the battered old Coast Guard buildings scattered across the land. Sometimes I thought about what my life would be like if I were back in the Bay Area as a young Christian. It was hard to imagine myself carrying around a Bible, witnessing to people from Bay High School. I knew they would scoff at my recent conversion, say Christianity was a crutch for the weak-minded. Honestly, I wasn't up to debating evolution versus the creation of the world in seven days; I just wasn't that intellectually nimble. When Andrea, an old classmate, wrote and asked if I was really happy and if I was planning on coming back to the Bay Area soon, I fired off a tense scripture-filled letter warning her to get right with the Lord. Andrea's letter gave me pause, underscoring the tension I was beginning to feel. My needs as an individual clashed with my need to belong.

Every night, we gathered in the dining hall for praise and worship, testimonials, music, scriptures. One of the elders would preach, and Leo and Rose, a young married couple, led us in song. Everybody noticed their charisma. During worship, tall, big-boned Rose sang and bopped from side to side, while Leo played the guitar, tossing his head like Gordon Lightfoot. They sang:

> *Blessed are ye poor!*
> *The Kingdom of God is yours!*
> *Blessed are ye that are hungry*
> *Ye shall be filled!*

Thoughts I'd had of leaving vanished. The air buzzed with holy electricity. And it felt dangerous, too. You never knew what was going to happen. Some nights, as the Holy Ghost swept through that concrete room, ions rearranged themselves, magnetic poles shifted, and the temperature rose by ten degrees. The fluorescent lights grew furry halos. When we raised our hands in the air, it felt like sparks flew from our palms. It was too fantastic to be true, and yet it was. I trembled because I knew I wasn't worthy. And I was scared. Something was happening. Jesus was in our midst! At those times, when the room was suffused with a rosy glow, it was easy to forget I'd been on laundry duty earlier that day, or that the next day I'd have to get up at five for a paper route. Children of God, that's what we were! We were saints, disciples. We loved Jesus, and we tried to love one another.

I floated back to the sisters' dorm, buoyant and lively, drunk with grace. In my bunk, I closed my curtains for privacy, lit a small gold candle and prayed: *I believe I believe I believe. Thy will be done. Thank you, Jesus! Lord, show me who You are. Show me Your heart. I believe I believe I believe.* Wax inched down the candle's flesh, hardening into tears. My Bible, my clothes, my clock, my diary – all my belongings awash in candlelight. But as I closed my eyes to pray, what I meditated on wasn't the Lord but wayward Madeline, cloistered and safe from the world's burning questions.

Little Flower

MY PARENTS WORRIED THAT I WAS INVOLVED IN A CULT. *Come home*, they implored. *Come see us.* But I wrote them that the elders frowned on my going home. I was too young in the Lord, I wrote, too tender a seedling to bear the winds of the world. I might have even used the King James word "spake," as in "The Lord spake to me." I was, I told them, a babe in Christ craving the "pure spiritual milk" of the Word. Taste and see that the Lord is good, I said, tossing in even more scriptures from the first book of Peter. To my parents, this was very strange talk. I sounded as brainwashed as that smart, high-strung kid who'd lived across the street from us before he joined the Hare Krishnas. True, I didn't shave my head or chant or wear a robe and beg for money in airports, but my missionary zeal and tendency to quote Bible passages made them very nervous.

But my conversion wasn't completely out of character. Every family has an anxious child who feels guilty, who feels responsible, who waits up late for the parents to come home, perched on the radiator watching for their car lights while the babysitter raids the refrigerator or talks on the phone with her boyfriend. I was such a child – chronicler, voyeur, pulse-taker, pint-sized drama queen. I believed myself misunderstood, unappreciated, yet somehow gifted with exquisite sensitivities.

When Mary pounded Brian, I intervened – through prayer. If my father muttered "Oh, Christ" when Blackie the Beer Man forgot his St. Pauli Girl, I crossed myself. Moping and sighing from the Little Flower: what else was new? One week I wanted to be "The Singing Nun," the next I was set on marrying Elvis.

Nuns were big in the movies in the '60s. In 1963 Sidney Poitier starred in *Lilies of the Field* as an unemployed construction worker who helped a group of no-nonsense East European Catholic sisters build their chapel in the desert. Two years later, Julie Andrews starred in *The Sound of Music* as a woman torn between celibacy and family life, and Sally Field, fresh from *Gidget*, starred in the ABC sitcom *The Flying Nun*. A nun from the Convent San Tanco in San Juan, Puerto Rico, Sister Betrille could fly whenever the winds picked up. Her dramatic headdress with its white points protruded nearly a foot from either side of her head.

I fantasized about being a nun, mostly because I liked the clothes. I liked the way a nun's habit billowed as she walked, the way her rosary beads clicked like mah-jongg tiles, the way her wimple made her head as sleek as a seal's. In fourth grade, I started referring to myself as Sister Rose, the Little Flower of Frankfurt, and walked around in our cramped apartment with a bed sheet over my head.

My parents weren't religious, although they tried to give us a moral upbringing, making sure we went to Mass and studied catechism. Before receiving my First Holy Communion, I learned about all the sacraments. Hell was real, although heaven wasn't a sure bet. I could work myself into a trance just thinking about spending eternity in a pit of endless fire, my parched, blackened skin falling off my bones like roasted chile peppers. Limbo was where the innocent little babies went who hadn't been baptized and still bore the stain of original sin. They flew around in a darkened room with flailing arms, bumping into walls and crying for their mothers. Purgatory was for people who died without going to confession. This was a spiritual holding pen where millions waited with a sense of dread, bellowing like cattle crowded into a dirty feed lot, standing ankle-deep in their own manure. In my imagination, everybody had his or her assigned place.

But when I got religion for real at the Lighthouse Ranch nine years later, my family took notice. This time it was more than wearing sheets. Candles, incense, Gregorian chants, Hildegarde of Bingen – hey, she was as classy and self-contained as a bottle of holy water, but "Jesus Loves You"? My conversion particularly flummoxed my mother, who'd started subscribing to Ms. magazine. I knew she considered St. Paul a first-class misogynist, a pious little prick with some deep-seated sexual hang-ups. She never used this kind of language, but if you got her started on that indefatigable bachelor saint, she would practically froth at the mouth. Her anger with him was tied up with Catholicism and the Church's stand on birth control. After Pope Paul VI's 1968 *Humanæ Vitæ*, in which he stated that contraceptive use was "intrinsically wrong," she mocked him by putting up a poster of him waggling his finger at the faithful, warning, "The pill is a no-no."

"Give me a break!" my mother said over and over, shaking her head in disgust. The summer that I left home and came to the ranch was the summer of Watergate, the summer of Dick Nixon's dirty tricks, the summer the GOP attempted to bug the Democratic National Committee headquarters. Every night on the news more baffling revelations came out about the affair. My mother sat glued to the living room couch next to our fifty-gallon fish tank, a cup of coffee in one hand, a cigarette in the other, glaring at the screen. As neon tetras darted through the water in bursts of electric blue, Nixon's pale scowl reflected off the glass. "Unbelievable." Perhaps that refrain was also an echo of her life's changing circumstances. Not long before, we had moved from a brick colonial-style house in Arlington, Virginia, to a suburban rancher in Lafayette, a small town not far from San Francisco. My father, after more than two decades in the military, had broken the news to her that he had an overwhelming desire to build his own boat and sail around the world. A native San Franciscan, he longed for the ocean.

My dad had been working sixteen-hour days at the Pentagon, assigned to the Joint Chiefs of Staff, where he wrote, rewrote, revised, and coordinated joint military policy. It was tiring and stressful work, top secret, very mysterioso.

Now he told my mother: I want to sell boats and sail them and I think I know how I can. My mother wasn't wild about the venture. In the end, the ocean won. My father worked for a year or so in an Alameda boat yard building boats – never drawing a salary from the job because he and his partners couldn't afford to pay themselves after rent and supplies. My mother took a succession of jobs, from a clerk in an insurance office to a teacher in Alameda. She was the one who was keeping it together. Slow work and slower money. The accusations flew.

One day on the job, as my father was helping set up a building framework for a customer, the hull of a cement boat fell on his kneecap, crushing it. He spent a month at a naval hospital and when he got out, the dream was over.

He sold his end of the business and desperately began looking for ways to support a wife and five kids – including one in private college. He sold jewelry in a city 100 miles away; he sold second-hand cars; he drove trucks for the county; he sold cleaning supplies for the Fuller Brush Company. After he had helped draft military policy at the Pentagon, it was hard to think of my dad selling detergent, shampoo, and little plastic key chains to impatient housewives.

Mary, nineteen, was away at college, although "away" was only across the San Francisco Bay, where she attended the University of San Francisco, studying to become a nurse. She was as single-minded about getting her education as I was about dodging mine. From the time she was a bitty girl, she always seemed to know what she wanted. Our roles were established in the womb, and there wasn't a thing we could do about it. She came first: tiny, intense, a furious hummingbird. Even as a toddler, she was opinionated, sure of the world and her rightful place in it. She was Florence Nightingale and Napoleon, caring and driven at the same time and always right.

She and my mother were very tight. There seemed to be an invisible circle around them that I couldn't penetrate. They were two women together, bound by gender – and genuine affection. They would sit in the living room talking quietly. I think my mother shared some of her worries about the rest of us kids with Mary, as well as some of her own frustrations about my father's career. Murmuring voices, the steady give-and-take of earnest conversation. When I'd enter the room, talk would cease. I felt like I was an intruder and feared, no, hated the idea that I was being discussed.

Sometimes during my LSD trips, I imagined being on top of a mountain. With my eyes closed, I fantasized about standing on the summit. Thin air, warm sun, a blazing blue sky wide and bright and deeper than chemicals. Tripping, nodding, feeling the rush, I imagined I would be able to talk to my parents. They would appear on the summit with me and we would be laughing and crying and breathing the thin air together, marveling at how good it was to be alive. And I would be able to tell them how much I loved them, how sorry I was for all the terrible things I'd done, and they would understand. They would forgive me and we would ... love each other. We would be happy together, like refugees who had escaped from a war-torn country. We would marvel at our good luck in escaping, congratulate each other, and when we looked into each other's eyes, we knew we would never revert to our old, critical selves, but always be able to speak the truth with love and perfect understanding. I dressed them in lederhosen with antler bone buttons, forest green knee-high socks, fresh white cotton shirts. I gave them boots and felt hats and hiking sticks and draped their necks with garlands of marigolds. Their teeth would be very white and they would be smiling and they would smell like peppermint Binaca. It was guilt, it was corn, it was one hundred percent LSD.

If my parents had really appeared in the flesh while I was tripping, it would've sent me into a heart-pounding freak-out so profound I would've curled into a little inchoate ball and tried to cover myself with that blanket of blue sky. In reality, they would not have looked at me with emotive, all-knowing understanding, but in horror and we're-taking-you-to-a-shrink shock. I would not have been with them on the mountaintop of understanding, but in a world of Very Deep Shit. But far from them, in the addled ether of my drug trip, I could pretend to connect with my parents, the people I loved, lied to, and hid from.

That Watergate summer, I missed Mary. I needed her as a buffer. In my mother's presence, I felt I had no skin. It was not enough to witness her exhaustion and disappointment; I had to bear it too. I was not the good daughter, not the one who had heeded our mother's urgings to be independent and self-reliant, to go to college, to make something of myself. Sometimes, hoping to ease my guilt, I quickly vacuumed the house. *See, I know you're tired. I understand. I love you. I want to be good.*

His Girl Friday

"PRAISE YOU, LORD, BLESS YOU LORD, HALLELUJAH, JESUS. Jesuuuuuuus. Jeeeeeeesus."

Ella slept in the bunk above me. She woke early and often spent the first half hour in bed Seeking His Face, sometimes aloud and always with great feeling. I lay on my bunk, staring up at the bottom of her mattress. Closing my eyes, I tried to burrow back into sleep. Her mattress shuddered.

"Thank you, Father," Ella said. "Oooooh, merciful Lord."

There was no getting away from Ella. I was breathing her air, she was breathing mine. Our molecules mingled. Once I gently reminded Ella of what Jesus said on the subject of prayer – that you should do it in your closet, with the door closed.

"I don't have a closet," Ella said.

"Then you should do it in your room."

"I don't have a room either," she countered. Her bunk was her room, the only private place she had. She was right, but I resented her tone. On five fog-bound acres of land, privacy was at a premium, rare as meat for dinner. Sometimes, so much forced intimacy felt like an endurance contest. Most of the women I lived with in the sisters' dorm were not my idea of perfect roommates. Some of them I tolerated, even loved, others were trials. Ella was my trial. The Lord was using Ella to humble me, and to help me work on my soul. Nobody but God or Satan could've placed that sister in my path so often. Kitchen duty, weeding the garden, sorting the mail—there was Ella, earnest and upright as a cowlick. Everything about her bothered me, from the little rickracked smocks she wore over her jeans to the Troll doll with purple hair she kept on the shelf in her bunk, right next to a tube of Avon hand cream.

Ella was a country girl; she came from a farming community in the Central Valley. She knew how to can vegetables and make grits and gravy. For such a short person, she gave off an intense vibe. She was moonfaced and stocky, with spaghetti-straight brown hair that hung down her back, and a little gap between her front teeth. A literal soul, Ella was completely lacking in irony, and she was living with us in the sisters' dorm until her husband, Chuck, was released from state prison in Vacaville. I don't know what he was in prison for, but I do know Ella was trying to honor her marriage vows and be a strong Christian witness to her husband. She hoped that when Chuck got out they could start over, basing their life on Christian principles. She could barely speak a sentence without invoking his name.

"Got a letter from Chuck," Ella would say, sitting in the dining room after the morning Bible study. "Oh, Jesus give me strength," she'd sigh, thumbing through one of his letters, scrawled on yellow legal stationery. Ella sotto voce during her morning devotional: "Help me to deal with him, Lord." Or in the kitchen, chopping onions for potato soup: "Chuck hates onions." *Whack, whack.* "No, Chuck never has liked them. Chuck's a picky eater." She'd put down the knife and stare out the window at the parking lot, as if expecting him to roar up on a Harley at any moment.

"Wonder what they're serving for dinner tonight in that place." *Whack.*

In some ways, Ella and I were closer than two people having an affair. We saw each other in our cotton underwear, when we were tired, when we huddled together warming our chilly backsides against the heater in the parlor of the sisters' dorm. Sometimes when the elders talked about how the Lord put difficult people in our lives in order to enlarge our hearts, I stared at Ella. But if the Holy Spirit was working on me, He was also working on Ella, who, I sensed, disapproved of me and Gretchen, the sister who slept across from us. Gretchen dyed her shoulder-length hair blonde, did Air Force strength-conditioning exercises in her pajamas and, in true communal spirit, sometimes borrowed our clothes without asking. In another life she'd been a musician and still played the violin during church services. She had so much heavy facial hair she had to shave every morning. I found it endlessly fascinating to see her in her baby dolls hunched over the bathroom sink, calmly running a Schick across her jaw. In the shower, as she soaped her *zaftig* body, she turned into Little Richard: "I am nothing! Jesus reduced me to loooooove! Jesus reduced me to loooooove!" Then she would cackle. I had never known anyone who fluttered their eyelashes on purpose, but Gretchen did. Maybe she thought it showed her sensitive side, or maybe she did it to be flirtatious, like a Christian geisha.

Some days Gretchen was flying so high, she couldn't stop talking. Other days, she took to her bunk with vague complaints about spiritual oppression. I liked Gretchen because she was out there; she had a sense of humor. Even in her lowest moments, she seemed campy, playing to a private audience: consumptive Camille with PMS; madcap Heidi with a five-o'clock shadow. But her mood swings grated on Ella, who was as self-contained as a baked potato. One afternoon as I sat in the dorm parlor resting after lunch duty, I noticed Ella stationed by Gretchen's curtained bunk.

"Are you in there?" Ella whispered.

Gretchen's voice was subdued. "No, I'm not."

"Can I share something with you?" Ella said. My heart always sank when people asked if they could "share" something with me. "Sharing" usually meant they were getting ready to make some cutting observation about me. The observation could be wrapped in sanctimonious language or

Bible verses but the result was always the same: a spiritual raspberry. I distrusted people who "shared" what was on their hearts and so, I suspect, did Gretchen. This didn't stop me, though, from "sharing" from time to time myself.

"Please just go away," Gretchen said. "Tell me tomorrow."

"Listen to me," Ella hissed. "You have the mind of Christ. Do you know what that means? You don't have to feel bad."

"Not today," Gretchen mewled.

"'Do not conform any longer to the pattern of this world, but be transformed by the renewing of your mind,'" Ella quoted. "That's Romans 12:2. You can look it up. The renewing of your mind, Gretchen. You need to renew your mind through The Word."

"Do we have any Pepto-Bismol?" Gretchen said.

"I'm going to pray for you."

"Why don't you leave her alone?" I said, walking over to Gretchen's bunk. "She said she doesn't feel well." I peered at her curtain. A faint light shone through the flimsy fabric. I thought I heard cellophane rustling. Gretchen often stashed bags of chips and cookies in her bunk.

"She's giving in to Satan," Ella declared earnestly. "Either that or she's faking."

From behind her curtain, we heard Gretchen suddenly and volcanically break wind. It sounded like a balloon deflating when you untie the end and, like a flabby pair of lips, it expels air in emphatic raggedy bursts. And it went on and on, like a bagpiper with endless lung capacity. Ella and I looked at each other, astonished. My eyes watered.

"Wow!" I said, reeling.

"That was stunning," Ella said.

"Thank you, Jesus!" Gretchen sang out.

At first I thought Gretchen's cheerful tone was an attempt to distract us from the fact that she'd cut such lethal cheese. I would've been mortified. Gretchen poked her head between the curtains. She didn't look the least bit embarrassed.

"That just slipped out," she said with a shrug.

"Ahem," Ella said.

Slipped was the wrong verb. Torpedoed, erupted, or ejected was more like it, but this wasn't the moment for a vocabulary lesson.

"Praise God," said Gretchen merrily. The diva was making a comeback. "It must've been the lentil soup."

"You are sick," Ella declared, her shoulders shaking convulsively. Giggling, she climbed the ladder to her bunk and drew the curtain. At that moment I forgave her everything.

IT WAS TIME FOR ONE OF ELLA'S VISITS TO SEE CHUCK. I WATCHED her closely as she packed. In my mind, those conjugal visits always seemed charged, mixed up with images of dangerous, violent sex, outlandish lingerie outfits, and postcoital crying jags. I imagined Ella and Chuck reuniting in a grim little motor home behind a thicket of razor wire, or having to tear themselves apart like breathless teenagers in time for roll call. The phrase "conjugal visit" sounds tawdry, conjuring up images of round-the-clock nooky, but I knew Ella was trying to throw her husband a domestic lifeline. Did they play Monopoly or watch *The Mary Tyler Moore Show*? (Mr. Grant to Mary: "You know what? You've got spunk. I HATE spunk!") Did Ella in her smock play Delilah to Chuck's Samson? Did she giggle and straddle his lap, run her fingers through his thick oily hair, or was she the picture of wifely submission, just down for a quick trip and a shot at witnessing to her man?

Off she went on Greyhound. My fantasies spun on and on. I couldn't turn them off, and I knew that when I saw Ella upon her return I would feel I'd violated them both in my thoughts.

DON'T HIDE YOUR LIGHT UNDER A BUSHEL, JESUS SAID. MY FRIEND Barbara didn't just shine, she was a human blowtorch. In the world, she'd liked speed, and now, at the ranch, the residue of that nonstop energy still clung to her like lint. I can't recall Barbara's salvation story, whether after meeting the Lord she quit doing drugs cold turkey or tapered off slowly. I don't remember if she'd once been married to her daughter's father, or under what circumstances she arrived at the ranch. But somehow her worldly résumé, that cataloging of past sins, didn't seem important. There was the immediacy of the here-and-now, of living in a world where we were all thrown like wet clothes into a dryer and spun together. It would take some of us years to sort ourselves out.

Although Barbara wore thick glasses and needed braces, she carried herself with slapdash confidence. In teetery heels she clomped to church, all skinny legs and big shoes, like Minnie Mouse. She had Minnie's exaggerated eyelashes, too, and favored kicky thrift-store ensembles. While most of us looked like hippies in our jumpers and peasant blouses, Barbara was His Girl Friday, a Southern California girl in a flared knee-length skirt and a pert jacket. She wore her ensembles with élan, living proof that a woman of God didn't have to be a drudge in a droopy calico sunbonnet, hoeing beans on the prairie.

Barbara and her young daughter lived in the Mothers' House, a wood-frame two-story building overlooking the ocean. The house, a duplex, was your basic box with a simple floor plan: kitchen and living room/dining room downstairs; two bedrooms and a bathroom upstairs. Each bedroom had two bunk beds; how much privacy a family had depended on the ranch's ever-fluctuating census. Sometimes two mothers and their children shared a room; sometimes, if they were lucky, a family had their own. A low-grade spirit of lawlessness reigned at the Mothers' House. Perhaps it was because motherhood – even single motherhood – was supposed to be sacrosanct, carrying with it a whiff of goodness. Along with the responsibilities of bringing up children in the ways of the Lord, there were privileges too. If you lived in the Mothers' House, you could cook a meal, take a long bath, make a batch of cookies, or stay up late with the light on. As I got to know Barbara, I spent a lot of time at the Mothers' House. In time I came to recognize the look of gleeful subversion behind her cat's-eye glasses, a look I immediately recognized years later when I saw John Belushi as the anarchistic frat brother in *Animal House*.

She made fun of some of the distracted-looking brothers who strutted around with their Bibles under their arms. "SMOGS," she called them behind their backs – Serious Men of God. Some of them affected a grave manner, emitting Old Testament disapproval that curled out of their sanctified nostrils like frankincense. In the Book of Ephesians, it says that we should put on the whole armor of God in order to fight the evil one. These brothers were so fortified they clanked when they walked. "We've got a SMOG alert in effect," Barbara would say, pointing her chin at Roland, the ranch mechanic, as he walked by in his greasy overalls, absorbed in his own thoughts. Though I laughed along with Barbara, Roland turned me on. The temples of his glasses were held together with masking tape; he wore heavy work boots and a distracted air. Somehow, I found this highly erotic. Sure, he seemed as distracted as Inspector Clouseau, but I suspected he was really intense once you got to know him. I once saw him lying on the grass near the edge of the bluff with his eyes closed and his Bible on his chest. He laughed and talked to Jesus as if it were the most natural thing in the world. He once said dreamily that the words "rose hips" sounded like they belonged in the Song of Songs. I couldn't tell if he was talking about tea or a woman's body, but after he said it I could certainly see his point. His goofiness and introspection fueled my fantasies; I imagined him falling in love with me, laying his tawny head on my lap in abject surrender. Rose hips.

That wasn't the case with Brother Leroy. Broad-shouldered, bearded, and always dressed in loose cotton pants and sandals, he seemed to float about on a holy magic carpet that rolled out before him. Did Jesus wear huaraches made from old tires and Irish linen shirts the color of rolled oats? Did Our Savior speak sternly and then only when spoken to, shunning women in particular, especially those who wore loud red corduroy pants? This was Leroy, a holy terror in baggy drawstring pants pretending to be Jesus. Of course people noticed his Old Testament ways. Barbara and I rolled our eyes at him, while others considered him a brother with a real heart for the Lord. There was a deeper reason for my scorn. Leroy bore a jarring resemblance to my cousin Sharon's old boyfriend, Phil: basset hound eyes, protruding upper lip, thick hairy wrists that conjured up cocked fists and a fighting stance.

Once as a teenager I'd spent the night with Sharon in Monterey. I'd been asleep when she and Phil staggered in drunk, knocking the princess phone off her nightstand. Her wallpaper was stamped with images of Holly Hobbie, the little girl in the blue-checkered dress and oversized bonnet. My cousin and her date wrestled on the shag carpet, grunting. The sound of jeans unzipping catapulted me into hyperalertness. "Aw, c'mon, kiss it," Phil cajoled Sharon. *Kiss it? "*Touch it." Heavy breathing filled the room. Phil shed his jeans like someone filleting a fish.

"It won't bite," he coaxed. I heard my cousin sigh. I imagined her considering Phil's one-eyed wonder. She bent over, then sat up.

"I cahn't," Sharon said. "It's gwoss." She coughed.

I giggled. Phil flicked on the light and glared at me, his Fruit of the Loom boxers around his muscular ankles. Sharon threw her head back and laughed. Smoothing back her tangled hair, she winked at me and lit a Kool. Fumes spiraled around the pink Holly Hobbie lampshade. Sharon inhaled deeply, pulled a hair out of her mouth and looked at it. She rolled her eyes.

"How droll," she said.

Now, as Leroy stood before me, I recalled those tangled limbs, the aproned pioneer girl, that single hair extracted from my cousin's mouth like an offensive bit of gristle.

"You loving the Lord? You seeking His Face?" Leroy asked. I had been making cookies in the kitchen and he had ... appeared. It was hard to answer readily; I had just shoved a big spoonful of peanut butter cookie dough in my mouth.

"Mumdgh," I said, nodding and trying to chew without moving my jaw. The dough stuck to the roof of my mouth. "Dugmgh."

"I don't even want to be around people who don't love Jesus." He peered into the bowl, sniffed. "What's this? What are you making?"

"Mookies."

His upper lip shot forward. "Mookies?"

"Cookies," I said, swallowing at last. "*Cookies.*"

"Ah."

Looking into my eyes, he dipped his hand into the bowl, and pinched off two fat inches of dough. Never wavering, he popped the mixture into his mouth.

"Hallelujah," he said sternly, chewing slowly.

THE FIRST DAY BACK FROM VACAVILLE WAS ALWAYS HARD FOR Ella. She was short and snappish with us, weighed down by private thoughts.

We watched as she slowly unpacked her overnight bag and placed her belongings back on her bunk shelves: King James Bible, hairbrush, hand cream, Troll doll.

"How's Chuck?" Gretchen asked, sitting cross-legged in her bunk, her hand in a bag of Pepperidge Farm Orange Milano cookies. "Is he still with the Lord? Did you guys get a chance to be together?"

"Chuck's fine," Ella said curtly, draping her good slacks over a hanger. "The Lord is doing a work in his heart."

"Just in his heart?" Gretchen teased.

Ella shook her head and sighed. I had crushes on some of the brothers and had indulged in a few motor-home-and-concertina-wire fantasies myself, but I would never admit this to Ella or anybody else. These were carnal, shallow, unworthy thoughts. It couldn't have been easy for Ella living with a bunch of moony women who liked to read the Song of Songs aloud and speculate about who would get married next (we were a regular marriage factory). Ella, who wasn't even twenty, was already well schooled in disillusionment and disappointment. Love wasn't some comely shepherd with grape leaves in his hair; love was sitting in a cigarette-strewn bus terminal waiting for a Greyhound that would take you to a grim room where you would be glumly searched and prodded for contraband. Love was unpacking your suitcase after a five-hour trip, smoothing out that blouse you'd bought on lay-away at Sears and asking your husband, "What's new?" even when you realized that nothing was new nor would be new for a very long time. Ella had character – she hung in there with Chuck and she hung in there with us – but that didn't make her my friend. Ella evoked in me a disdain so deep that even now I barely understand it. She was simple and plain and vulnerable, completely without artifice. Why did I scorn her for that? Because she frightened me. She was trying to follow Jesus, serve Him, honor her vows, do the right thing. While Chuck was doing his time in Vacaville, Ella was doing hers at the ranch. Was this the kind of perfect obedience the Lord required, this passive, animal acquiescence? Ella was being broken, bit by bit, her will bent into a shape beyond her reckoning. I did not want to turn into Ella.

Aunt Clarissa

FIVE ACRES. THAT WAS THE SPAN OF THE LAND WE ALL LIVED ON. It was two miles to the nearest house, five miles to the highway, twelve miles to town. Below was the pale brown sand of the beach and across the road, the pretty meadow with its fairy-tale toadstools and flowers. The cypress with their wild branches hugged the bluff. Room enough for everyone, one might think. However, it was easy to feel claustrophobic because there was no simple access to town. This world at the edge of the world felt isolated. Sometimes, working in the middle of the day, maybe sweeping out the dining hall or scrubbing the toilet on my knees, I could feel the heartbeat of the place, the pulse of sweat and prayer. Time alone was a gift I stole, working at it slowly like a lock picker.

Everybody had a job, whether at the ranch or in town. The ministry supported itself through several businesses, including a bakery and a newspaper, *The Tri-City Advertiser*, a weekly shopper delivered on foot by ranch residents to the good people of Eureka, the nearest town. The *Advertiser* was the junk mail of newspapers – everybody complained about it, and nobody wanted to admit that they actually read that fish-wrapper. At the same time, readers bitched if they didn't get it. It was a fact of life, like toilet paper. As much as the locals sneered at it, they read it faithfully, selling hunting dogs, buying rebuilt alternators, snapping up miracle algae that promised renewed sexual vigor and enlightenment. Short on editorial content, it spanned twenty finger-smudging pages of want ads, interspersed here and there with pithy proverbs. Scanning its pages, someone might read: *Wanted: used oboe. Will trade for pygmy goat.* Beneath it might be this Bible verse: "The words of a gossip are like choice morsels; they go down to a man's inmost parts" (Proverbs 18:8). During my first months at the ranch, I was kept far from the vulgate of the world. I was a baby Christian who needed protection back on the land, where I could grow hardy on The Word. In the mornings, I watched as a few of the brothers who sold ads for the *Tri-City Advertiser* readied for their daily trip to Eureka, swinging their faux leather briefcases and strutting in their wool blend suits from J.C. Penney's. The day beckoned and they planned to seize it, selling ads for hot tubs and time-shares in Maui and witnessing to dolorous housewives too. God has a plan for your life! Sign on the dotted line! With a spring in their step, the men sallied forth, leaving many of the women behind to tend to the babies, make the pumpkin bread, weed the Swiss chard, and wash endless loads of laundry.

"Cripes, these guys go through their clothes faster than a newborn in diapers," a new sister might complain, and I would silently agree. The only break in the work routine was on Thursdays – the day every able-bodied person from the ranch delivered the free paper. That's when we broke up into teams and, armed with sack lunches and maps, hit the streets and pitched papers. Eureka symbolized the world, lost souls who needed Jesus. When somebody in town called the ranch elders and complained that a shaggy-haired paperboy (a babe in the Lord, no doubt) had dumped a load of *Advertisers* into a backyard creek, there was hell to pay. Temptation was everywhere; best to step smartly, stay vigilant. Be friendly, share Jesus, and get those papers on porches!

The mornings were often cool and foggy, smelling of wood smoke and the ocean. As I walked, tossing my papers, the sky turned a greasy gray. Dogs barked. A light flickering in the window triggered fantasies about the people inside. I pictured a teenage boy in his undershirt drinking orange juice out of the carton in front of an open refrigerator, or an old woman with knobby hands absentmindedly stroking the tabby cat on her lap. People looked hard at me and I looked back, hardly looking.

"Morning," I called as I sailed down the sidewalk, saluting them with a rolled up *Advertiser*. "Jesus loves you!"

My heavy canvas vest – loaded down with newspapers and rubber bands – bumped against my chest. Walking the streets of Eureka, waving to strangers, throwing newspapers, I prayed to Jesus. Are you real? Give me faith. I believe. Am I really saved? Is this my life now?

WHEN I WAS ASKED TO HELP OUT WITH THE NEWSPAPER, I WAS ready. The *Advertiser* operation was on B Street, in Jim's old real estate office, Sequoia Realty. The editor, Leo, knew nothing about the business end of newspapering, but he quickly absorbed the rhythms of ad deadlines and showed a remarkable flair for layout and design. By my lights, Leo was an old-timer in the Lord. He'd been saved two years earlier and lived at the ranch in a dinky beige and brown trailer with his pregnant wife, Rose, and Rose's young daughter. Rose and her daughter had come to the ranch seeking distance from a difficult husband as well as from the cops in San Francisco, because Rose had been busted for dealing marijuana. One look at the handsome Leo and she was loop-de-loop over the moon. Blood called to blood. He sang. She sang. There was so much sexual electricity between them, you almost expected them to crackle.

The elders at the ranch finally consented to their marriage after it was clear Rose wasn't going to reconcile with her first husband and her divorce became final. Or perhaps they suspected the lovers were sneaking off to a Eureka hotel once a week on their day off.

Everybody got one day off. Sometimes, if someone had a car, we'd ride around on the back roads, exploring the Victorian village of Ferndale, nosing around in the old-fashioned mercantile store. Or sometimes in our cut-offs and halter tops, we went swimming in the south fork of the Trinity River. Clambering over the hard oval river stones, we flung ourselves onto the sand, angling ourselves just so under the burning sun. Inhaling the redwoods, we sucked our stomachs in. The idea was to do something, go somewhere – anywhere – before the hours vanished and we were back in harness. Like the rest of us, Leo and Rose didn't hang around the land on their day off. I don't know where they went but I like to think they checked into a hotel, where they ate hash brownies and made tantric love for hours, then slipped back to the ranch, fragrant with pheromones and chocolate, limber as Gumby dolls.

Leo, who wanted me to help out reading copy, advised me to read a skinny little volume, Strunk and White's *The Elements of Style*, and to learn copyediting symbols. He'd typeset the ads and on Tuesday nights, after downing cinnamon rolls from the bakery next door, we'd set about cutting and pasting with razor-sharp, pencil-sized X-acto knives and jars of sticky glue.

On Wednesdays, Leo drove to Crescent City, where the camera-ready pages were printed. On Thursdays, we delivered. On Friday evenings, the deadline for ads was five o'clock, and so began another cycle: used baby clothes, lost dogs, and *"The sluggard craves and gets nothing."*

Working downtown one day a week was a refreshing change from the ranch routine, where chopping thirty heads of cabbage for cole slaw and making a dozen loaves of banana bread could consume a morning. Working in Eureka meant shops, the library, and Woolworth's up the street. It meant having your own desk, a desk that actually locked, and being seen as someone who had ideas and maybe even a little talent.

As the months went by and Leo became more familiar with writing headlines, cutlines, and editing, he began to fancy himself a real newspaper editor, not some backshop hack. Why not run articles?

"We could be more," Leo said to me one Tuesday night, expertly lining up a column of ads. The bottom one said: *Young bunnies. Good for eating or as Easter pets.*

"More than what?" I said.

Leo looked dreamy, deftly holding the X-acto in his hands like a surgeon's scalpel. Little did I know that in fifteen years' time, both he and Rose would be doctors. "More than what we are!"

"And what would that be, Leo?" I said, exasperated.

"A real newspaper."

"Real newspapers have reporters," I retorted. I took a swig of tepid coffee, then made a face.

Leo looked up at me and grinned. A lock of curly brown hair fell over one eye.

"What about you?"

"What *about* me? I don't have any experience."

Leo was silent for a long moment. Then he snapped his fingers and strode over to a large book filled with clip art and photographs of people's faces.

"Experience, huh?" he grunted, flipping through the pages. I peered over his shoulder. A vampy-looking woman with Veronica Lake hair flew by, followed by an aproned Aunt Bea type. The pages made a slapping sound. I saw an ashen-faced pharmacist with a pencil behind his ear chased by a gap-toothed freckled girl in pigtails. Then my eyes fell on the face of a woman with snow white hair piled high in an elaborate bun.

"Hold on," I said. "Just a second."

The woman's eyes shone behind her steel-rimmed glasses, as if she had a secret. A cardigan draped around her narrow shoulders was fastened with a pearl clasp. Somebody's eccentric aunt? A former nun gone sour on the world? No, wait, look closer. See the way the corners of her mouth turn up in a saucy smile? A godmother, perhaps, in sneakers and pedal pushers, who hands out boxes of chocolate-covered cherries and crisp twenty-dollar bills. A kind face, lined and mild, not easily shocked, quick to laughter. A real friend.

"So what do you think?" Leo said.

"Who is she?" I asked, squinting at the picture.

Leo laughed. "That's the beauty. She's anybody you want her to be. You tell me."

"She is pretty," I said.

"So are you," Leo said loyally, and I remembered all the reasons why Rose fell in love with him in the first place.

"Not like her. She looks like somebody's aunt. Classy."

"We could make her a food expert. You know, with recipes and stuff. She could have a regular weekly column." Leo was getting excited. "We could print recipes, letters, and maybe have, like, an ongoing saga about cooking. Bake-offs, cookie contests. A column would be great for ad revenue. Oooh, it would be fun!" I stared at him in disbelief. I'd never seen this domestic side of him before.

"But who is she, Leo? I can't just make her up out of thin air!"

"Oh, sure you can," he chuckled, deftly cutting the woman's head out of the clip art book with his X-acto. As he held her in the palm of his hand, his wedding ring caught the light. It was two in the morning and we were zombies, strung out on caffeine and sugar and the possibility of Real Journalism.

"Can I see her for a sec?" I said.

He handed the little paper oval to me. I stared at her face.

I could be you, I thought. Let me be you. Let me have your life and all it holds, good or bad. The woman's eyes beamed back at me, the way car headlights seemed to bounce and shimmer on a foggy night. I don't know how long I stared at her. Five seconds? Twenty? A minute? Leo yawned and cleared his throat. He ran a hand through his curly hair.

"I'm dead," he said.

He turned off the lights.

I left the woman on my desk, propped up against a Boston fern, dreaming in a pool of moonlight.

Shy Hotdog Pie

AS THE NEW *TRI-CITY ADVERTISER* FOOD COLUMNIST, AUNT Clarissa was supposed to come up with exciting new recipes for our readers. Of course, the modest newspaper office at the corner of 5th and B Streets in Eureka was nothing like *Sunset* magazine's sprawling headquarters in Menlo Park. Sunset boasted a gleaming 1,000-square-foot test kitchen where senior editors and "guest chefs" could test 2,000 recipes a year. We had no test kitchen, no hair net–wearing "researchers" whipping up new variations of Pineapple Upside Down Cake. Aunt Clarissa didn't believe in research. She lifted recipes from library cookbooks or back issues of *Good Housekeeping*, sometimes changing the ingredients to fit her mood. It never occurred to her that she should at least try the recipes first or, failing that, get permission from the cookbook publishers. Copyright infringement? Plagiarism? What was the problem? After all, with a simple modification or two – a teaspoon more of baking powder, a skosh less Crisco, give or take a few other key ingredients – the recipes would be utterly original.

Aunt Clarissa had an imaginary sidekick – a pet hamster with twitching whiskers named Alfred. She carried him in her floury apron pocket. He kept her company as she whirled around the fictional kitchen, box stepping from canister to canister. She was a bit of a space cadet, a nut, a dreamy rebel, although judging by her appearance – the silver hair, the bun, the wire-rimmed glasses – she certainly wasn't a victim of typecasting. My alter-ego had a secret self, another life. She was quirky, a blend of Miss Clavel and Auntie Mame. Like me, Aunt Clarissa wanted to be good, but she also wanted to have fun. I tried to keep her on the straight and narrow, but Aunt Clarissa wasn't really interested in cooking. She wanted to wander off the page with her bad self, really bust loose, maybe float over the Grand Canyon in a hot air balloon or race Siberian huskies in the

Iditarod. With every column, she grew bolder. She was becoming whacked, strange, weird on a stick.

It never occurred to me that a cooking column featuring a made-up spinster with a pet rodent – a palm-sized doughboy that might actually poop in the cook's pocket or leave Raisinette-sized turds on the counter – would turn some readers off. I was seldom troubled by thoughts about Aunt Clarissa's relationship to her alleged readers because they seemed hypothetical at best. I doubted that anyone read "Aunt Clarissa's Kitchen." During the few short months she appeared in the paper, wedged between camera-ready ads for lawn mowers and Bible verses, she never received as much as a postcard. Mail was for people with fans and critics. Aunt Clarissa had neither. But in the laboratory of her soul, she experimented and flourished, coming up with catchy names for the recipes. Companies like General Mills invest millions to come up with the right word combinations so their products will appeal to a mass audience. This was Aunt Clarissa's forte. She had a natural feel for words – and more than that, she had whim. One of her favorite recipe names was "Shy Hot Dog Pie," a dish that included a frozen pie crust, a 16-oz. can of Van de Kamp's baked beans, and 2 cups of sliced hot dogs. The hot dogs were baked in a sea of legumes until they plumped up nicely, their tips poking up through the crust like little foreskins.

After a few months of "Aunt Clarissa's Kitchen," Leo suggested we drop the column (it hadn't generated any additional ad revenue) and develop another one instead: "The Bargain Lady." It would be a fantastic advertising tool, he said. Think of the potential! As the Bargain Lady, I could browse through the shops in downtown Eureka, talk to the storeowners, and write a little column on the week's bargains. And of course I could witness to people in town. I hated to kill off Aunt Clarissa, but she had started to seem a little unpredictable, even to me.

Leo and I came up with a slogan for "The Bargain Lady," which we ran under a photograph of me in a brown tam-o'shanter. The slogan said:

Something new,
something old,
something for you

that hasn't been sold!

Carrying a notebook, I moseyed around the town, browsing in head shops and hardware stores, boutiques and cafes. There was no trick to writing "The Bargain Lady"; I just wrote about what I would've bought if I'd had a few dollars. I was ghost-shopping, pretending to be a tourist on vacation, or a big-city reporter on assignment. After I introduced myself to a woman who ran a clothing consignment store on 4th Street, she gave me the once-over and said she wasn't interested.

"But I'm not selling anything!" I said.

"I know all about you. I even know where you live," she said with a dry chuckle.

"How can you tell?" I tried to summon a smile.

"By the glazed expression on your face," the woman snapped. Her streaked blonde hair was styled away from her face in golden wings, like Farrah Fawcett's on *Charlie's Angels*. "All of you people have that ... look. All you brainwashed freaks live at the Lighthouse Ranch."

At the lunch counter in Woolworth's, I felt led to witness to a bearded man in a Harley-Davidson jacket. He was eating a toasted cheese sandwich and reading the *Eureka Times-Standard*.

"Excuse me, but do you know the Lord?" I said, fingering the religious tract in my pocket.

"Oh, buzz off," he said, barely glancing up from the sports page.

"Sir, I bring you the Good News."

"Get bent, lady."

I remembered the scripture from the First Book of Corinthians about becoming a fool for Christ. By God, I'd be that fool. Gingerly I slid a tract next to his coffee cup. It said: "Getting Right with God." The man looked up. I was staring into the face of someone Truly Perturbed.

"What is it with you people?" he said, leaning forward. His nose was three inches from mine. His breath smelled like Copenhagen chewing tobacco mingled with a spicier note: marijuana. The pores on his face seemed to expand and contract with each word he spoke. "Worry about your own soul, why don't you?"

"OK, OK," I sputtered, noting his matted hair and large wrists. The image of an angry water buffalo on an African veldt floated through my head. I could almost see the outline of anger shimmering around his body as he pawed the dusty ground, preparing to charge. *Whomp, whomp, whomp, whomp.* Through clenched teeth the biker said, "Do not think. For one moment. That you can fuck with me." He took the tract and ripped it up.

"I apologize profusely," I said, backing away.

"Go to fucking hell."

No apologies were necessary at the Eureka Public Library on 3rd Street. Walking down the narrow aisles, staring at the titles, my heart rate slowed. I wasn't a Jesus Freak or the Hound from Heaven, I was a reader, a seeker of knowledge on equal footing with all the other seekers. I looked at the people settled in chairs reading magazines and books. They seemed like contented grazing cows, munching the pages under the calm fluorescent lights. I was part of this herd. Brain food. If you held your breath, you could hear the sound of mental mastication. The library provided a breather from the ranch. The atmosphere there was tinged with an end-time, purple twilight. We all seemed to be in a state of heightened awareness. The rapture was near. In the twinkling of an eye, Jesus would come like a thief in the night. This made me anxious. I didn't want to depart this world, not for all the cotton clouds of glory in the next.

Sitting at the oversized oak table near the card catalog, I opened my Bargain Lady notebook, read over my scribblings from the day. *Natural fiber dresses on sale at Nell's. Thirty percent off. Rice paper lampshades, two dollars each at Home Connection. Cards, stuffed animals, pens, stationery. Big liquidation at The Stationery Store!*

And then I wrote: *This morning at breakfast in the dining hall, eating yogurt, suddenly the room was full of sun. Light streamed through the thin curtains, creating a glow, almost a shiny mist. There was something in the air. The room had a restless quality to it. I felt like I was waiting for something to happen.*

I sighed. It felt so good to write; writing was more real than religion, more satisfying than scripture. I bent my head over my notebook and wrote about what that biker had said to me, and what I wished I had said in response. *I should've said God Loves You instead of I'm sorry, but I thought he was going to pop me.* I wrote about what I felt, what I knew, and what I feared to be true about myself. Writing, even in the public library, was private; it was mine. Writing meant I was alive, separate, wholly myself. Writing made me pay attention to my life, allowed me to utter what if? *I know I should be spending time in The Word but the Bible bores me. Heresy!*

Closing my notebook, I tracked down the books I'd read years before – *Franny and Zooey*, *Tender Is the Night*, even Mary McCarthy's steamy coming-of-age tale, *The Group*. Once more I read about Dottie getting fitted for her diaphragm at the Margaret Sanger Clinic, then losing her virginity to Dick. These books comforted me in ways that The Word or worship could not. God seemed silent, but these books actually talked back. They didn't bear the *Good Housekeeping* Seal of Approval from the Lighthouse Ranch elders; they weren't Christian allegories like *Hinds' Feet on High Places*, but they pointed me toward a better world – in this life. Books filled me with hope; they spoke, they were holy, they were dangerous. Books said "yes, step right this way, you are not alone." Trying to read myself into existence, I bent over Anaïs Nin's diaries and heard the clink of absinthe glasses in a Parisian cafe. Curled up in a big leather chair with *Cannery Row*, John Steinbeck stirred up tendrils of yearning as he described the foggy wharves I knew so well. I glanced at the clock by the checkout counter, but failed to note the placement of its hands. Instead I was transported back to my grandmother's lush garden in Monterey, a toddler wandering along its labyrinthine path under climbing yellow roses, pink hydrangea clusters, cherry trees, boughs of red fuchsias. Squinting at the pages, I saw my small bare feet slapping against bricks. I smelled juniper, mint, lemon, thyme, tangy salt air. I looked up through the roof of the library into the atmosphere of childhood, where I saw a break in the clouds, the promise of sun. I remembered. It came at me in sharp licks.

Rocks in a Tumbler

I WAS HOMESICK. MAYBE MY SOUL WAS EMITTING A HIGH-PITCHED mosquito hum of desperation without my knowledge. All of us send out unconscious signals that attract or repel. It's the timbre of somebody's voice calling up memories of a schoolyard bully, the shape of a lip that seems to curl in a sneer, the involuntary desire to touch a strange woman's shoulder because she smells faintly of gardenias and gardenias remind you of your grandmother singing as she gets dressed for church. We are sponges, all of us, blotting and absorbing, tasting and erasing. Are you sweet? Are you bitter? I don't like you, and I don't know why. Or: I don't know why I'm confiding in you, I've never seen you before in my life. Neurons fire, molecules spray like pollen, the mind turns like a kaleidoscope.

We tried to love one another with a holy love, but we were like rocks in a tumbler, constantly knocking against one another. The problem – then as now – was ego. Everybody had one. In the midst of that striving, it was helpful to think that those collisions could serve a spiritual end: all that knocking could chip away the soul's rough edges until we were as smooth as polished glass. But then again, we were people, not rocks, and some of us had a low tolerance for friction.

One rainy winter day, as I stood in the kitchen elbow-deep in bread dough, I glanced up and noticed a white Rambler pulling into the ranch's parking lot. A tall, broad-shouldered woman built like a phone booth and a pudgy teenage boy clambered from the car. One eye on the window, I fought with the dough, trying to subdue it into the smooth softness of a baby's bottom. And then the wooden door burst open, pushing in cold gusts of air.

"Glory to Gawd," the tall woman proclaimed, stepping across the threshold. A lumpen shadow followed her. I raised a sticky hand. She said her name was Nedra; she and her seventeen-year-old son, James, were from Crescent City, a small California city just south of the Oregon border. They'd come down this way because they felt "led" by the Holy Spirit, she said, nodding with approval as I punched and slapped at the dough.

Gretchen looked up from washing the Chinese cabbage, wiped her hands on her apron and curtsied. There was high color in her cheeks. Her eyes were shining too brightly. Sweat collected in the black stubble above her upper lip. "We welcome you to Munchkin Land," Gretchen said in a helium-pitched voice. "His mercy endureth forever."

"Do the elders know you're here?" I said, wiping my hands on my apron.

"Dear one, I called them as soon as the Lord gave me the word." Nedra's eyes never left my face. It was hard not to stare back. A black widow's peak accentuated her white skin. She carried her Bible with the sky blue leatherette cover tucked under her armpit, the gilt-edged pages riddled with bookmarks. Her white crepe-soled shoes squeaked on the cold cement floor as she shifted her weight from foot to foot. A polyester dress fluttered around muscular marble calves.

She strode over to the counter and peered into the bowl. "My, that's quite a job," she said, clucking her tongue. Her voice was definite and strong. I blew a strand of hair out of my eyes. She ran her eyes over my hair, my shoulders, down the length of my stooped body, considering, weighing, measuring. "But you ... seem up to the task." Her words were layered and mysterious. It was as if her sentences had been dredged in that bowl of flour; a powdery residue clung to the underside of her vowels. Even the most banal things Nedra said to Gretchen and me – "There's a cold wind blowing" or "That soup smells good" – came out sounding like someone reading tarot cards at midnight.

"How long are you staying?" I asked, pressing and pushing on the dough.

"Well, that's up to the Lord," Nedra said, glancing at her calf of a son. He stood next to her with a lowered head, breathing through his mouth, arms limp at his sides. He must've felt shy and a little awkward standing there, waiting to take a cue from his mama. This boy was so different from my three younger brothers, who were all druggy attitude and slouchy insolence. To my parents' despair, my brothers partied, smoked potent Hawaiian hash, cut school, and consorted with fast, older girlfriends. They didn't take cues from anybody.

It was hard to imagine James giving his mom any teenage guff. With a roll of flab around his middle, the faintest hint of a blonde mustache, and an intensity that I surmised had more to do with hormones than holiness, I found James more than a little strange. Later that night at Deliverance Temple, I studied him with covert fascination. When he sang, he cried. When he danced, spittle formed in the corners of his mouth. When he spoke in tongues, he brayed like the donkey in *Pinocchio*. When he prayed, he blubbered and lifted his milk-white arms like a frightened infant who wants the breast. He rocked on the balls of his feet with his eyes closed and said, "Praise you, Jesus! Praise you!" Like his mother, he was fired by some unfathomable candlepower. Jesus commands us to love one another, to lay down our lives for one another, but in church, as I watched James from the corner of my eye, I felt distinctly queasy. All I could see were tonsils.

People like Nedra and her son came to the ranch all the time. It wasn't unusual to find yourself sitting across from a family at breakfast who'd been homesteading in Alaska for a spell before deciding Jesus had other plans for their lives. Silent women with dead eyes and compressed lips showed up at the ranch seeking direction (and protection) from the men who beat them. Single dads alighted here too, as well as teenage runaways, ex-cons, potheads, and edgy loners with dog-eared copies of *Siddhartha* in their army fatigue jacket pockets. All that was required was a repentant heart, an unflagging work ethic, and submission to the ranch's rules. This was no vacation for Nedra and James. They were like clouds; they gusted about the land, forming and regrouping, doing chores like the rest of us. But in the back of my mind, I wondered what they were really doing here.

Every Thursday morning at the ranch, we got up at five and gathered in the chilly dining hall to collate *Advertiser* pages. By six, our thumbs were black with newsprint. By nine, abuzz with caffeine and sugary oat-meal, we'd been divided into delivery teams. Armed with sack lunches, cardboard street maps, and canvas vests, we headed into Eureka, ready to begin our routes. One morning James and I found ourselves sitting together in the ranch van, squashed by stacks of newspapers.

"How's it going?" James said. He punched me in the shoulder.

"Ow! Cut it out."

"Sorry!"

We rode on for a few miles without speaking. Then James said, "I used to have a paper route."

"That's nice," I said, looking out the window.

"Did you ever have a paper route?"

"Why aren't you in high school?" I said, turning to him. "What are you doing here anyway?"

"My mom is home-schooling me," James said.

"Sure she is," I said snidely.

"She doesn't trust the public school system. She thinks the teachers are godless people."

"Or mindless idiots," I murmured. I'd hated school.

"No," James said, "she never said that."

"So are you getting home-schooled while you're here at the ranch?" I said, needling James. "Are you studying?"

James gave me a big hungry smile. "Oh, I'm studying. Don't think for a moment that I'm not."

"So when do you graduate?"

"Whenever I have a mind to." *Then that will be never,* I thought. James yawned and stretched his arms up. His hand grazed the back of my neck. I shivered and sat forward. It was hot in the van now. The windows were all steamed up. In the condensed moisture on the glass I drew a cross.

"And then what will you do?" I asked James. "After high school?"

"I want to start a church," James said, breathing through his mouth in that irritating way of his. "I want to be a pastor."

We rode on in silence. It started to rain. I studied the ads in the *Advertiser.*

"What do you think about that?" James said. "Do you think I'd make a good pastor?"

"Boy, I don't know. I think you really have to have a calling."

"I really, really want to start a church though," James said.

"So where's your dad, James? Is he a pastor too?"

James swallowed. He looked forlorn.

"Is he up in Oregon? Or did he —"

"Jesus is my dad," James said slowly.

The van pulled over to the curb. We got out and started walking, pitching papers in the rain for James's dad.

JAMES KNOCKED ON THE DOOR OF THE SISTERS' DORM AND SAID he needed to see me. He stood at the door in a pair of cream-colored chinos and a pale blue sweater, breathing hard, fogging up the glass window in the door. Behind him, the elders' little house loomed in the fog.

"It's urgent," he hissed, his blond hair plastered to his forehead. He looked feverish. "I need to talk to you." I stared at James.

"James, I, uh, was reading The Word. Can we talk later? Maybe tomorrow?"

James shook his head and stamped a sneaker. "Trust me, it's got to be now."

"Why?" *You big baby.*

He pressed his lips together. His jaw became tight. "You'll see," he said. I thought he was going to cry. I was about to say "No" and close the door when James put up his hand. "Please," he whispered, spreading his fingers.

"OK, hang on, give me a minute. I'll meet you in the dining hall."

I shut the door. Gretchen, sitting cross-legged on the couch, a pair of tweezers in her hand, said, "What's he want?" Depression, that black dog, had been herding her for days.

"I have no idea," I said, sighing.

"Ugh, he's a child, a repulsive little child," Gretchen said, then added, "bless his heart."

James and I sat side by side in front of the heater in the dining hall. I could hear sounds emanating from the kitchen, laughter and the clanking of industrial-sized pots being stirred with a metal spoon. The fragrance of steamed kale, rice, and soy sauce floated over the heavier odor of heating oil. James inched closer to me and took one of my hands. I sniffed: Clearasil.

I took my hand back. "So what's up, James?"

"God," he croaked and swallowed hard. "God spoke to me. God ..." His chin quivered. The word "God" swam between us as his mother squeaked into the dining room. Her crepe-soled shoes pivoted. She beamed at us. James shot her a pleading look and Nedra melted into the kitchen. Laughter floated from behind the door. Was she talking about us?

James cleared his throat and started again. "Do you know why we came to the ranch? God told me ... I would find a wife here."

"Really?" I said, and thought *Jesus, you wouldn't dare!*

James nodded. His eyes were shining. "He did. He showed me. He showed me it's you!"

"He *what?*"

James nodded through the tears coursing down his cheeks. He began rocking back and forth in his chair, chanting: "He showed me! He showed me! I had a dream! He said: 'Behold your bride.' And it was you!"

Oh Jesus, I prayed, *don't do this to me.*

"James," I said, hating myself and hating him. "Jesus may love you, but I don't."

"Oh, you will," he chirped.

"Not like that."

I looked at James and saw myself mirrored in his eyes. His loneliness, his fumbling eagerness, his desperate fantasies about finding a mate, finding somebody to love him, that was me too. I had crushes on brothers all the time, especially the devout ones who wouldn't give me the time of day, because they were so spiritual.

"All I'm asking is that you pray about this," James said, reaching for my hand again. He snuffled a little.

"OK, I'll pray about it, but I already know the answer."

"God," James promised, "will change your heart."

Bardo-matic

THE PRAYER ROOM WAS WHERE WE HOLED UP WHEN WE REALLY needed to seek God's face. It was a windowless musty room overflowing with bags of second-hand clothes, stacks of yellowed newspapers, and moth-eaten army blankets. The room had a mysterious aura. It was like the proverbial overflowing hall closet: when you opened the door, you were never sure what would come tumbling out. Sometimes when I walked by the room, I heard shouting, clapping, or muffled laughter. Once I saw a brother who'd been fasting for a week emerge from the Prayer Room in a radiant daze, tears streaming down his wan cheeks. What went on in there? Had he seen a burning bush?

After James's declaration, I decided to devote an entire day to praying and fasting in the Prayer Room. At six in the morning I stuck a "Do Not Disturb" sign on the door, got down on my knees, and pressed my face into a ripped orange Naugahyde couch. I was listening for that still, small voice, but all I heard was the roaring of my own thoughts – and the day unfolding on the other side of the door: pay phone ringing in the hall, metal breakfast gong clanging, toilet flushing. Jesus! Where are you, Lord? Quiet. Darkness. Shut up! Jesus. In the inky gloom, I pictured God's heart radiating love, pulsing kindness, enveloping me with a holy protoplasm. Was this my own fanciful imagining or was the Holy Spirit really in the Prayer Room? My heart felt like a fist wrapped in sandpaper. Still, I tried with a kind of desperate energy to leave behind the here-and-now, the world of palpable details, and listen to what God wanted to tell me. But again and again, the tangible reeled me back. As I burrowed my face in the cushions, all I could think about was how many butts had ever rested on the couch and whether Naugahyde could be dry-cleaned.

"Dear Jesus," I began again, "please show me a sign if I'm supposed to marry James." The pay phone in the hall rang again. "I don't love him, Lord. He's … disgusting. I'm sorry. I know, I know, you love him. And that's really great," I babbled on. I retreated under the ledge of that prayer to where I thought Jesus couldn't hear me and tacked on this unspoken addendum: *He's such a freak.* I tried to imagine what it would be like being in bed with James, James with his mayonnaise skin and quivering chin. I shivered.

"Lord," I begged, "please show me if this is your will." I needed to silence my own will, become as yielding as pummeled bread dough, so that the Lord could speak to me. The flesh, my ego, needed to die. As I tried to settle into prayer, my mind kept seizing on the first time I took acid with my old boyfriend Mark. A psychology student at the University of Maryland, he was constantly trying out psychology phrases on me, such as "defense mechanism," "passive aggressive," and "latent hostility." In addition to psychology textbooks, Mark was studying *The Psychedelic Experience: A Manual Based on the Tibetan Book of the Dead,* co-written by LSD guru Timothy Leary. Mark believed – as did Leary – that psychedelic drugs were a way to achieve a state of illumination. Tripping wasn't about getting stoned; tripping was a holy act. You could find spiritual liberation, awareness, absolute purity through cosmic voyaging. Mark talked often about the *bardo*, an element of Tibetan mysticism that describes the series of stages through which a spirit must pass to be reborn. Transcending the first *bardo* (there were three) was the hardest, fraught with hallucinatory peril as you struggled to silence the ego's yammering. Peaceful or wrathful visions could appear, and those visions could be overwhelming, but the idea was to remember they were all ego projections. Mark was so into *The Tibetan Book of the Dead* that he called his car, a dented red Lincoln that transported him from place to place, the Bardo-matic.

Tripping, we sat in his basement apartment in College Park, listening to Bob Dylan and staring at Mark's black-light posters. Under the ultraviolet light, the colored lines of the posters drifted like tufts of cotton candy, melting onto the walls. The drug gathered momentum and pushed in short shallow waves in the tidal basin of my brain. I was holding on, maintaining. Mark and I sipped Mateus Rosé out of Loony Tunes jelly glasses as Dylan's craggy voice sang about the Girl from the North Country. "She once was a true looo-oove of mine, a true love of mine, a true love of mine," Dylan sang, and I felt inexplicably sad. Mark had taken off his shoes and socks. His toenails were yellow, long, and curved. They looked like potato chips. I panted like a dog. I closed my eyes and thought about my parents across the Potomac in Arlington. I'd told them Mark and I were going to see the movie Z in Georgetown. Now I was tripping out of my mind. God, did it never end? The lies? The sneaking around? I was sixteen and way over my head with Mark. I closed my eyes and imagined the blood inching sluggishly through my veins like a long tapeworm.

"Mark," I said, "I'm scared."

"Shh," he said sagely, "don't worry. Go with it."

"No, I can't," I said, suddenly sitting up.

"Just rest. Don't worry about it."

I gripped my stomach and leaned back again. Mark's Bean Bag chair … Was it? Oh, god, it was. It was breathing in and out. I wasn't imagining it. The chair was … moving. I sat up again. "I can't do this."

"It's all a projection."

"I'm dying, Mark!"

"Go ahead, babe. Die. It's all right."

"How can you say that?"

"Hush," he said.

The colors from the black light drifted onto the rug. I blinked, studying the way they pooled and shimmered next to Mark's boots, like mercury dancing on an oil slick.

Let's go outside and walk around for a while, the LSD in me suggested. *Maybe that will stop my heart from hammering so hard.*

"Stop fighting it," Mark soothed.

"Why?"

"It's all in your mind."

The mercury gathered into a single silver ball and formed into a sleek comma, a long pause that turned into the shaved head of a monk. The monk's face had no eyes, no ears; it was as smooth as an egg. Dylan was singing about if dogs run free, why can't we, and someone was scatting along in the background. I wanted to go home, but I was in no shape to get there.

"Mark, I can't, oh shit, what's my name? I can't remember my name! Turn on the lights."

Mark lit a candle. He looked stern and rumpled, a cranky owl with ruffled feathers. Where had he flown in from? "Don't worry," my boyfriend said. "It's just your ego talking."

It's just your ego talking. Two years later in the Prayer Room, my ego was still nattering on. My brain itched. I fumbled for the lamp switch. Spots ran before my eyes as I tried to adjust to the light. Sitting on the couch, I closed my eyes again, opened my Bible at random and flipped open a page. I caught my breath. It was the Book of James! My index finger landed on this verse: "But when he asks, he must believe and not doubt, because he who doubts is like a wave of the sea, blown and tossed by the wind" (James 1:6).

What was *that* supposed to mean? As I pondered those words, I felt strongly that God was rebuking me for doubting Him, doubting His love for me, doubting that He had everything under control. James was just a projection, a symbol of my own lack of trust in the Lord. James was just, well, a manifestation of *bardol* transition. "Relax," Jesus told me. I breathed easier. By mid-afternoon, I was in a better frame of mind. The Lord and I,

I felt, were in accord about James. I was off the hook. I was even able to regard James without active dislike. Then I heard something outside the door that made my heart quail. James and his mother were standing in the hallway, and it quickly became obvious that they were talking about me. They were picking me apart, analyzing my hair, my appearance, the way I spoke, the way I couldn't carry a tune – "not even in a bucket!" – according to the chuckling Nedra.

"Once we're married, I'm not going to let her wear those tight sweaters," James said. The adenoidal way he talked made everything sound like snot being strained through a sieve. *Glubba glubba glubba.* "Or those little strappy shoes with the heels," Nedra said. "Mercy, they're loud. And dangerous. That girl could hurt herself." They were talking about my sandals, a pair of pointy-toed Candies I'd fished out of the Free Box last month. "Mama, I do love her though," James said. *Glubba.*

I sat very still on the orange couch, listening to them talk, afraid they would open the door and find me on the other side with a twisted grimace on my face. All the progress I thought I'd made that afternoon, the equanimity I'd achieved in coming to a place of tender peace about James, vanished, replaced by inexhaustible frustration.

Gretchen was right. He was a repulsive little child. Another hour dragged by. Two. I stayed inside, too proud to break for dinner.

At seven o'clock, I left the Prayer Room. In the garden, I drank in the fresh cold air. I stank, even to myself. My breath had fins. I exuded sweat and musk and hair oil. After hours by myself in that room, red hours, hot hours, pacing inside my brain, worrying about James and Nedra, it was good to be outside. I stood on the bluff and watched the black waves, steady as my heart, beating, beating. There was a presence on the bluff. God was everywhere – in the sky, on the beach below, in the rippling grass beneath my feet. The wind caught my sweaty clothes, and I raised my arms. It felt like Jesus was bathing me with that cool, cleansing wind. At that moment, my ego felt as small and ordinary as a rock in my pocket. But even then, I knew it was alive, hard and round and of this world.

Nedra never acknowledged me after I told her son I couldn't marry him. Telling James wasn't hard, I didn't like him. I didn't like Nedra either, but she scared me with her spooky way of interpreting God's will. A few weeks after I rebuffed James, they left. Perhaps the Lord was leading them on another wife-finding mission for James. Or perhaps the original message from God had gotten scrambled in the translation. In that superheated atmosphere, it was easy to do. Sometimes now I think about James, his fervor, his tears, the way he raised his arms in praise at Deliverance Temple and danced in the Spirit. Did he ever find a wife to match his intensity? Did he ever become a preacher? I wish I could see a man who has finally grown into the fullness of himself, but James is frozen in time for me, chubby, gonadal, pale, and earnest – a teenager with a fierce mama. In memory, through the years, he drifts on an ice floe, speaking in tongues and dancing. He sweats. He cries. He brays and dances. His nuts are swollen. Lips open, teeth bared, through his mouth, into the wetslick cavernous maw at the back of his aching throat, I glimpse his red, raw essence. Tonsils.

Glazed Raised

WHEN MY LOVE AFFAIR WITH JESUS EXPANDED TO A FLESH-and-blood infatuation with Forrest Prince, my parents realized it was time they paid me a visit. Change was in the air for all of us. My father had just taken a job with the Army again, this time as a civilian. In a matter of months he would be moving to Germany. My mother and the boys would stay behind until the house was sold. I wanted them to meet Forrest, although I wasn't sure exactly how to explain our relationship. Forrest grew up in Plumas County, in the foothills of the Sierra Nevada Mountains. His parents were hardworking country people, modest and unassuming and unpretentious. Forrest mustered that simple ancestral spirit when he sang and played the guitar in church. He didn't sing or play particularly well, but what he lacked in melody, he made up for in enthusiasm. Everything about Forrest was larger-than-life, from his broad shoulders to his baguette-sized feet to his piercing blue eyes. Forrest's rich baritone soared at church services in Deliverance Temple while he strummed his guitar, repeating a few simple chords. His eyes roamed the congregation until they locked on mine. His powerful forearms were something to watch, hard and ropy, tendons dancing under the skin. Sitting among the swaying, arm-waving, clapping crowd, I tried to keep my mind on Jesus as Forrest played.

Ha na sham ma lo. Koti boti ma. Thank you, Jesus! *Harem mesh a la.* Praise you, Lord!

Forrest and I shared a secret, a burden. One day, soon after we had become close friends, we were doing our laundry in the basement beneath the Mothers' House. I wanted to confide in him right then that I was often plagued by impure thoughts and actions. But making the leap from pairing cotton knee socks to talking about hand jobs was very daunting. Self-abuse was a no-no – we all knew that. Yet orgasm felt holy too, a gift from God. You gasped and quivered like a fish, twitching against the inevitable reeling in of ecstasy. You fought, you flopped, you came, you died and were reborn. The psalmist writes of being "fearfully and wonderfully made" and I was, by God, I was. I was a regular marvel.

"Listen," I said, "there's something I need to tell you. I feel really bad about this. Sometimes I, well –"

Forrest's blue eyes didn't waver. He nodded his head knowingly. Gazing back at my friend, I knew he'd been a fish too. He'd been a gasper.

He held up a palm as if he were about to testify. "It's something I struggle with," I said.

"Hey, everybody does," he said.

I stared at the heap of clothes on top of the dryer, suddenly feeling shy. So now he knew.

"I hope you won't think less of me because of this," I said.

"Are you kidding?" Forrest pulled me to him. I burrowed into his chest. His flannel shirt smelled like Tide. I could feel his loyal heart pumping. Was that a bump in his jeans? "You're a godly woman," he said.

"No, I'm not."

"Don't argue with me, Miss Fallon."

I looked up at him. "What are we going to do about it?"

He squeezed me tighter. "Give it to God."

So we gave it to God. And sometimes we took it back. Forrest was seventeen; I was eighteen. Hormones had the upper hand. I knew the body was a temple, a sacred vase, and that the Holy Ghost, like a rare orchid plucked from a steaming, tropical rain forest, was supposed to dwell there. I prayed to keep the container pure, filled up with God's living waters. And if that didn't work, I prayed that my bunkmates wouldn't hear my sighs of wonder and pleasure. At those moments, I felt strangely… edified. Afterwards, doing chores on the land, I was centered and content; my heart brimmed with well-being, even though I knew I was probably going straight to hell. Even when I hadn't succumbed in weeks, I would sniff my fingers, searching for traces of myself.

It was good to have someone to confide in. I wasn't in love with Forrest but I liked the idea of having a boyfriend. Somebody – a guy! – who would sit with me on the bus on the way home from church and cradle my hand, a person I could confide in and, sometimes, with whom I could discreetly neck on starry nights down at the beach. He was sweet and devout, and even now I believe that high-octane sincerity – a potent mixture of lust and faith – can propel us out of our sorry selves, if only we can harness it. Forry!

In a few years' time, my friend would reject the idea of a supernatural god and life in the hereafter. Embracing the Humanist philosophy, he would come to believe that the here-and-now is the only life anyone ever gets, and you might as well live it as deliberately as possible. He would settle near Fresno, marry, father a son, divorce. In his forties, he would trade his desk job for work as a truck driver.

But as a teenager, Forrest was gung-ho for Jesus. He worked as a deliveryman for the Donut Shop, one of several ministry businesses run to keep the ranch afloat. Every weekday morning, he and several other brothers hawked donuts door to door in Eureka. In their white slacks, white shirts, and white paper hats perched rakishly on their heads, the brothers were supposed to be godly witnesses, bright beacons in a dark and craven world. The Glazed Raised were one dollar a dozen, but God's love was free and always on special. Jesus loves you! Yes, ma'am, we're fresh out of the Maple Bars, but here's a proverb to sweeten your day. This one's on the Baker Upstairs.

Each Donut Brother was assigned a route. In the rain, through the fog, they pushed their wooden carts down driveways, past barking dogs, taking care not to get the wheels stuck in mud or excrement, whistling, singing songs, praying. I imagine them hitching up their pants, adjusting their hats, ringing the doorbell, getting ready to witness to that face at the door. Like Kabuki dancers acting out time-honored roles, the housewife in curlers stares at the gap-toothed young man with the 1,000-watt smile. He's grinning and holding out a sweaty package of Glazed Raised.

"No!" she says, shaking her head, tightening the belt of her bathrobe as she starts to close the door. And then, showing that while she means business, she does have manners: "No, thank you anyway."

Sometimes the tempo changes. The man in the hat proffers donuts, money changes hands, then his cute butt – high and rounded from so much walking – recedes down the street. Or sometimes, invited in for coffee, he waltzes over the threshold. *The Price Is Right* is blaring on TV, the drooling baby in the highchair is covered with oatmeal and sports a diaperload so potent it causes the Donut Brother's eyes to tear up. No matter, because he's being called to minister to this lost woman. She's not just lonely or bored, she's being led to hear the Good News. The brother holds her hands as she bows her head and prays the Sinner's Prayer, asking Jesus to come into her heart. Salvation, a sugar fix, a curt word, or a lunging, hyperactive Airedale: the brothers never knew who or what was on the other side of the door.

Those of us left behind at the ranch prayed for these men and all the souls they would encounter on their routes. Men of God. Men of white cotton. Men of lard and lemon glaze. When Forrest returned after a hard day selling Buttermilk Bars, smelling faintly of cinnamon and dusted with powdered sugar, he entertained me with stories.

"You'll never guess what happened to me today," he said one fall afternoon. It was an Indian summer and the weather, after a few depressing days of drenching rain, was finally clear. Light streamed in through the tall narrow windows. Forrest sipped a cup of Swiss Miss in the dining hall, shaking his head in bemusement.

"What?"

"I met this woman today on my route. She said, 'Would you mind coming in for a minute?'" Forrest cleared his throat.

"And you led her to the Lord," I said, smiling.

"Not exactly."

"But you prayed with her, right?"

"No, not that either." Forrest's cheeks reddened. His blue eyes blazed in their sockets. "Hoo, boy," he said. "Thank you, Lord."

"And?" I prompted. Forrest was a flaming extrovert. It was hard to understand how selling donuts could rattle him.

He wiped his face with a napkin. "She wanted to know all about the Lighthouse Ranch, what life was like here, and why I was so … zealous."

"You witnessed to her?"

Forrest looked off into space, the cocoa forgotten. He said slowly, "She said this weird thing. She said, 'You know, if you ever feel the need for a woman, up close, I'd be willing to do that for you here, right now.'"

"Oh, dear God," I said, stifling the urge to laugh.

"I'm serious," Forrest said. He bit his lip and tried not to smile.

"What did she look like?"

"Oh, average-looking. She looked like somebody's mom."

"A *mom* propositioned you?"

"She said, 'You're such a fine young man, and I'd hate to see it go to waste. I'd like to … make love to you.'" My heart beat a little faster.

"Yikes." I tried to picture a woman in sweats and sneakers making a pass at Forrest. Maybe her hair was tied up in a bandanna like Lucille Ball's on I Love Lucy. It was hard to imagine a middle-aged woman flirting with Forrest Prince, not because he wasn't cute, but most people in town made fun of the Donut Brothers. To be honest, they looked a little ridiculous in their white uniforms and paper hats. A guy with a Bible wheeling a cart full of Maple Bars isn't the sexiest sight in the world. Maybe that housewife was the spawn of Satan. Maybe she got a perverse thrill from seducing young male Christians who were trying to stay pure. Maybe Forrest had been tempted too.

"Were you tempted, Forrest?"

"I ... of course I wasn't tempted. What a thing to say!" Forrest looked down at his high tops.

"I'm sorry." A few seconds passed. A brown skin had formed on the top of Forrest's cocoa. "So then what did you say to her?"

"I said thanks but no thanks."

"What did she say?"

"Actually she was very polite about it. She smiled and said, 'No hard feelings.'"

"'No hard feelings'? That's it?"

"No, she bought two dozen custard-filled Maple Bars."

"Well, that's good," I said, a little curtly.

"She said the offer still stood. She said I could come back any time."

"That certainly was nice of her."

"Are you upset?"

"Why should I be upset?"

"You sure?"

I shook my head. Forrest's story made me feel small and unattractive. I knew I shouldn't feel that way but I did. Nobody out in the world ever wanted to make love to me. Nobody worried about my body going to waste. Not that it mattered. Most of the time, it seemed like I was just lugging my body around anyway. It was just like a picture frame surrounding the real me, the spiritual me.

"By the way, you got a letter from your mom," I said, fishing around in my apron pocket for the unopened letter. I tossed it at him and resisted the urge to say, "Here you go, stud."

Forrest's mother was a faithful letter writer. Her letters were penned in a wobbly hand and filled with motherly concern. She was worried about us "going all the way," she confessed, after Forrest had told her the Lord had "introduced" him to a Wonderful Woman of God who might possibly be Mrs. Forrest Prince someday. I shuddered to think what else he told her. Mrs. Prince's letters were honest and direct and filled me with hot embarrassment as I read them: "I know that what you two are feeling for each other seems right and natural, I know your bodies must be urging you into the completion of a beautiful act, but it's best to wait. Love, Mom."

The completion of a beautiful act? My mother would've sooner turned Republican than write a letter like that. Forrest and I. What did we have? If we'd been in "the world" we might've hung out, either by ourselves or in a group, but we wouldn't have felt the pressure to justify our attraction. In the fishbowl that was the ranch, where every relationship was scrutinized and weighed for its godly intentions, Forrest and I needed to hurry up quick and find out if we should marry or just be friends. There was no room for dalliances, ambivalence, flakiness, or for mysterious ambiguities of the heart. And now my parents were on their way to see me and Forrest. I had no idea what we would tell them.

Into the redwoods they drove north in their ancient VW bus. On windy Highway 101 they passed lumber mills, tourist traps that sold cheese logs and salad bowls and cases of Chablis. I can only imagine the conversation between them.

My father (lighting up the first of many unfiltered Camels): "So are we going to see the Dalai Lama, Jim Durkin? Do you think his excellency will be in residence at the summer palace?"

My mother: "Hell if I know, honey."

My father: "What's the boyfriend's name again?"

My mother (snorting): "Forrest. Prince."

My father: "Oh, good Christ."

My parents were wiser and more tolerant than most people. They understood irony and they appreciated a good joke, even if it was on them. But this trip couldn't have been fun for them. When they arrived, it was raining. Again. Still. Stepping across the sodden grass, I showed them around. Even as they made small talk with Forrest and me, I knew they were taking it in: the crude dining hall; the austere, windowless Prayer Room; the rustic "office" filled with bins of dried lentils, millet, whole wheat flour, and granola; the paint-by-numbers mural of the Last Supper; and most of all, the telling smell of poverty that hovered above the Cloroxed floors. I was fat, too, fatter than I'd ever been, with tight braids and a tugboat high ("Proud Mary! Rollin' on the River!") butt. It was alarming to them to find their daughter transformed into a grinning 144-pound Brünhilde, quoting Bible verses about a land of milk and honey.

My parents took Forrest and me out to a smorgasbord near Eureka famous for its authentic pioneer atmosphere, costumed help (Early American), trestle tables, and homemade bread. You almost expected to see Betsy Ross toting a kettle of beans or pulling a wagonload of pumpkin pies.

"Son, how long have you been at the Lighthouse Ranch?" my dad asked.

Forrest, beaming: "Well, sir, it's been about six months."

"Ah, and what do your parents think about this, Forrest?" My father leaned forward across the table, nose to nose with him. Forrest blinked in surprise. He wanted to please my father. I did too, but it was far too late for that. Was there a right answer? Was this a trick question? Forrest smiled uneasily and pulled on his earlobe. I felt sorry for him.

My father was in military mode. I knew it well. For years he'd been the front-door court-martialer, grilling pimply Lotharios. "And you say you're going where?" he'd ask my dates. "Have my daughter home no later than 2200 hours." He suspected (and rightly so) that we were up to no good. As my date and I crab-walked away from him, my father flung last-minute advice: "Don't smoke any funny cigarettes!" "Keep a quarter between your knees!"

"Well," my mother said, glancing around the smorgasbord, "this is certainly something!" It certainly was. The decor was an astonishing blend of Paul Revere and Herman Melville: pewter mugs, harpoons, tricornered hats, and fishing nets.

"This sure is a festive spot, honey," she said to me. A waitress sidled over. "Can I get you anything from the bar?"

"Let's have some of your house white," my dad said.

"Just iced tea for me," Forrest said quickly. "I'd love a beer but … "

"Let me guess," said my dad. "You're not twenty-one?"

"No, sir, I'm not."

"How old are you, son?"

(Proudly): "I'm seventeen, sir."

"Any college plans?" my mother asked, hungrily reaching for the bread. It occurred to me that all of us were starving. We tore into the bread, chewing as nervously as squirrels stocking up before a blizzard.

"It's up to the Lord, Mrs. Fallon," Forrest said. "I'm waiting on Him."

Now that a carafe of the house white had appeared, my parents seemed more chipper. "How will you know?" my mother said playfully. "I mean, will He mail you an application?"

"Ha, ha, Mom," I said.

"Tell me, young man," my dad said, "what do your parents think about you living at the Lighthouse Ranch?"

Forrest had just tucked a big piece of buttered bread into his mouth. His teeth were working hard. "Well, Mr. Fallon," he began earnestly. I watched him chew. His ears were moving up and down as he chomped. I stared at his Adam's apple, transfixed. Finally he swallowed. And spoke. "My dad thinks this is all a bunch of baloney. My mom, well, she's a Christian. She loves the Lord and all, she's saved, she just doesn't understand why I can't serve Him at home."

"Understandable," my dad said, tapping one end of a cigarette on the wooden table, then reaching for his lighter. Oh, brother, I thought. Now he's slipping into his Socratic mode. Ask him what time it is and he'll give you the history of Big Ben.

"Why can't you?" my dad said.

"Why can't I what, sir?"

My dad inhaled and regarded the young man in overalls sitting across from him. His face was impassive as he plucked a piece of tobacco from his tongue and studied it for a second before flicking it away. "Why can't you serve the Lord at home?"

Forrest closed his eyes for a moment. I gripped the edge of the table, willing him to answer. Forrest's eyelids snapped open.

"Mr. Fallon, have you met the Lord?"

"I believe I have," my dad replied evenly, "although I know him by a different name, many names, in fact. Buddha, Krishna, Mohammed, Jehovah…"

"Sir, actually, it's" – and here Forrest coughed. "It's Jesus. King of Kings. Lord of Lords. The Lily of the Valley, the Bright and Shining Star, the –"

"Understood, son, understood, and it's also Yahweh and Allah."

"Mr. Fallon, I don't mean to –"

"*Om Mani Padme Hum*," my dad interrupted.

"What?" said Forrest.

"*Om Mani Padme Hum*. 'Behold! The jewel in the lotus.'"

"Jesus loves you," Forrest whispered.

The expression on my father's face was pained. I could tell he'd had a bellyful. He smiled and scratched his head. I knew this gesture, too, from the countless times he'd tried to teach me to play chess. Patience wasn't my father's strong suit. Game's over, baby. I'm done. Gently, my father said to Forrest: "I'm sure he does, son, I'm sure he does."

My parents glanced briefly at each other, and in that second, I saw Forrest through my parents' eyes: a beefy hick playing at religion. They didn't see him as a godly Donut Brother saving souls and strumming his guitar; to them he was a dumpling in denim who needed to grow up. In the refraction of their gaze, I saw myself as they must've seen both of us: two teenagers living in an airtight bell jar, believing in angels and demons, miracles and prophecies, predicting the end of the world – and running out of oxygen.

My parents drove us back to the Lighthouse Ranch. Forrest and I sat in the back seat holding hands. Maybe my mother made small talk; maybe it was painfully silent. What was there to say, really? Have a nice life? I wasn't the same daughter who'd been warned to keep a quarter between her knees, who cried when Joni Mitchell sang "Blue" and kept a dog-eared copy of Richard Brautigan's *In Watermelon Sugar* on her nightstand. I had never been easy for them, but they never could've predicted that their wild teenage daughter would be hijacked by religion, only to get in exchange someone so humorless and judgmental.

My dad pulled into the ranch's ramshackle parking lot and turned off the engine. On the double, Forrest sprang out of the car. Hoping for a graceful end to the evening, he leaned over to kiss my mother through her open window. Instead, he miscalculated the distance and whomped his head on the side mirror, really whacking it hard.

"That's got to hurt," my dad said, biting his lip.

"Are you OK?" my mother cried.

Forrest balled up his fists, then staggered against the front of the van and leaned his face against the windshield. From the inside of the car, he looked like Casper the Friendly Ghost. His eyelids fluttered and an imbecilic smile creased his pale face.

"Thank you, Jesus!" Forrest said, raising up both his arms. "Hallelujah! I'm claiming the victory," he shouted. Then he kissed my disbelieving mother goodnight.

That was it. It was curtains for Forry. If he had uttered a "fuck!" or "shit!" or even a mild "ouch!" he could've redeemed himself with my parents. They would've forgiven him for all his preaching platitudes. He was just a big sweet horny kid with a sunburned forchcad. But Forrest – like all of us at the ranch – had to turn a bump on the head into a sign from God.

2.

So Late, So Soon

I LAY IN BED LISTENING TO THE WAVES CRASHING ON THE BEACH, and the *splat-splat-splat* of rain on the sidewalk. Clouds over the ocean. Wind in the twisted cypress. If I closed my eyes, I could hear mold growing. The ground was a humid sponge that never dried out but kept decomposing underfoot. The windowpanes by my bed sprouted hairline fractures of dark green. It was so moist, the linoleum sagged like mushy Rice Krispies. Even clean cotton sheets fresh from the dryer quickly assumed the sweet-sour fragrance of curdled milk. Nature was a magician: it caused wood to bend and glass to sweat.

Listening to the steady rain, I wondered if it was raining on my parents' house in Lafayette too. I was in a tight cocoon, bound by worship and work. Time was ticking by, cycling through season after season. Years later, reading Dr. Seuss to my two-year-old son, I would feel a sharp pang of recognition, so perfectly did it capture the ranch's state of missing time:

How did it get so late so soon?
It's night before it's afternoon.
December is here before it's June.
My goodness how the time has flewn.
How did it get so late so soon?

It was easy to drift in a fugue of isolation; no newspapers or radios alerted me to the world outside. As isolated as I felt, I could've been living on an atoll in the Pacific. In 1973 – my second summer at the ranch – the Miami Dolphins won the Super Bowl, Billie Jean King beat Bobby Riggs in a tennis match billed "The Battle of the Sexes," Kurt Vonnegut published *Breakfast of Champions*, and "streaking" became a fad across U.S. campuses. While the space probe *Pioneer 10* was transmitting television pictures from within 81,000 miles of Jupiter, women in consciousness-raising groups were clambering up on tables with plastic speculums and mirrors, hoping to get a glimpse of their own inner space.

"I'm in the hollow of His hands," I wrote my parents on Lighthouse Ranch stationery featuring a neat little garden overshadowed by a cross. And then quickly, God spread his fingers, and I was allowed to scamper briefly back into the world – chauffeuring a troubled woman back to her home in the Bay Area. Helen had driven to the ranch, but she was in no shape to get herself home. In her early twenties, Helen's heart seemed – there's no other word for it – *flayed*. She'd recently given birth to a baby girl, Zooey, whom she'd given up for adoption. I don't know why Helen had come to the ranch, but her kinetic presence in the sisters' dorm made us edgy. I read once that sharks never sleep but have to keep swimming to move the water through their gills, or they'll drown. Helen was like that, a trolling blur of restless limbs, with reddened eyes that never shut. How tired she must've been; how tired she made us all. What kept her swimming was Zooey. Helen was bereft, inconsolable, continually on the verge of tears. Talking nonstop one minute, nearly catatonic the next; she was losing it.

Her parents were wealthy intellectuals who lived in the Berkeley hills. I had the distinct feeling that they wouldn't have approved of their daughter's sojourn among us. In the Bible it says: "Whosoever will may come." Helen had come and it was now clear she could not stay. We couldn't help her. We'd prayed over her, laid hands on her, asked Jesus to lift the spirit of oppression that plagued her. But Helen didn't improve. Probably because I was single and childless, knew how to drive, and was semireliable, I was recruited to drive Helen to her parents' house in Berkeley.

Helen handed me the keys with a gloomy air.

"Ready?" I asked.

She shrugged.

"OK, let's go," I said.

Helen stood by the door, looking across the sprawling garden, to the wooden cross on the bluff.

"Okay, here we go," I prompted.

She nodded absently. We stood there a minute longer.

Barbara clip-clopped out to the car in her silly little high heels. The wind caught at the hem of her madras skirt, exposing knobby white knees. "Praise the Lord, Helen, we'll be praying for you," Barbara said, trying to hurry her along.

Helen fixed her distracted eyes on the horizon. A tear glistened in the corner of her eye. Barbara looked at me. I looked back, imploring her with my eyes. Somebody had to take charge.

"We'll miss you, Helen," Barbara said, brisk as a nurse. "*Goodbye.*" She put Helen's suitcase in the trunk and slammed it. Finally Helen got in and I drove out of the parking lot with a heavy heart.

Lurching down Highway 101 in Helen's Volvo, I kept a sweaty grip on the wheel. I glanced over at my passenger. She sat slumped against the door, chin trembling, hands folded tightly in her lap. Towns rolled by: Fortuna, Rio Dell, Scotia, Pepperwood.

"Want to sing a song?" I said. "How 'bout 'The Joy of the Lord Is My Strength?'" Helen shook her head. I didn't blame her.

"Helen, what's wrong?"

"I'm fine," Helen said. Sniff, sniff. And then the skies opened up and the rains came. Helen wept and babbled rapid-fire about Zooey. Zooey! She wanted her baby girl back. Why couldn't she get her back? She was a good mother, wasn't she? Where was Zooey? Couldn't she at least visit her baby?

"I don't know," I answered, feeling helpless. "I'm so sorry."

Placing her hands on her doughy abdomen, Helen bent over and sobbed. "I should never" – *gasp* – "have let her out of my sight." I tried to keep my mind on driving, but by the time we'd reached Ukiah, about 150 miles from the ranch, I was ready to turn back. Chauffeuring Helen was a job for someone with a hardier, less permeable personality. I was becoming as hopped up as she was, twitchy, hungry, homesick for a child I'd never known. My mind was echoing: Zooey! Mama! Baby! Gimme! I chewed the inside of my cheeks, and tried to stay within the white lines. Think of those lines as stitches, I told myself. Stay within the boundaries. Neat and tidy, in and out. Sew yourself to Berkeley and keep the thread taut. As we reached the outskirts of Ukiah, Helen started hyperventilating.

"Stop the car!" she said, bracing herself against the dashboard. I hit the brakes and the Volvo shimmied.

"Are you sick or something?"

Helen put her hand on the door handle. She unrolled the window. "I need to get out for a minute."

"Do you have to pee?"

Helen opened the door and swung her legs out. She lurched away.

"You know, Helen, we're never going to get you home at the rate we're going," I called to her back.

"I need some air," she said. You and me both, I thought.

Helen stopped at a grove of redwoods. I watched her clutch at a tree branch and shake a finger at it, as if lecturing to a naughty puppy. I was trying very hard not to be terrified of Helen. We had been thrown together in the most basic way, without the buffer of small talk, just two people hanging on by our fingernails. There was really nothing I could do except pray and that I did in the most direct way: Oh-shit-God-help, oh-shit-God-help, oh-shit-God-help. Row, row, row your boat. Oh-shit-God-help. This was my mantra, a four-word invocation I mindlessly repeated as Helen talked to the trees. At that moment, Jesus seemed like a figment of my imagination. Helen was gathering steam for what seemed like a real meltdown. The river rushed over the rocks, cold and frothy. Helen required so much vigilance. I didn't know if she was going to impale herself on the car's radio antenna, fling herself into the Eel, or start singing "Three Blind Mice." I was nineteen and childless. What did I know about postpartum depression? I watched her from the window, thinking: Why are you doing this to me, Helen? And then I stopped, convicted down to the soles of my feet. *Helen.* I'd been flogging her with her own name, a name that was not only familiar but cherished by God. I thought about that scripture that says the Lord knows us and has called us *each by name.* That scripture, so intimate, so personal, always gave me chills.

I got out of the car and walked over to Helen. She was sitting on a tree log.

"What's wrong, Helen?" I squatted beside her.

"I feel sad, that's all," she said, flinging in a handful of pine needles. "I'm sorry I'm such a mess."

"You're not a mess, I promise you."

A few minutes later we walked back to the car and drove on. When we reached Helen's parents' house that night, they plied her with anxious questions as they fed us tofu and stir-fried vegetables. Had she forgotten to take her medication? Where exactly had she been? Did she need to make an appointment with her psychiatrist? No one mentioned Zooey.

I spent the night at Helen's parents' house. The next day I met my mother in the Berkeley Rose Garden on Euclid Avenue. I had wanted to see her but was also dreading it. I wore a pair of knee-high leather boots I'd found in the Free Box. They were two sizes too big but the leather was nicely broken in. I chose a dress for the occasion, one of the few store-bought items I owned, a long-sleeved blue and red plaid mid-calf dress with strawberries on it. My mother and I sat in the stone amphitheater, surrounded by terraced, climbing roses. I wanted to cry, but I was here to witness to my mother, show her God's anointing of my life. I wanted her to see that I'd changed.

"So how have you been?" my mother said.

"I am so blessed."

My mother sighed. "How's Forrest?"

"We broke up a few months ago."

"He seemed nice. Nutty but nice." My mother clucked her tongue. We sat in the sunlight. "Mmmm," my mother said, closing her eyes, "smell those roses."

"He *was* nice."

"What happened?"

"It just wasn't God's will, Mom." My mother shook her head and plucked at the pleats on her skirt.

"Are you mad or something?" I said.

She folded her arms across her chest, crossed her legs. "Listen, cookie, why don't you come home for a while? Think about college."

My chest ached. I shook my head. I couldn't contain all the grief I felt.

"Why are you crying?" my mother said in alarm.

"I'm just so happy."

"Honey, what's wrong?"

"The Lord loves you, Mom," I said softly.

I was crying for more than my mother's salvation. I was crying for the missed cues between us. I wept for Helen, mentally unhinged by grief; I wept for adopted Zooey; I wept for myself, a daughter who had left her mother's house and been adopted by another family. I had been in retreat and now I was back. Everything that day now seems exaggerated: the garish plaid of my dress, the Bunyonesque bigness of my boots, the cloying scent of the roses, and of course, my mother's presence. My mother was the most important person in my life, more real than Jesus, more powerful than all the ministry's elders combined. I'd thought that living with other people would dilute her mighty power, but here we were, once again caught up in each other's gravitational pull. Next to her, I felt large and ugly, unlovable and weird. Like Helen, I felt like a mess.

I boarded a Greyhound bound for Eureka that evening. Still in my dress and lace-up boots, I got a seat by the window. Travelers clutching bags of fruit pushed down the aisles, faces full of hope as they looked for empty seats. The choking odor of diesel mingled with the smell of urine and orange peels. My mother and I had parted hours before, hugging awkwardly. I didn't know when I would see her again. I looked out the window as the passengers climbed aboard, then reached for my Bible. I was eager to lose myself: palm fronds and donkeys, loaves and fishes, lepers and alabaster jars of perfume. The engine rumbled and hissed. Then the driver released the hand brake and we were off, away from the brown, sun-scorched hills.

Somewhere around Healdsburg an older woman got on and sat next to me. She was short and had a bad perm that was growing out. She pulled out a ball of yarn and began knitting. I glanced over at her and then looked away, feeling clearly that God wanted me to witness to my seatmate. I didn't want to. Several miles passed. I argued silently with God. Do I have to? Why can't I just ride the bus like everybody else? What do you want me to say, anyway? Frowning, I snapped open my Bible. The page opened to Psalm 130:1, which said:

> Out of the depths I cry to you, O Lord;
> O Lord, hear my voice.

I stared at the lines and meditated on them. God was telling me to call on Him at all times, even on a Greyhound.

As James's mother had pointed out, I couldn't even carry a tune in a bucket. I was tone-deaf and tune-challenged. But as dusk came on, I flicked on the overhead reading light, cleared my throat, and took a deep breath. I sang:

Oh God, hear my cry
Attend unto my prayer!
From the depths of the earth
I will cry unto thee
When my heart is overwhelmed.
Lead me to the rock
That is higher than I!
Jesus is the rock
That is higher than I!

I sang those verses as my stone-faced companion didn't drop a stitch. After a few minutes I stopped, flicked off my light and turned toward the window, burning with embarrassment. Neither of us said a word. When we stopped in Cloverdale for more passengers, she moved to another seat.

A Babe in the Lord

MY FRIENDS WERE GETTING MARRIED OFF AT AN ALARMING rate. Almost every month there was a wedding. God paired people up like socks, and there I was, mateless. Pretty soon I'd have the whole dorm to myself.

"I'm never getting married!" I told Priscilla, one of the sisters in the dorm. Pris was tall and had a regal bearing. When she wore nylon headbands, she reminded me of the TV commercial for Pond's face cream, where a woman with very blue eyes is always patting her smooth face with a little hand towel. Priscilla had recently announced her engagement to Eugene, an earnest "older brother" who seemed to wear a permanent scowl in my presence.

Pris's mom often sent her money. "Use it to buy some good shoes," her mom would write, enclosing a check for fifty dollars. I knew it bothered Eugene. He wanted to be the sole "provider" for his wife-to-be, but he had no outside job, and drew only a small weekly stipend. Just how many pairs of shoes could a woman buy? Eugene had put this question to Priscilla a number of times. They were getting married in a week. Soon they would be a matched set, salt and pepper shakers for Jesus, Mr. and Mrs. Elder.

"I have no desire whatsoever to be a wife," I told Priscilla, sitting on the rim of the bathtub. Priscilla was brushing her thick, honey-colored hair in the mirror and humming a little. She caught my eye.

"Sure you don't," she teased, smiling a little. She put on some Chap Stick. She was wearing a wool jumper and low-heeled Ferragamo pumps.

"I mean it," I said. "I'm happy with my life."

Pris sighed and turned around. She draped an arm around me. "Look, your turn will come."

We were constantly reminding each other to keep our eyes on Jesus. "Seek ye first the kingdom of God and his righteousness, and all these things will be given unto you," Jim Durkin preached from the Book of Matthew, and the emphasis was always on "first." But what if your eyes were on Jesus and you still had a powerful attraction to someone else? Then perhaps it was a godly thing, the way you kept daydreaming and fantasizing about that person, right? Perhaps Jesus had planted that seed of desire. Perhaps the relationship wasn't of the flesh but of the Lord. But how could you know for sure?

THE FIRST TIME I SAW HIM, HE WAS STANDING BY THE SIDE OF the kitchen door, bent over and breathing hard. A small fluttery hand clutched his throat. "Help me!" he gagged, slapping at the strangling hand, which turned out to be his own. "Stop it!" *Slap, slap.* "Leave me alone!"

"What are you *doing?*" I said.

"Nothing," he said, laughing, holding out his hand. "I don't think we've met. I'm Henry."

"You're silly."

A day later, I bumped into him at breakfast sitting at one of the long Formica tables in the dining hall. Taking an unpeeled banana from the fruit bowl, he was Elvis singing in Las Vegas:

I'm in love! Ugh!

I'm all shook up!

We all stopped chewing our Corn Flakes, transfixed by this ... utterance. Gretchen batted her eyes and took a baby sip of her tea. "You know," she said, "I'm all shook up too." She glanced at us. "Oh, come on, you guys. Shook up in *the Lord*. Shook up for *Him*."

"Help us, dear Lord," Ella muttered, casting her eyes up to the ceiling. She continued mumbling, "Deliver us ...ways of foolishness ... on your paths."

"Thank you," Henry said in his Elvis voice. "Thank you very much."

The next time I saw him, he was singing in Deliverance Temple. His eyes were closed and his palms were upright. His head was bobbing. Corkscrew curls gleamed under the overhead lights. A sweet smile played across his lips, lips that were full and sensuous and ... Henry's blue eyes opened, as if he could hear my thoughts. I closed mine. We sang about having peace like a river in our souls. I peeked at him. He was swaying with the music. I wasn't sure I had peace in my soul. It felt more like an otter.

Henry wasn't one of those shy, tongue-tied guys who puttered in the garage in baggy grease-stained overalls, quoting scripture while changing the transmission fluid on an old pickup. He wasn't handy with tools and he didn't stammer and blush around sisters.

He was clearly different from the rest of us. He was Canadian for one thing. And Jewish. He had that finger-in-the-light-socket hair. He spoke four languages, including Yiddish. His exotic-sounding *"oy vehs"* stood out among our rote "hallelujahs." Music to my tired ears.

Barrel-chested, slim-hipped, Henry loved to dance, a talent he'd inherited from his mother, Lea. He grew up in Montreal, tarried briefly in college, and then launched himself into that extended '70s adolescence known as "finding yourself." This included spending a season on an Israeli *kibbutz*, traveling through Europe on a Eurail pass with a buddy, hitchhiking through Mexico, and reading lots of pseudo-spiritual books, including *The Teachings of Don Juan*. He was a nonpracticing Jew, although his mother kept a kosher house, and his older brother, Felix, would eventually marry an Israeli woman and settle on a *kibbutz* in the Negev. By his mid-twenties

Henry had smoked marijuana, mastered the art of juggling, spent a few lackadaisical semesters in college, fallen in love several times, and worked off and on for his father. In Mexican woven sandals and hip-hugger jeans, he exuded the aura of someone at home in the world. When he told me he loved to travel, I paid close attention.

"Tell me something," I said. "Do you think you're going to stay here?" We were sitting together—riding back from church just like Forrest and I had done several months earlier.

Under the jumble of Bibles and coats, Henry reached for my hand. I stared out the window as the streetlights of Eureka glimmered in the distance. Two thoughts ran through my mind simultaneously: He-is-so-cute-Lord-is-this-your-will?

Henry shrugged. "It's up to God. And whether I can get an extension on my visa."

"Do you want to stay here?"

"Sure I do," he said, running his hand through his hair. "God willing."

"If you don't get an extension on your visa, will you go back to Canada?"

"I'll have to pray about it."

His Romanian parents had fled their communist homeland in the forties. Now divorced, they lived in Montreal. Cosmo had a sewing machine business and worked in the industrial part of town that had been immortalized in Mordecai Richler's novel *The Apprenticeship of Duddy Kravitz*. Lea lived off a pension. Unlike other members of his extended family, Henry had slipped the bonds of responsibility. Settling down, getting established in a career, taking on the encumbrances of middle-class life—none of these things held any attraction for him. While his counterparts had been going to college, making mortgage payments, and paying for their kids' braces, he'd been wary of settling down. He'd converted to Christianity in Mexico, after meeting up with a group of zealous Christian men who lived together and pooled their slender resources as they preached God's word.

"They were a happy band of brothers," Henry said. "Their lives seemed so simple." His eyes grew moist. "I was touched." It was moving how easily he cried.

"What do your parents think about this?"

"Oh, boy," Henry said, wiping his eyes. "They think I'm crazy." He laughed a little. "Maybe I am a little."

"Crazy for God," I said.

"That would be me." He blew out his cheeks. "Jesus is the Messiah. Who knew?"

By the time Henry arrived at the ranch, he was ripe for the harvest. He was received the same way I'd been greeted, with hallelujahs and hosannas, welcomed as another spiritual wayfarer drawn here by God.

WE TALKED ALL THE TIME ABOUT DYING TO OURSELVES – OUR carnal minds and senses – acting on the truth of God's word, rather than relying on our petty feelings. Feelings were loose puppies: fickle, wayward, messy. I hadn't been housebroken yet. I lived in my feelings; I was emotional to the core. But revealing how I felt could be a sign of spiritual immaturity. If I had ever gotten up the nerve and said to the brethren, "You know, I'm going to skip church this Sunday and worship the Lord my own way – maybe in the bathtub if there's any hot water," they would've said: "Sister, those are just your feelings, you know you can't rely on them." Then I would've said, "Thank you, I realize I've just stepped in something nasty, and if you'll excuse me now, I'll go scrape off my shoes."

But I had feelings for Henry. Was it God? Was it lust? Was it loneliness? He was a little goofy, but full of joy too. It was hard to decipher what I was supposed to do. I felt far from the Lord so much of the time, and then sometimes, I felt swallowed up in His radiance. For those moments, I stopped striving. I didn't want for anything in the world, not even Henry. My heart's desire was to stay balanced with God, right in the curl of the wave that never breaks.

DANIEL, ONE OF THE ELDERS, SAW US WALKING UP HOOKTON ROAD picking blackberries. I was going to make a pie if we managed not to eat all of them before we got home.

"It seems like you two are spending a lot of time together," Daniel said when Henry and I wandered into the dining hall out of breath. "What's going on?"

Henry's purple lips parted in a smile. "We're not sure."

"Is this of the Lord?" Daniel said, crossing his arms. "What do you think?"

"I'm praying about it," I said.

"Hmnn," Daniel said, raising an eyebrow. He stroked his chin. "I think the Lord is doing a work in your hearts."

"A work in your hearts." Promising words from an elder. This meant Daniel "bore witness" to the relationship. If he thought our relationship was of the flesh, he would've advised us to break it off. I prayed for and about Henry. My prayers clicked their heels, did undignified cartwheels, showed their grass-stained undies. *Hallelujah, praise the Lord, hot diggity dog, yessiree, thank you Jesus!*

If I had been really honest, I would've admitted to myself that there was something else mixed up in my desire to be with Henry: If there was ever anyone I could honorably leave the Lighthouse Ranch with, it was him. He was Canadian, he had visa problems, and he liked to travel. My old self, the Army brat who craved reinvention, came alive with him. My life, my supposedly blessed life in the Lord, the spiritual life I'd bludgeoned my parents with was being supplanted by a new restlessness.

And They All Said Amen

I CALLED MY MOTHER FROM THE RANCH PAY PHONE.

"How are you?" she said. "What's new?"

"I'm wonderful," I said. "I'm getting married." Silence. "God has blessed me and Henry," I added.

"Oh, honey. Don't you think you're rushing things just a little? How long have you known him, twenty minutes?"

"Listen, he's a wonderful man. We love each other. He's standing right next to me. Let me put him on the phone."

"Wait a –" my mother said.

"Praise the Lord!" Henry gushed. "How are you?" He put his arm around me. "Can I call you Mom?"

"_____."

"I'm so blessed! Your daughter is a Virtuous Woman of God."

"_____."

"I'm looking forward to getting to know you!" Henry said. "Dad too. We love you, Mom!" Henry handed me the phone.

"Doesn't he sound neat?" I said. "Mom?

"He sounds great," she said faintly. I could hear Timothy Leary barking in the background.

My mother cleared her throat. "Well, for god's sake, whatever you do, don't get pregnant."

"Right," I said.

"Have you met his family yet? Have you set a date?"

"Not yet," I said in answer to both questions. "But I will. We want it to happen soon."

"Well," she sighed, "this is certainly some news."

"Are you happy for me?"

"You're too young to get married. You're not even twenty. You should be in college instead of living in that goddamn commune."

"But you're happy for me, right?"

"I'm happy that you're happy, but I've got to tell you, I think you should wait."

"I'm going to marry him, Mom."

"Do what you want," she said, and sighed again. "Just don't make me the heavy."

When I hung up the phone, I felt like crying.

HENRY'S DAD DIDN'T TAKE THE NEWS WELL EITHER. WHEN COSMO got wind of our wedding plans, he flew out to visit. He reminded me of Boris, the cartoon spy from the *Rocky and Bullwinkle Show*; his stiff pointy mustache looked like it had been drawn on with a stubby black eyebrow pencil. He was short, intense, and very European.

"Hallelujah, Praise the Lord, Jesus Christus," Cosmo said in a guttural tone, leaning against his rental car in the Ranch parking lot. He made the sign of the cross, tossed his head back and laughed.

"So how are you, Pop?" Henry said, towering over his dad. He hugged his father.

"Could be better but it costs more," Cosmo said with a shrug.

I stood at Henry's side, beaming. Cosmo sized me up, taking in my crocheted apron, brown braids, shapeless long blue skirt and embroidered peasant blouse. I sucked in my stomach and stood taller.

"Pop, this is my, ah, fiancée," Henry said, tightening his grip around my shoulder. Cosmo made the sign of the cross again, then steadied himself against the car. I wondered if he'd had a few drinks on the plane.

"Hi there," I said, holding out my hand. For some reason, I had an almost overpowering desire to curtsy.

"*Bonjour, mademoiselle*," Cosmo said. He ran a little hand through his thinning hair and patted the top of his head, as if to make sure it was still there.

I smiled back at him so hard my braids ached. From the corner of my eye, I could see Ella dithering in the garden.

"Come on, Pop," Henry said. "Let's go in and eat."

Cosmo looked pained at the prospect of sitting down with a hundred *goyim*. And what was on the menu? Why, any fool could smell it. Swiss chard and Spanish rice!

"Hen-ri," Cosmo said, punching the first syllable of his son's name and rolling the r. "Let's go out." He straightened his cuffs. "Let's ... celebrate, yes?"

Going out to dinner sounded good to both of us. Henry fairly skipped as he went to get our jackets.

"So," I said, turning to Cosmo, really looking at him for the first time. He had long, giraffish eyelashes and his brown eyes were merry. Rayon trousers and a sleek silk shirt marked him as a man with very different sartorial tastes than the Lighthouse Ranch brothers who favored overalls and flannel shirts. The gold medallion around his neck burrowed in his gray chest hair like a happy tick.

"So," Cosmo echoed. "You believe in Jesus Christus too?"

"Oh, yes," I breathed.

"And you want to live here? Here?" *Herrreee.* Cosmo gestured toward the broken-down cars and the dilapidated lighthouse, badly in need of another coat of paint. He wrinkled his nose, as if he smelled something foul. "Why?" he asked, spreading his hands wide. "This is no place to live."

Henry huffed up, all business. "OK, Pop, let's go."

I sat between the men in the car. Cosmo lit a Gauloise and began speaking in rapid-fire Romanian. He waved his right index finger in his son's face.

"Pop! In English, please, for my fiancée's sake," Henry said. *Fiancée* gave me a little thrill. Cosmo ignored him. On and on they talked; I couldn't understand what Cosmo was saying but his tone was stern. He mentioned Montreal and Lea, and something about immigration. Henry seemed to shrink inside his cardigan. I could feel him balling his hands up in the pockets. As the Cadillac nosed away from the ranch, I watched the late afternoon sun rake across the hills.

At Volpi's Restaurant off Highway 101, Cosmo knocked back two quick Vodka tonics, then ordered a bottle of Beaujolais.

"None for us, Pop," Henry said. "We don't drink."

"Oh, live a little," said Cosmo.

The waitress brought three glasses. Cosmo poured.

"What are you doing at this Lighthouse Ranch?" he asked Henry.

"I'm a salesman," Henry said. "I sell ads for our newspaper, the *Tri-City Advertiser.*"

Cosmo snorted. "You, a salesman? How much they pay you?"

"Five dollars a week." Henry flashed a self-deprecating smile.

"An hour, you mean."

"No," Henry said, shaking his head, "I mean a week."

"You're smarter than that! Henrico, look, they're stealing from you!"

"It's honest work, Pop." Henry reddened. "I know what I'm doing."

"Who's going to pay for the wedding? The cake? The dress? The orchestra?"

"The Lord will provide," Henry said flatly.

"You are a man, Henry." Cosmo drained his glass. "Stop this foolishness."

"I love Jesus, Pop," Henry said quietly. "It's not foolishness."

Cosmo rolled his eyes and lit a cigarette. He inhaled deeply. Smoke curled around his head. He looked over at me as if to say, *Kids. What can you do?*

I played with my lasagna.

"Come work for me," Cosmo said, hitting the table as if the idea had just occurred to him. "I'll pay you more than five dollars a week."

"It's up to the Lord." Henry's lips were tight.

"Bullshit!" Cosmo glanced at me, gave a little bow, "Forgive my language, mademoiselle, but sometimes a father must speak this way to his son."

"No problem," I said. I took a sip of wine. "I understand."

Cosmo put on his dark glasses. He leaned into Henry's face. "I say bull"– he paused –"shit."

"Pop," Henry began, "I–"

Cosmo swatted his words away like they were little buzzing gnats, glanced over at me and winked. "D'Arcy," he implored, "you want to live in Montreal with Henrico and me, yes?"

I drained my glass. I glanced at Henry. He looked unhappy and raw in his cardigan, as if the wool were chafing his neck. "Cosmo," I said, turning to the little man in the silk shirt, "it's in God's hands."

Côte St. Jew

"CALL ME *MA*," HENRY'S MOTHER SAID, FLUTTERING HER EYE-lashes. Cosmo, hoping his son could be induced into moving back home, had impulsively sprung for a trip to Montreal a few weeks after his visit.

"Are you sure?" I said, gazing at the birdlike woman with stiff blonde hair sitting primly on the edge of her plastic-covered sofa. A short wool skirt revealed slim legs, and a clingy turtleneck sweater displayed a high, proud bosom. Next to her, I felt gigantic. She projected – despite her years of unhappy marriage to Cosmo – the image of a happy-go-lucky single gal all on her own. But I was soon to learn that Ma wasn't an innocent airhead. Behind those lashes, she was taking measure. Her tape measure was her European background, her religious roots, and her sow-bear love for her youngest cub, Henry.

I stumbled over "Ma." My mother was "Mom," plain and simple, not "Mommy," "Mama," "Mum," or "Mother." "Ma" complicated things, con-juring up the image of a toothless, jug-swigging dustbowl granny from *The Grapes of Wrath*. Calling my mother "Ma," the selfsame woman who read literary best sellers and sewed chic dresses from *Vogue* patterns, would've seemed disrespectful, just the thing a snotty teenage daughter would do to get under the maternal epidermis. But Lea insisted on Ma and so Ma it was. I was in another country now, far from the redwoods of Northern California and the shallow politesse of my family, farther still from the emoting, moist-eyed saints at the Lighthouse Ranch who automatically called each other "brother" and "sister." Deep in the heart of Montreal, Jewish Montreal, Côte St. Jew, Lea was Ma, and Ma was the reigning queen. And I was the last person in the world to stand on ceremony. So desperately did I want her to like me, I would've genuflected before her scuffed white go-go boots and kissed her little nyloned knees.

Lea lived in a tiny, one-bedroom apartment in Côte St. Luc, a neighborhood she and her friends jokingly called Côte St. Jew because it was a popular Jewish enclave. The bakeries sold challah bread and poppy seed cake, and the shelves of Steinberg's, the local supermarket, brimmed with lox and bagels, gefilte fish, matzoh bread, and other kosher staples. It took me several days to realize that Steinberg's welcoming motto, *oui*, meaning *yes* in French, was not *oy*, as in *oy veh* in Yiddish.

"What do you do?" Ma asked.

Good question. Somehow my putative career as a cooking columnist for our free, throw-away shopper didn't translate well. Neither did my other incarnation as the Bargain Lady, sniffing out *schmattes* on sale in Eureka. My other jobs at the ranch – sandwich maker, toilet scrubber, laundress – sounded like grunt work. Oh, how to sum up a life?

"I cook and write," I offered.

Ma smiled encouragingly. "Uh huh. What do you write?"

"It's a long story."

HENRY AND I BROWSED IN OLD MONTREAL, POPPING INTO ANTIQUE stores, boutiques, and cafes. He introduced me to his old friends, fast-talking, outspoken Jews never at a loss for words. With his slender, strong arm around my waist, I felt invincible. The city was the antithesis of gloomy, wet Humboldt County, where everyone seemed permanently welded into long underwear from October until May. Life at the ranch was routine, enforced by a spiritual alarm clock that never stopped ringing. Montreal in the fall was sharp-edged and full of sly surprises. Spiky red and golden maple leaves crackled underfoot, and the air was infused with the heady scent of ripe apples. And then there were the French – beautiful, stylish women and slim, mustachioed men in leather jackets and tight jeans whose asses seemed sculpted in denim.

The French-Canadians spoke French like they were slowly exhaling cigarette smoke from the corners of their mouths: the words came out terse and cramped. Every sentence sounded like a sexy, gangsterish aside. Compared to the French, the English-speaking natives were earnest and chipmunk cute, the Canadian version of Donny and Marie. They spoke in a sing-song cadence, each sentence suspended on the point of a questioning "eh?" Perhaps they sought reassurance.

Secession was in the air in Quebec. A few years earlier, the charismatic René Levesque had founded the separatist *Parti Québécois*, with the hope of eventually cutting Quebec's national ties to the rest of Canada. The divorce never took place, but both sides were still smarting. In the early '70s, Montreal was a city roiling with issues of identity and independence, a place where everybody's differences became more exaggerated. In that city, I became more aware of my otherness too. I was someone who would never be able to "pass" for anything except an outsider among dissenters: American *shiksa*, backslidden Catholic, Army brat, the Yankee with Mick blood. After a childhood of repeated moves and constant upheaval, this sensation of being an outsider was all too familiar.

IT WAS A TIGHT SQUEEZE IN LEA'S ONE-BEDROOM APARTMENT, made tighter because Henry's easy-going older brother, Felix, was visiting. But we were all on very good behavior—at least for a while. I was assigned to share a bed with Ma, while Henry and Felix doubled up on a foldout couch in the living room. Usually Felix was traveling in Europe or visiting friends who lived on *kibbutzim* in Israel, but he came home from time to time when he ran out of money. The brothers had that same luscious thick curly hair. There must've been a stubborn corkscrewed gene in the Romanian family, and with these brothers, it literally went to their heads. But that's where the similarities ended. Felix's face was square and ursine, set off by an inquisitive blunt nose that seemed to be sniffing a stash of honey. In contrast, Henry's features were chiseled and refined, betraying no hungers. One of Felix's legs was shrunken, crippled by childhood polio. He was matter-of-fact about walking with a limp. The essence of his personality was revealed in his casual rolling gait. *Hey, don't sweat it. I'm getting by just fine.*

I discovered Henry had multiple personalities and changed when he was with his mother. Little by little, he reverted to a younger, fussier, more indecisive self. His parents called him "Hentsle" – Yiddish for Henry – but even that metamorphosis wasn't final. His short, roly-poly, rheumy-eyed grandmother, Magda, who lived nearby, would run her floury fingers through his thick curls and call him *mouton* – her little mutton, her little lamb. Henry, Hentsle, Mouton: was there another character waiting in the wings?

Henry had told me about Ma back in California, and I thought I'd understood the subterranean push-pull of their relationship. She smothered, he retreated. She guilt-tripped, he confessed. She grew distant, he sulked. He still hadn't cut the cord with his mother, and in truth, I hadn't cut the cord with mine either. But the family dynamics were radically different. In my family, we didn't raise our voices unless really provoked. Until then, we seethed, pouted, and talked behind each other's back. We became bitter. We gossiped, we plotted, then we made our move. But in Ma's house, it was always a frontal assault. Mealtimes were miniature psychodramas playing out in Ma's Kitchen Theatre in the Round.

Felix: "Ma! Where's the mustard?"

Ma: "What?"

Felix: "Mustard! You got any?"

Ma: "In the fridge." She took a bite of her sandwich and chewed. "Hold on a minute."

Felix: "I'll get it already! I just asked!"

Silence descended for a moment as we chewed our egg salad sandwiches. Felix speared a pickle. I winced as his teeth made a hollow crunching sound.

Henry spoke up. "Ma, do we have any horseradish?"

"No." Lea patted her flat tummy and flashed a tiny smile. "Gives me gas."

"I thought I saw a jar in the fridge."

"I'm telling you" – Ma started to raise her voice in mock annoyance – "I ought to know what's in my own house!"

"I just asked!"

"Felix," Ma said. "Tell him. Do we have any horseradish?"

"We don't have any horseradish, Hents."

Soup followed sandwiches. Carrots in a beefy broth, and then poppy seed cake and tea, slurped noisily. Little poppy seeds, like black love beads, winked from between our teeth. I looked at Lea and Felix and Henry chewing and thought, wow, we're practically family. I'm going to grow old with these people. The radiator ticked. Ma drummed her orange lacquered nails on the Formica table. I tried to imagine my parents sitting at the table with Ma and the boys. What would they say to each other? I looked around the table. The more I thought about it, the clearer the answer became: Nothing. Plenty.

"So, you're really going back to California?" Ma said.

"Don't start with me, Ma," Henry said.

"Can't I ask a simple question?"

"Don't start."

"Who's starting?"

"You're starting, Ma. Let's just have a nice meal together, OK?"

"What's the matter with him?" Ma implored Felix. "Is he deaf? Can't I ask a question?"

"Leave me out of it," Felix said.

Ma sighed. "Let me try this again," she said. "Is it absolutely necessary for you to go back to that place in California?"

"Yes," my beloved said.

"Why?" Lea said, hitting her palm on the table.

"Do you have to yell, Ma?" Henry said.

"Pish, I'm not yelling."

"You're yelling."

"Felix," said Ma. "Am I yelling?"

"Ma, leave me out of it," Felix said. He caught my eye and there was a smile in his kind brown eyes. Was this a game?

"Pheh!" said Ma, waving her hand at her eldest son. Turning back to Henry, she said, "I don't understand why you can't stay here."

"Ma," Henry said, "it's God's will that I return."

Ma stood up abruptly, brushed the crumbs from her lap and gathered up the plates, shuffling them as if they were cards and she a dealer in Vegas. She trudged over to the sink and dumped them into the water. Then she spun around to face us. I felt like I was watching TV. The Lea Show.

"What about your will? Are you brainwashed? You should come home and get a job! Enough of this Jesus! Look at you! You're twenty-five."

"Twenty-six," Felix said, raising a finger. "Just in case anybody's keeping track."

"Thanks," Henry said.

"Ma," I said, choking on the word. "Let me help you. How about if I wash?" She shook her head. I was part of the problem. The prodigal son had come home, but oy, with such baggage. Who knew he was bringing a *shiksa*?

THE REST OF THE FAMILY DIDN'T KNOW WHAT TO MAKE OF US. Henry's cousins' reactions ranged from disbelief and incredulous laughter to outright scorn. Hey! Hentsle's a Jesus freak now. He's here with his American girlfriend. Check it out. Yeah, he's been living in some commune in Northern California and reading the Bible! Jesus H. Christ on a raft, the kid's always had a screw loose but now he's a certified nutcase! His male cousins – pale, short versions of one another – had their wingtips planted firmly on the ground. They had bills to pay. Who had time to think about heaven when Eli's bar mitzvah was next month and Rachel wanted violin lessons? Hentsle had escaped all that, they concurred with bemusement. Always the dreamer, that one. Never married, always traveling, reading weird books, living in strange places. Now he was "serving the Lord." The goofball.

During those times in Montreal when I felt scrutinized and dissected, I clung to one of my favorite proverbs: "He who finds a wife finds what is good and receives favor from the Lord" (Proverbs 18:22). I wanted to be that good thing, not an odd interloper, a ridiculous object of gossip that threatened the family. I had fantasized about being welcomed into the bosom of a warm and colorful family, a bunch of gesticulating Bohemians who laughed at the dinner table and later danced in whirling gypsy skirts and knee-high boots after imbibing many liters of wine. Maybe, I'd thought, I could pick up the tambourine. Maybe I could learn to dance the hora.

"What about children?" Henry's cousin, Stefan, asked me one night when we met for dinner in Old Montreal. Stefan sold Mr. Coffee makers out of the back of his car for a living. He was still single, didn't have a girlfriend, but wanted to get married. "Will they be raised Jewish or Christian?"

"Both," Henry jumped in. "Look, it's not like I'm forsaking my Jewish roots."

"I wasn't talking to you," Stefan said slowly as he lit a cigarette. "I was talking to your… girlfriend."

"If we have children, we'll raise them in the ways of the Lord," I said, glancing at Henry for his approval. That answer had boiled up right out of the ether; it floated straight from the lips of some humorless elder's wife I never wanted to become. I hated using that kind of robotic Godspeak – it was something I reverted to when I felt cornered – but Stefan had no way of knowing that.

"Oh, right, the ways of the Lord," Stefan said sarcastically, exhaling a thin stream of blue smoke. "And which ways are those?"

I smiled at him as if to say, hey, I'm not the enemy, I'm on *your* side. I already knew I didn't want to live at the Lighthouse Ranch with Henry. I didn't want to share him with one hundred needy souls. Was it possible to tell Henry that I hoped we would move away as soon as we got married? No, it was risky. Too much intensity might scare him off. I wasn't sure he loved me – or even really knew me. Secretly, I was afraid he couldn't envision me away from the ranch, that he believed the commune and I were one, that I came with the property, human real estate as inseparable as the fog and the rain.

AS I UNDRESSED IN MA'S BATHROOM THAT NIGHT, I LOOKED AT myself in the mirror. A windchapped face with bushy eyebrows stared back. I was no Pond's girl. I vowed to buy some makeup as soon as I got some money. As I brushed my teeth, I could hear Felix and Henry talking in the living room. Johnny Carson was on.

"You know, Pop thinks you're crazy living in California," Felix said. "Seriously. He thinks you've flipped out."

"So what else is new?"

"Are you really gonna get married?"

"Lord willing."

I opened Ma's medicine cabinet. Hairpins, laxatives, and Avon lipsticks crowded the shelves. One of the lipsticks was called "Desire." I drew a thick orange-red line across the back of my hand.

"So what do you think of D'Arcy, Felix?"

"She seems like a nice kid. She's ... nice."

"Nice? Is that all you can say?"

"She's OK, Hents."

"Can you see us together?"

What kind of question was that? What difference did it make whether Felix saw us together?

"I don't know, Hents. I just think you're rushing into things."

I could hear Johnny wrapping up his monologue, then Ed McMahon's booming laugh. Carefully, I drew Desire on my lips.

"Look," Felix said, "don't get mad. You could change your mind about everything next week. This isn't the first time you've come home fired up about God and religion. What's it going to be next week? Buddhism? Mormonism?"

I rubbed my lips together.

"Felix, I—" Henry stuttered.

"Look, I don't have anything against your girlfriend or your religion or how you live your life. It's just you seem so uncertain, so shaky about what you're doing. It's hard to take you seriously."

"Well, I am serious, Felix." Henry's voice had a smarting edge to it. "I love her." Slowly, I kissed myself in the mirror. It made a perfect imprint. Rose hips, I thought.

"Love! What's love?" Felix said scornfully.

"She's a godly woman," Henry said.

"Look," Felix said, "if it's just a sex thing, go ahead and do it. Why do you have to get married to do it?"

"It's not about sex," Henry said. "Believe me, it's not *that*." I reached for a Kleenex to wipe the mirror clean.

"This relationship," Henry said, "is of the Lord."

"Yeah, right, and the Holy Ghost lives in my pants." My arm paused in mid-wipe.

"Shut up!" Henry hissed. "Lower your voice."

Somebody got up and turned the TV off. I started wiping the glass again. There. The mirror was clean. Silence seeped into the corners of Ma's apartment. Then Felix's voice cut through the quiet.

"Will D'Arcy want to stay at the ranch after you're married?"

"We never talked about it."

"Well, you'd better, buddy boy, you'd better."

"We both really love the Lord," Henry said. "We want to be in His will."

"Sure you do," his brother said. "Hallelujah."

I turned off the light and tiptoed into Ma's room. She was snoring softly. I eased under the covers. I folded my hands across my chest and tried to pray. I wasn't sure what I wanted Jesus to help me with specifically. I just needed generic, all-over coverage. "Whatever blessings you're handing out tonight, Jesus, I'd like some," I prayed. In another part of my mind, I imagined the wedding. Was this really God's will or my own? The ranch seemed so far away, like a remote land inhabited by trolls who needed dental work and cartoonish angels with neon yellow halos. Black or white, bad or good, there was no in-between. *Ding!* One minute I felt blessedly confident, the next I was toiling in a mineshaft of doubt. Ma turned over and pulled the covers over her shoulders. I closed my eyes. "He who finds a wife finds what is good and receives favor from the Lord." Was I good? Would Henry find favor with Jesus because of me? It never occurred to me to wonder the same thing about him.

Good Hand, Bad Hand

I LAY IN MY BUNK FOR A LONG TIME, STARING THROUGH THE mildewed glass at the pink morning sky. During the past year and a half that I'd been at the Lighthouse Ranch, as more sisters left the dorm and others rotated in, I had slowly worked my way back to this prime piece of real estate – a bunk in a rear alcove that actually had a window. In this narrow private space, partitioned from my sisters with a blanket curtain, I had dreamed and prayed. I had pondered The Word, scarfed maple bars, tried to reverse the damage with sit-ups, and scolded myself in my diary. I had argued with God – and myself. I had been tranquil. I had been afraid. I had touched my body in wonderment, wept, and listened to the murmuring rain, steady as the hand of God. Now, on a February morning as I lay in my bunk for the last time, I looked at the cypress trees that clung to the steep cliffs. In a few hours Henry and I would be married. I would never come back here. Somebody else would have a turn in this coveted corner, someone who would listen to the wind and wait for morning's light.

I glanced at my watch. Seven-thirty. My grandmother Mary, my mother, my sister Mary, and two of my younger brothers were staying at a motel in Eureka. I wondered if they were up yet. As I brushed my hair, I remembered the way my grandmother used to stroke my head when I was little. I used to curl up with her in her bed on foggy Saturday mornings in Monterey. We'd play a favorite game; one of her freckled hands would assume a personality of its own. If it was the "good" hand," it would clumsily stroke my head, like Helen Keller mindlessly patting a Labrador. "Good girl, that's a girl," my grandmother would croon in her gravelly voice. If it was the "bad" one, the hand would flutter about my ears, pinching and tickling until I batted it away and shrieked, "Stop!" You never knew which one was hidden in the covers. As her wrinkled, bejeweled hand crept out from beneath the flannel sheets like a heavy human spider, I faced it, giddy with dread and pleasure.

DANIEL, THE RANCH ELDER WHO'D COUNSELED US ABOUT GETTING married, stood in front of the Eureka Veterans' Hall in his cowboy boots, leaning against the podium. Wearing a bolo tie and a shirt with snap pearl buttons, he looked more like he was ready to preside over a cattle auction than herd us into matrimony.

My mother sat in the first row, flanked by the two Marys. These women created a formidable triad. What was my mother thinking, sandwiched between her mother and her oldest daughter? Her stiff body language – the way she folded her arms across the bodice of her silk dress during the ceremony – spoke volumes about her mood. I come from a line of strong, long-lived women who don't believe in keeping their lips buttoned. They don't believe in letting people have the last word, unless they happen to be those people. All three women loved me, wanted me to be happy, but as they sat on uncomfortable metal folding chairs that Sunday afternoon, I didn't feel I had a place among them. Many years later, my mother would tell me she had been heartsick about the wedding because she feared I would get trapped in a fundamentalist lifestyle that stripped me of my options. I knew they'd been talking about this. I could imagine the conversation:

My mother: "She's ruining her life, you know."

My grandmother: "Boy oh boy, I hope this turns out OK."

My mother: "Let's hope she's on the Pill."

My sister: "What does she see in him?"

Henry's father must've been thinking the same thing about me. Cosmo's youngest son was marrying a chatty gentile who had tracked his boy like an Indian scout. In wedding photos, Cosmo sits a few seats away from the Marys. I remember his eyes – at times looking thuggish, then merry, then sad – glittering behind his glasses. My younger brothers, Chris and Mike, were also in attendance. My oldest brother, Brian, was already in Germany with our father. My mother and the boys would follow as soon as she sold the house. Other cousins rounded out the ensemble, as well as a handful of Henry's friends from Santa Barbara.

"You look nice," Chris said, gagged in a coat and tie as he stood at the back of the hall with me. We were about to walk down the aisle.

"Thanks," I said.

"How do you feel?" he said.

"Actually, a little queasy. You?"

"Oh, I'm just high on life."

"I hope that's all you're high on," I whinnied. My voice was pitched too high; I sounded like a race horse stoked on laughing gas. "Remember what Dad always used to tell us: 'Just keep a quarter between your knees.'"

"'And don't smoke any funny cigarettes,'" Chris retorted.

"Yeah, well, you don't have to worry about me smoking any," I said.

"You don't want me to roll you and Henry a couple of fat ones for your honeymoon? I've got some weed in the car."

I stared at my brother.

"Just kidding," Chris said. "Mellow out, will you?"

But I felt high. Dear Jesus. I *was* high. Distant. Outside myself. Like a balloon with a slow helium leak, I felt like I was bobbing along the Veteran's Hall ceiling, barely touching the walls. I closed my eyes and prayed: Jesus, please help me get through this.

Leo hit a few chords on the upright piano in the corner, and some members of the congregation hummed in response. Then a longer piano riff. *Hmmmmmm!* Somebody picked up a fiddle and Naomi, Daniel's wife, began tuning her guitar, expertly finding the right key with a few adjustments. As I stood at the back of the room, I saw a short guy with curly hair and hip-hugger slacks do a little improvisational folk dance step, like an Israelite rejoicing before the Ark of the Covenant. Henry!

Leo, pounding the keys, launched into "I've Got Peace Like a River" and a few members of the congregation raised their hands and began swaying. A man sitting near my mother started speaking loudly in tongues. "Praise you, Lord! *Ah-kea-sundra. Ak-kea-sundra-la.*" Shoot, it was Leroy, the holy terror, in his linen drawstring pants. Oh, praise you, Jesus! This was out of my hands. Leo leaned into the keyboard and starting pounding out the melody as the congregants, human boats, bobbed and rode a rising wave of refrain:

I've got love like an ocean!
I've got love like an ocean!
I've got love like an ocean
in my soooooo-ooouuuul!

"Cool," Chris said, snapping his fingers and cocking his head. "That piano player really wails."

I've got Jesus as my savior!
I've got Jesus as my savior!
I've got Jesus as my savior
in my soooooooo-ooouuuul!

Leo segued into "The Wedding March" and Daniel cleared his throat. Chris patted his pockets nervously, as if he'd forgotten something. Rolling papers? Harmonica? Ah, the ring, Cosmo's ring.

Back in Montreal, Cosmo had given me a thick gold ring with a microscopic stone in it. "It's a diamond, D'Arcy," Cosmo had told me, putting his index finger to his lips. "Very valuable." He acted as if the ring had been purchased at great peril. "Put it on!" he commanded.

I wrenched it onto my left ring finger, forcing it over the joint. The little diamond – it couldn't have been bigger than the head of a straight pin – winked back at me.

"Do you like it?" Cosmo asked.

"Love it!" I said. My finger looked like an overweight dachshund wearing a rubber band necklace.

Daniel nodded at us, then Chris gave me his arm and we made the long walk across the waxed wooden floor, past the saints with their manic smiles, past my sad and nervous mother, to the front of the hall. Henry took my hand as I bounced next to him, nervously rocking in my pumps. Chris glanced over at me as if to say, *Whoa, sis, don't fall over.*

This was no drive-thru ceremony. Daniel wasn't in a hurry to give his benediction, not without a sermon first. When he cleared his throat, Chris tapped his foot and sighed.

"Before I marry these two, I have a few words of advice for this young couple," he said. The sun exploded behind Daniel's head. He glowed for a moment. Motes of dust swam through the filtered rays and drifted toward the floor. I looked at Henry; his eyes gleamed behind his glasses.

"Wives, like plants, need warmth, light, and a sheltered environment," Daniel said. "But every now and then you've got to … prune them. Trim them. Nip them in the bud." He looked down at his notes on the rostrum. "You have to water them, fertilize them, and, if aphids appear, *you must pluck them off.*" My mother sat stiffly in her chair, her mouth pursed. A photograph taken of her during the sermon shows her glaring at the preacher with *pluck this* written all over her face.

Daniel continued. As for the woman who worries about keeping her beauty – and thus her man's interest – Daniel reminded us that it was more important to train her eyes on the Lord. In the First Book of Peter 3:3–5, it says that a woman's beauty shouldn't come from fancy hairstyles, jewelry, or designer clothing, but from the gentle, quiet inner self, which is of great worth in God's sight. The sun skirted behind a cloud and the room darkened momentarily.

"Henry, are you ready to feed D'Arcy, tend her, shield her from the wind and expose her to the sun?" Daniel said. "Will you help her grow hardy on the Word, invigorated by the Spirit and refreshed by Living Waters?"

"Amen," Henry said, unblinking, earnest.

Daniel turned to me. "As for you, D'Arcy, are you ready to submit to your husband's authority and respect him as your rightful head? Will you, in other words, allow yourself to be pruned from time to time?"

"I will," I said, "I mean, I do."

"Then, by the power vested in me, I now pronounce you man and wife," Daniel said.

The saints cheered and I felt lifted up on a cloud of loving approval. Henry took me in his arms and kissed me on the lips. I put my arms around him, ran my fingers through his hair, and caught my brother's eye. Chris raised his eyebrows and waggled his fingers near his lips, like Groucho Marx smoking a fat stogie.

Cosmo chucked me on the cheek, fumbled in his pocket, and handed Henry a handful of bills.

"For the trip," he said gruffly, rolling his r's. The *treeep*. "Have a good time with Jesus Christus."

"Pop, please, you don't have to –" Henry began.

Cosmo shrugged. "Go ahead. Live it up."

"Congratulations, honey," my mother said, kissing me on the cheek. "I love you."

"Wow, you're married," my sister said, popping up beside us. Henry hugged Mary for a millisecond longer than I thought proper for a spanking new brother-in-law and an infinitesimal flash of jealousy flared in my blood.

"Thanks so much for coming," I said, throwing my arms around her, taking in the very Mary-ness of her: stubborn curly hair, little wrists, sharp angles, pointed chin, and high cheekbones. She was so tiny and so strong.

She was going to be a vet or a doctor or maybe a nurse. Why was she so smart? Who taught her that the world was hers for the taking?

"Be happy," Mary murmured. "I hope you guys have a great honeymoon."

"Oh, we will," I said, suddenly fighting a wave of panic. Things were out of sequence. It seemed like I was always leaving, or thinking about it. I had been the first child to really leave home. Mary had gone only thirty miles away, across the Bay Bridge, to college in San Francisco. Goodbye was in the air. Marriage felt final.

My grandmother, looking smart in her Chanel leather mini-skirt, enfolded me in a freckled hug, exuding Evening in Paris perfume and Halo shampoo. She stroked my hair, then stood back to look at me. Her blue eyes filled with tears.

"Oh, honey, I wish you two the best," she warbled.

"Thanks, grandmother," I said, sniffing.

"Come visit us, OK? Bob and I can't wait to see you in Sedona."

"I will," I whispered, nodding.

The Veterans' Hall was emptying out. Henry went to get the car. As the shadows lengthened on that cloudy February afternoon, I waited on the curb with my family. My new husband pulled up in the old VW bus my parents had given us and honked. All the ceremonies were over. A last hug, then I climbed in the passenger seat and we drove away, waving.

Good hand, bad hand.

Day-o!

WE PASSED THE HUMBOLDT BAY NATIONAL WILDLIFE REFUGE just after two in the afternoon. I took a deep breath and held it in. Beyond the salt marsh grasses, beyond the jetty, the ocean foamed and pounded. I turned on the radio, heard static, flicked it off. Henry kept both hands on the wheel. The bus's tires hummed on the pavement. We had all the time, all the room in the world.

"We did it, sweetheart," I said.

"Yeah, I know," Henry said with a nervous giggle.

"Your dad looked like he was going to keel over during the wedding." I scooted closer to him, looped an index finger through a curl.

"He always looks like that."

"He does?"

"Pop's a tense guy."

I was tense too. We'd planned to spend our wedding night at a hotel in the redwoods somewhere near Garberville. As we homed in on our cabin, my stomach lurched. After I accepted Christ, I believed I was *New In Him.* Did that make me a born-again virgin, with a resurrected, hermetically sealed hymen? Sex as sacrament.

My head throbbed. Had I packed the birth control pills? The new nightgown from Penney's? Why wear a nightgown anyway? Sex. Praise God! But godly sex. In the spirit. And the flesh. Becoming one. Did we pack aspirin? The redwoods along the highway stood thick and close. A pallid sun flickered between their green quills. The cold Eel River splashed and bubbled over unyielding rocks. I turned to Henry and studied his profile: that unapologetic, strong Roman nose, those full lips, that hair.

Love was holy, sex was good, marriage in the Lord was blessed. In the Song of Songs, the Shulamite besotted with the King proclaims:

O daughters of Jerusalem, I charge you –
if you find my lover,
what will you tell him?
Tell him I am faint with love. (5:8)

Faint with love. And getting tiny rushes, pinpricks of anxiety. Was it hot in the car or what?

Henry put an arm around my shoulder. "Are we there yet?" he said.

I looked away. "Pop gave us money for the trip?" I asked, knowing that he had. "How much?"

"Oh, about $43."

"It sure looked like a big wad of cash."

Henry took his arm back to steer. Then he poked me in the ribs. "With Pop, it always looks like a big wad."

"I mean, a really big wad," I said. "A really huge, humongous wad." My tongue felt like a slab of liverwurst.

"A wad of ones," my husband said.

"Well, it was nice of him anyway."

"Sure."

I glanced down. My seat belt was on. We had a full tank of gas, a carload of unopened presents, and a five-gallon bucket of fresh granola, praise God.

"Pop's got a good heart," I chattered.

Henry snorted. "Tell that to Ma."

"Well, I like him." It was true.

"He can be a devil, trust me."

"There's some good in everybody."

"He needs the Lord."

I tried to imagine Cosmo saved and filled with the Holy Ghost. I couldn't picture him as a scripture-quoting businessman witnessing to the bald, shuffling men who browsed in his store in Montreal. His store was a monument to stone-age technology, filled with industrial sewing machines that perched on the showroom tables like mummified pterodactyls. My father-in-law. Dancing in the Spirit at Deliverance Temple in his sleeveless undershirt, his eyes moist with joy behind the gangster shades. Or sitting next to us in a church pew like a ventriloquist's dummy, his little feet barely brushing the floor, listening to a sermon about training his soul.

We pulled up to a rustic motel nestled in the redwoods. The sin-red vacancy light shimmered in the February fog. A blinking arrow pointing to the office pulsated *yes!*

"I think this is it," Henry said.

"OK," I said.

"I'll get the key, honey. You coming?"

"In a minute."

I sat in the car and watched him lug our bags over to the office. The imperturbable trees, a cold river running over sharp rocks, the glimpse of the gray sun through the window made me feel ancient and impossibly juvenile. We had crossed a threshold earlier in the day when we took our vows and we were about to cross another one. "Pretty is as pretty does," my mother used to tell me. I got out of the car, stood up straight, and aimed for pretty.

AT FIRST, IT FELT STRANGE TO BE AWAY FROM THE CLAMOR OF the ranch. Strange in a good way – like the sudden abeyance of fierce wind. We didn't know what to do with ourselves. No heavy brass gong summoned us to the dining hall for Bible study or breakfast, no voice cajoled us to rise and shine. For the first time since we'd met, we were together and utterly without supervision. We could do anything we wanted. Anything. And I wanted, I wanted. What did I want? To eat the world, drink the sky, inhale the sun. Dance barefoot on wet grass in a batik sarong. Love. I was faint with it.

AFTER TWO DAYS ON THE ROAD, WE STARTED FOR MY GRAND-mother's house in Sedona, Arizona. So far we'd been staying in little hotels, but knowing there was a mattress in the back of the car gave the trip an illicit *frisson*. Sex could happen at anytime, anywhere. It was literally right around the corner, in the next copse of trees. One afternoon we pulled over off the highway in the desert and drove into the sagebrush. As the engine ticked and cooled under the hyacinth sky, we closed the curtains and made sweaty love, then fell back into sleep as if slain in the spirit. When a highway patrol officer rapped smartly on the window an hour later and demanded some ID, we scrambled for our clothes.

Sometimes when Henry flicked on the car blinker and eased into the exit lane, I turned to him expectantly. It took me a moment to register that he was pulling over for gas, not love.

"We're running low, babe," he said, kissing me on the check. He got out, whistling sexily, and washed the windshield. Itchy, restless, I hopped out after him. After gassing up, he pulled out the dipstick to check the oil, wiped it with a rag, and said, "She's runnin' low. Probably could use a quart or two."

"Me, too," I said, blushing.

At a Howard Johnson's outside of Kingman, I ordered a cheeseburger and a plate of French fries and held a private conversation with Jesus. *Give us a plan, Lord, help us be happy, help us forget about time.* I dipped a French fry into a Dixie cup of ketchup and looked over at Henry. He was studying a map of Mexico.

COCKTAIL HOUR. MY GRANDMOTHER AND BOB SAT ON THEIR BACK deck, grinning in the sunset. Sedona's bright apricot rocks glowed in dusky light; Ancient Age bourbon and ginger ale paddled through my bloodstream. I let the alcohol do the steering, happy just to drift for now.

My grandmother wore white cotton slacks, a pink blouse, an apron, and one of her heavy turquoise necklaces. Bob was in his usual attire: crisp, creased shorts, moccasins, and an immaculate Polo shirt. Henry, drinking apple juice, sat in a wicker chair under the hummingbird feeder, strumming his guitar absentmindedly. His sandaled feet kept time to a tune I couldn't follow. Hawks drifted above us, surfing on the thermals.

"Shoot, Mary, before you know it, I won't even be able to drive my own Cadillac!" Bob complained to my grandmother before petulantly flinging a handful of Planter's nuts into his mouth. Slender, worldly, dapper, Bob was a stock market whiz. He aligned himself with the Republican party and the NRA, while my liberal grandmother loathed Ronald Reagan.

The gasoline shortage was a pain in the butt, he snorted. We're down to rationing! How infuriating that he couldn't gas up whenever he wanted, that some teenage kid at the corner Shell station could have veto power over him.

"Pretty soon they won't let people drive at all," he fumed, his tanned, lined face pleating with disapproval.

"You think so?" my grandmother said, winking at me. Men. She pulled on her earlobe and smiled. "I don't think it'll come to that, Bob."

"Hell if it won't," he growled, lighting the Tareyton in his long elegant cigarette holder. Smoke curled over his balding head. He sipped his bourbon. At that moment, he looked like the right wing's answer to Hunter S. Thompson.

In her more playful moments, my grandmother admitted she liked having a "fella" around. Bob was her fella, but they were very different people. Of course, people were probably saying the same thing about

Henry and me. I glanced over at him. His mouth was pursed in concentration. He was so handsome, but when he got that faraway look of elastic concentration, he reminded me of Harpo Marx. He should've been a mime. Maybe after dinner he'd do his strangling act for everybody. It was a guaranteed showstopper.

My grandmother got to her feet. "Well," she said, clapping her hands together and rubbing them on her apron. "Who's on the dinner committee with me?" It was a rhetorical question. Her fella popped another peanut in his mouth and looked off in the distance, chewing slowly. My fella looked equally preoccupied. I bounced up and started setting the table. My grandmother pulled the pan of enchiladas from the oven. I thought back to Aunt Clarissa and Shy Hot Dog Pie. Maybe I could finally try out that recipe.

"Boy, that smells so good," I told my grandmother.

"Natch," she said, smoothing her hair back like a bathing beauty.

"It's great being here," I said.

"Well," she said, drawing out the word, "it's a treat for us."

We stood together by the sink, looking out the kitchen window at our men. Bob was immersed in the *Wall Street Journal*, his tortoiseshell bifocals perched on the bridge of his nose. Henry still strummed his guitar, frowning with concentration as he searched for the right chord.

Elbowing my grandmother, I said, "He's cute, don't you think?"

"Why, of course he is! Is he having fun here?"

We'd been in Sedona four days and gone to church twice already.

"He's having a wonderful time." I paused. "If he's not, he's missing one heck of an opportunity."

"Right-o!"

"Shall we have wine with dinner?"

"Why not?" my grandmother said gaily.

LATER THAT NIGHT HENRY AND BOB PLAYED POOL UNDER A LOW-hanging Venetian cut-glass lamp that flooded the room in a pale yellow wash. My grandmother was stretched out on the couch reading Lawrence Sanders's *The First Deadly Sin*. I put on one of my grandmother's favorite albums – *An Evening with Harry Belafonte* – and looked around the room.

We're all married, I thought. Two couples. A foursome. Grown-ups. We could play bridge, just like my parents, except I never learned the game.

I wandered down the hall and paused in the doorway of Bob's and my grandmother's room. Their twin beds were covered with matching lavender coverlets. Portraits of my mother and her younger sister stared back at me from over the headboards. Both of them wore simple off-the-shoulder gowns. My aunt, with short bangs and enormous blue eyes, looked straight ahead; my mother's face, framed by thick long auburn hair, was featured at a slight angle, a quizzical smile tugging at one corner of her mouth. Her eyes followed me as I touched my grandmother's expensive perfumes on her vanity table. I spritzed myself with Chanel No. 9 as Belafonte's honeyed voice came floating down the hall like a breeze whispering through the sugar cane:

> *Work all day on a drink a'rum*
> *(daylight come and he wan' go home)*

Bob growled, "Well, goddamn, son! You beat me, you little Canuck!" Henry laughed politely.

"*It's six-foot, seven-foot, eight-foot bunch!*"

I slipped on one of my grandmother's heavy silver bracelets and curtsied in front of my mother's portrait.

Coral-colored toenails smiled up at me. I danced. We weren't due back at the ranch for another ten days. Perhaps the rapture would happen first and we'd never go back. I danced myself back to the living room and poured two inches of crème de menthe into a sherry glass. Henry was reading the Bible; my grandmother and Bob were out on the deck, looking at the stars.

"How you doin'?" Henry said, looking up at me as he marked his place with a finger.

"I'm wonderful," I said, dancing in front of him. Bobbing, swooning, shaking my hips, snapping my fingers, I said, "Come, Mr. Tallyman."

Henry rolled his eyes. "Oh, boy, what's she been smoking?"

"Stack bananas till the morning come."

"Day-o," Henry sang along.

"Day-ay-ay-o," I said. "How is your banana?"

"You're goofy," he said. "Are you drunk?"

"Actually, yes. A little. Dance with me, honey."

He set his Bible down on the table next to *The First Deadly Sin* and looked at me with a raised eyebrow.

"Come here," I said, bobbing and weaving like Muhammad Ali. He stood up, his arms by his side.

A beautiful bunch of ripe bananas!
(Daylight come and he wan' go home)
Hide the deadly black tarantula

Henry began shuffling slowly, deliberately across the satillo tile floor. He snapped his fingers and twirled slowly. There were so many things I didn't know about him, starting with how he saw me. It doesn't matter, I told myself, out of breath. When my shins bumped the coffee table, I kept dancing.

In the Desert

WE SLEPT IN THE BACK OF THE VW. CROSSING THE ARIZONA desert on our way to Baja Mexico in our microbus, I thought about the early American settlers who plodded west in Conestoga wagons, bumping through the sagebrush as they scoured the horizon for a new home, a new way of life. I felt happy to be away from the people who would compare the new me with the one I used to be. At night, the sky burned with so many stars we could see each other's face without flashlights. It was almost bright enough to read The Word by moonlight. Almost but not quite. Henry and I lit candles and sang, ate cold cuts and crackers, toasted each other with lukewarm Pepsis. I wanted us to keep driving forever.

I'd gotten my license two years earlier, but I needed practice with a stick shift. Henry winced when I tried to downshift.

"Don't strip the gears!"

We bounced down a rutted two-lane road, bobbing past the cacti, dead armadillos, and old tires.

"Easy, easy," he said, gripping the side of the window, as if that would make the ride smoother. The bus shuddered as I slowed, stuck behind a slow-moving farm tractor.

"I *am* easy," I shot back. "*You* be easy."

In a poor fishing village at the north end of the Sea of Cortez, we camped on the beach. Henry was anxious to speak Spanish to the natives; me, I wanted to lie in the sun and sleep, maybe swim. I awoke every morning with a sharp pang as light streamed through the van curtains, realizing we were spending our honeymoon days like money we didn't have. The bill would come due when we returned to the ranch, payment required for freedom and sunshine. Henry's mood was light; he noodled along the beach in his sandals, talking with the bronzed fishermen about the Lord as they mended their nets. He pointed to me, grinned. He said, "*Mí espousa.*"

Be happy for what you have, I told myself, watching him. I remembered what it said in Matthew 6:34: "Take no thought for the morrow, for the morrow shall take thought for the things of itself. Sufficient unto the day is the evil therof."

On Sunday Henry said, "Let's go to church."

"We're on vacation."

"Not from God."

"The only church in this town is the Catholic one," I said.

"How do you know?"

"I'm just guessing."

"OK, let's go to the Catholic church then."

"Forget it," I snapped. "We can worship the Lord outside. I've had enough of the Catholic church to last a lifetime."

"I think we should go to church," Henry said, rubbing his jaw thoughtfully.

"I'm not going," I said.

"Suit yourself."

Kneeling in church, I studied the Mexican flag, which stood out against the turquoise walls. Behind the altar, Jesus writhed on the cross in frozen agony, flanked by his mom and dad. Mary stared at me in tight-lipped reproach, reminding me of all the nuns I'd ever known. Her ceramic face was clouded with skepticism, as if to say: *Get with the program, Missy.* I turned from her, and appealed to Joseph. His eyes were fixed on the back door, as if he couldn't wait for Mass to be over so he could bolt past the heavy wooden doors and smoke a cigarette in peace. Neither of them were any help. There was only Jesus, the dying Christ, whom I kept crucifying through my disobedience and willfulness, only Jesus, my spiritual husband, whom I drew back from in guilt.

I WATCHED A FISHERMAN IN SAN FELIPE CLUBBING AN OCTOPUS, trying to tenderize its flesh. Henry and I fought. He wanted to head back to the ranch, stopping on the way to see friends in Santa Barbara. I didn't want to return to the United States. I wasn't ready to share him.

"Honey, we've got to go back sooner or later," Henry said. He took my hand, patted it. "Don't worry."

I looked up at the sky. The clouds were rippled, like the sand dunes. A rooster crowed. "Do we have to go back?"

"You mean *ever?*"

"No, yes, I mean, can't we stay awhile?"

Down by the shore, a shirtless man hammered his boat. Seagulls circled over the beach.

Henry bit his lip and then said: "We *have* stayed awhile. It's time to go home."

ON THE TRIP NORTH, WE STOPPED TO SEE MY MOTHER IN CONTRA Costa County.

"How-are-you-how's-the-trip?" my mother quizzed as we walked through the door. "What's-your-news-what-have-you-been-doing?"

I took a breath. "Well, we were in Mexico and –"

"Oooh, was it fun?"

"It was, Mom. We stayed in this little village and ate seafood –"

"Seafood? You're kidding. Are there any art galleries down there? What are the locals like? Did you –"

I gulped for air. "We didn't see any galleries, but we weren't really looking for any."

Henry stood next to me, smiling widely. I smiled. My mother smiled. Timothy Leary thumped his tail on the carpet. He'd gotten so gray around his muzzle. Maybe redheaded canines didn't age well; maybe I'd lost track of time.

"Good to see you, Mom," Henry said. He put his arm around her and gave her a squeeze.

"Good to see you too," my mother said. "Tell me all about everything."

It occurred to me that my mother was nervous; all this chatter was like a team of sled dogs pulling us safely through vast stretches of snowy, dangerous silence.

I remembered the time my old boyfriend Mark from Virginia had visited me in this house; he had been staying with us while he looked for a place to live in nearby Berkeley. Early one morning he had been meditating in the lotus position on the living room rug, next to an antique Chinese chair once used in a local theater production of *The Mikado*. He'd startled my mother, who almost stepped on him in the dawn gloom as she made her way into the kitchen for coffee. Later, she laughed about it with me. "Good god, you know what the scariest part of it was? He was nekkid as a jaybird!" she'd said, clutching her hand to her heart in mock horror.

Standing in the backyard, I gazed at the hills of Lafayette, the new March grass so young and green it almost hurt to look at it. The apple trees in the backyard had yielded little green fruits, smaller than jawbreakers and just as hard.

The first movement of Bach's *Brandenburg Concerto No. 5 in D Major* floated out the window, lively familiar harpsichord notes tripping like a baroque princess dancing among her subjects, the notes trailing behind her in an elaborate veil. My mother stood in the kitchen looking out the window, transfixed by the music. Although I couldn't hear her, I knew she was humming.

Setting out for Eureka early the next morning, the VW had a flat before we even reached the highway. At the Shell station in town, impatient motorists queued in a long line for gas.

"Maybe God's telling us today isn't a good day to travel," I said.

"Maybe He's telling us to persevere," Henry replied in a steely tone.

AT THE RANCH, WE MOVED INTO A LITTLE ROOM IN THE UPSTAIRS section of the main building, where the married couples lived. The roof leaked and the walls seemed as flimsy as balsa wood. Henry began working as an ad salesman for the *Tri-City Advertiser*. I hung up curtains and put a coleus plant in the window. After a week, the room started to feel like home. In the evenings after Bible study, Henry and I giggled as we padded down the hall to the communal showers in our bathrobes. Afterwards, damp and clean, we read The Word. I had made a vow: I would be happy here, no matter what.

My Mexican tan faded. On St. Patrick's Day, Henry was appointed a "group leader," overseeing a small group of ranch residents who met once a week to talk about their relationship with the Lord. When spring officially started, it had been raining nonstop for a week.

3.

The Married Club

"GOD WANTS TRUE DISCIPLES, NOT HALF-BAKED ONES," BROTHER Caleb preached, restlessly pacing back and forth in the dining hall. His enormous brown eyes bulged out of the sockets. Caleb used to be a surfer in Los Angeles; if I closed one eye, I could imagine him kneeling on his board, long arms stroking through the water as the Malibu sun pummeled his broad, tanned shoulders. I began counting his steps, anticipating how many foot lengths it would take before his sneakers turned.

"Jesus wants it all," Caleb said, still pacing back and forth in front of the piano while all of us, 130 tired saints, listened, rapt. Mist pressed against the long, narrow windows. "He doesn't want us to be on some sort of a *trip*."

Caleb stopped suddenly and stared above our heads, as if trying to decipher words written on the dingy ceiling. He seemed disdainful at what he saw. "He doesn't want us to be on a Jesus trip, some kind of a *phase* we're going to grow out of."

"Amen," chorused a few of the SMOGS.

"Praise you, Lord," said Marion. She and her husband were the new elders at the Ranch.

"Hallelujah!" said Henry with a faraway smile. He was getting that Harpo look. After Caleb's Bible study, Henry was supposed to sing a few folk songs he'd learned while staying on a *kibbutz* one year. There might be some edifying talk about his travels in Israel.

Caleb shuddered. And spoke. "*Hana-to-macki*. Praise you, Lord! Oh, hallelujah, Jesus! *Hee-pan-da. Sha-habba. Habba-rabba.*"

Listening to him speak in tongues, I thought of Fred Flintstone. *Yabba-dabba-doo!* I replied behind a small, locked door in my mind. Out of nowhere, the cartoon theme cranked up:

Flintstones, meet the Flintstones,
They're the modern stone-age family!
From the town of Bedrock,
They're a page right out of history!

The pacing began again in earnest. Caleb was so long and tall, so sinewy and quick, I half expected him to vault over the table and shake his finger in my face.

Wil—ma!

His eyes bugged out. Maybe he had a thyroid condition. Every few minutes I glanced at the clock over the piano and sighed. I was twenty. I had been married for three months. I was wearing a long wool skirt, a sweatshirt, and a pair of hiking boots. I held a Bible in my lap, and I was trying to remember if I'd taken my birth control pill that day.

I wasn't the same person who'd left the ranch for a Mexican honeymoon. I was different. Marriage whetted my appetite for solitude and privacy. Feelings I'd kept under wraps during our courtship—anger, impatience, sadness—re-emerged those first weeks after our wedding. I cried for no reason. One rainy night, I ran through the dark hall upstairs past the married couples' rooms, crouched and hid in an empty shower stall, laughing for no reason behind a moldy plastic curtain. After lunchtime chores, I could barely keep my eyes open. Upstairs in our bedroom, I fell into bed and flung myself into sleep like a steel suitcase tossed into an algae-filled pool. Down, down, I sank, until I hit the murky bottom, where I lay curled in suspended, fetal animation. When I woke up, I felt hungover and exhausted.

In the late afternoon, like a bored concubine, I readied myself for Henry's return, spritzing myself with the free, finger-sized vials of Estée Lauder's Youth Dew that my sister had sent me from I. Magnin in San Francisco, where she worked while attending nursing school.

"Jesus doesn't want us to hold back," Caleb said. One, two, three, squeak and kickturn. "Are any of *you* holding back?"

I fought a strong impulse to raise my hand and tell Caleb and the rest of the body of Christ that yes, I *had* been holding back, but I wanted to turn myself in. I had been hanging out in my soul, thinking rebellious evil thoughts but now I was ready to return to the land of the living. I wanted to come clean. I knew I wasn't the only person going through trials. The week before, in the middle of the night, without a word to anybody, Raoul and Bridget slunk away. I knew Raoul had been unhappy—he had trouble submitting to the elders' authority, and he had a temper. Bridget had recently asked us to lift him up to the Lord during a prayer meeting. Where had they gone? I stared at the knotted laces in Caleb's shoes.

Henry loved the ranch. It fed into his sense of self, and propped up his idea of who he wanted to be. He was popular. He was cute. He was smooth. The elders at the ranch told him he was a "mighty man of God," that the Lord was "raising him up" to do good things. Affirmations made him preen. Younger brothers and sisters liked to hang out with him, hear his songs, listen to him talk about life in Israel. I was jealous, although I was expected to respond with hot-diggity-dog enthusiasm. Who was he really, without the validating onlookers? Alone, just with me, he seemed diminished, mortal, ordinary. On those rare occasions when we dined out together, he had trouble deciding what to order. The simplest choices concealed land mines.

"What do I want, what do I want?" he mumbled one day as we sat in Denny's, raking his fingers through his hair. I stared at my husband and thought, Yes, my darling, what *do* you want?

The hovering waitress paused, pen in hand. "Shall I come back?" Carla said hopefully.

"No. Just a minute." Seconds ticked by. Make a decision, beloved. Did he know I was silently counting to myself? Could he intuit my mounting exasperation?

"How's the snapper?" Henry asked.

"Snapper's good," Carla said, shifting her weight from one foot to the other. Coins clinked in her apron pocket.

"Fresh?"

"Excuse me?"

"Is the snapper fresh?"

"Oh, I'm sure," she said, glancing over at her customers at the next table. They were signaling for her. Henry consulted the menu again. "Decisions, decisions," he muttered, stroking his chin.

It's just food, I thought, and then felt guilty about my impatience. This is my man. We're married. I should support him in all choices, even an entree at Denny's. Godly wives don't roll their eyes or drum their nails on the table. They don't feel the urge to yell, or lob cellophaned packages of crushed saltines across the room. They don't have to suppress the urge to scream, "Oh, for Pete's sake, order everything, why don't you? Bon fucking appetit!" My anger surprised me; my impatience seemed out of proportion, but it was difficult to muffle the critic within.

"I'll come back," Carla said. "Just wave when you're ready."

"I'm ... ready," my husband said.

"Good," she said faintly, snapping open her order pad. "So what are you having?"

A nervous breakdown.

"I'll have –" Henry paused and stroked his chin again. He peered at the menu like Galileo gazing into a telescope, on the verge of discovering a new planet. "I'll have ... the chicken." I took a deep breath.

"Okie dokie," Carla said before turning to the next table.

I leaned forward. "So how's your day going? How are you?"

"Oh, I'm OK."

"What is it, honey?"

"I'm fine."

"You seem down."

He paused a few beats. "You know, I should've ordered the spaghetti instead," he suddenly burst out, smacking the table with the palm of his hand.

"Really?" I said.

"I always choose the wrong thing." He smote his forehead. "Why do I always choose the wrong thing?"

"Look, change your order before it's too late."

"Naw, I'll just have to live with it," he said.

"Honey, it's not a big deal," I said.

"Then why don't you quit talking about it?" Henry said. "Let's just enjoy ourselves."

BEFORE THE WEDDING, I THOUGHT THAT HENRY AND I WOULD join that throng of wholesome, popcorn-popping, Bible-quoting young marrieds who lived upstairs over the ranch kitchen. I used to think of them as members of the Married Club. They always seemed to be laughing and pulling pranks, like a retinue of extras from a Frankie Avalon and

Annette Funicello movie – call it *Beach Party Disciples* or *Surfing with Our Savior*. I believed that once we were wed, Henry and I would be transformed into better, more loving and beautiful versions of ourselves. Now that I was in the Married Club and a dues-paying member, I saw all of us for who we really were, a collection of too-human souls trying to work out our own salvation. And now I was impatient with the club members, especially Henry. What did I want?

Playfulness. Leisure. Joy.

I wanted to be wooed and courted. I wanted a decisive man who wasn't afraid of my feelings – or his own. I wanted a talker, a ravisher. I wanted to be drawn out, and not by a tentative, soft-spoken man in sandals and hip huggers who agonized over what to have for lunch. I wanted Henry to lead us away from the ranch, cutting and hacking through the jungle of protestations and prophecies ("God won't bless your life if you leave!" "The Evil One is tempting you!") that barred every exit. I wanted him to be Paul Bunyon brandishing an electric weed-whacker, blazing a trail out of there.

Slugabed

IN THE MINISTRY, THERE WAS NO SUCH THING AS A PERSONAL question. All parts of our lives were supposed to be open for scrutiny. But what had once seemed to me like a charming frankness, a willingness to lay bare one's soul, now felt like a psychological laxative. It was a constant purge. There was no physical or psychological privacy – particularly if you were a married woman – because so much time was taken up with child rearing. To pursue any of life's other options, such as college or an outside job, seemed an act of rebellion. Better to fall in line. Biology was destiny. My friend, Beverly, who had come to the ranch with a young son from another relationship, now lived next door to Henry and me. Like us, she was a new member in the Married Club. Recently wed to a handsome, mustachioed ranch resident, Beverly was now pregnant with their first child. This baby filled her up. Wide-hipped and bosomy to begin with, pregnancy transformed her into an earth mother, the Lord's odalisque. I watched her widen and expand, grow huge with private satisfaction. Most of the married women at the Lighthouse Ranch had children or were pregnant with their first one. It wasn't uncommon to witness a wedding and then, forty weeks later, see the young bride nursing her baby in a back pew in church. Fecund young women, waddling across the land, would quote Genesis – "Be fruitful and multiply" – and inquire why Henry and I weren't pregnant yet. Were we using birth control? (Yes.) What kind? (The Pill.) Why didn't we just trust the Lord? (A tight smile and a shrug. The real answer: I was petrified of getting saddled with a child so soon after my wedding, and no, I didn't believe Jesus had anything to do with whether or not I got pregnant.) I wanted to reply that this relentless line of inquiry was nobody's business, thanks all the same. But I didn't.

I swept the floor in our room and tried to dislodge the toast crumbs wedged in the cracks of our burl table. Fog swirled around the cypress, enveloping the squat, gray water tower. Millet for breakfast. Tuna sandwiches and soup for lunch. Vegetable stew and whole wheat bread for dinner. *The Lord is my shepherd, I shall not want.* Yes, but chocolate would be a blessing. Bible study. Gardening. Sorting the mail. Shopping at Wholly Foods, the health food store in Eureka, for oats, honey, oil. During the day, many of the men and single women scattered to jobs in town, leaving the ranch largely populated by married women and young children. By six, when the men came home, the ranch was suddenly awash with testosterone. It was as if we'd been holding our collective breath all day, and finally, as the cars pulled into the parking lot and expelled briefcase-toting husbands and sunburned Donut Brothers, we could finally exhale. Daddy's home!

When some of the brothers brought three tons of tomatoes from Marysville, I was charged with canning them. I didn't know anything about canning, and I hoped we all wouldn't get botulism. That's how it was at the ranch. Even if you didn't know what you were doing, you just grabbed an apron, read some instructions and hoped for the best. Pretty soon there were hundreds of ruby red jars lined up in the pantry cupboard with little labels bearing the date.

I kept track of the days in my diary. The pages were underscored by scolding self-criticism and painstakingly copied Bible scriptures. "The wise woman builds her house, but with her own hands the foolish one tears hers down"(Proverbs 14:1). The pages contained pep talks and seasonal observations, meditations about Jesus, sugar cookie recipes, dreams, and the Dr. Atkins diet regime (hard to pull off on the ranch's low-protein, high-carb diet of pasta and potatoes).

HENRY WAS MR. COOL BREEZE. PEOPLE LIKED HIM. HE WAS SWEET, funny. He didn't try too hard. He was open with others. He loved to sing and he wished I could sing with him. Henry had been asking the Lord to give me a good singing voice. I had a lot of feeling when I sang. I was sincere. I had volume, but I was frequently off-key. One time when Henry and I got up before the brethren after dinner and sang a little song Henry had written, some people smirked. Nobody asked for an encore.

"I have other talents," I told Barbara.

"Really? And what might those be?" she said.

A FEW MONTHS AFTER OUR HONEYMOON HENRY AND I LAY IN BED. Soon, I would have to get up. But on this particular morning I lingered, listening to footsteps going down the hall to the bathroom. A slamming door. A long hard piss. A flush. The creaking of rusty pipes as lukewarm water poured into the sink. It was Joel, whistling "This Is the Day That the Lord Hath Made." God may love a cheerful heart, but for the rest of us, someone else's cheer is excruciating before six in the morning without coffee.

I'm so sick of this place, I thought, deathly tired as I pulled the covers over my head.

"We've got to get out of here," I told Henry. "I can't take another day."

Henry sighed. "I don't think that's God will for us."

"How do you know?" I whispered.

"Because God didn't tell me. I think I'd know before you did."

Calvin rang the wake-up bell. "Arise, slugabeds!" he shouted as he walked across the front lawn.

"Hallelujah!" Joel shouted from the bathroom window.

"Praise God!" Calvin replied.

"Praise Him in His Firmament," Joel yelled back.

"What is this, a contest?" I said.

"Praise Him with psaltery and harp!" Calvin boomed.

I rolled over and groaned. Joel still wasn't finished with his ablutions. Hard honks reverberated from the bathroom. It sounded like his brains were being pushed out through his nostrils. What was Joel doing in there, anyway? Examining the evidence?

"I wish he'd hurry up," I said. "I'm about to wet my nightgown."

"Patience."

"He's probably going to use all the hot water too."

"You're a regular ray of sunshine."

"Do you have to go to work today?"

"I have a job, remember?"

"Oh right."

"What's the matter anyway?"

"I hate this place."

"You're just being selfish."

Joel rapped on the door. "Praise the Lord, you two! Bathroom's free."

"Thanks for your compassion, Henry."

"Try being happy for a change. Try being grateful for what you have."

"Right. And your life is perfect."

"I can do all things in Him."

"Come on, get real."

"I am real."

"You're such a phony. You suck up to everybody and pretend to be spiritual when I know you're afraid to be real."

"Why can't you be like Marion? Why can't you just support me for a change?" Marion was a couple years older than I was and had two children, but she always looked chipper. Marion. Candy-striper for Jesus.

"You're such an asshole."

"I can't believe you just said that," Henry said. His face flamed scarlet. "Please just calm down."

"Wimp," I said, starting to cry. "You have no spine. I hate you."

"If you're so unhappy, leave." Henry put on his bathrobe and cinched the sash. "Nobody's stopping you." He crossed the hall to the bathroom.

"Certainly not you, right?" I called after him. He didn't answer.

When he came back, he dressed quickly, buttoning up the shirt I'd ironed the day before.

"You honestly don't care if I leave?" I said.

"It's between you and the Lord."

"It has nothing to do with you? Nothing?"

He reached for his tie. "I'll pray for you."

I raised my hand. It moved of its own accord in a swinging arc, made meaty contact with the side of his face. Henry's glasses flew against the wall. A lens popped out.

"You, you …" Henry gasped, rubbing his cheek. "You bitch."

"Go to hell."

Wide-eyed and pale, he tip-toed out of our room. Ten paces away, I heard him pick up his stride, moving with a jaunty step, a man clearly in charge of his life – and his wife. I heard the brothers greeting him.

"Praise the Lord, Henry," they called. "How are you this morning?"

"I'm fine," he said. His voice shook a little. "The joy of the Lord is my strength!"

I dried my eyes on the sheet, put on some Chap Stick, and went downstairs to start boiling water for the oatmeal. In half an hour, I would lead the sisters in prayer. In the name of Jesus, I would ask His blessing on the day.

Bad Dog

I LAY IN BED, THINKING OF THE SALT MARSHES ALONG THE coast and how the tides both inflated and eroded the natural world. In, out, in, out, the water pulsed. It was as natural as breathing. I was trying not to think about leaving. That was dangerous. The more I fantasized about leaving, the further I felt from God. And if I spent the day fully dwelling in the idea, embracing the possibility of starting afresh somewhere else, Henry would know. When he came home from work, I would be a different woman from the one he'd left that morning. I would be distracted, teary, impatient. (Perhaps he wouldn't know the difference.) But my heart was canted toward that direction, no matter how hard I tried to keep it from tilting.

Just breathe. Think about now! Praise God! Get your eyes on Jesus!

There was a sharp rap at the door. Marion stood in the doorway, looking disheveled in a flour-dusted apron. "Look," she began, waving the spoon at me. "You're not doing your job!" Her kerchief was askew. A wooden spoon dangled from her left hand. She panted. For a second, she reminded me of a Keystone Cop instead of an elder's wife.

Marion was pregnant with her third child. I knew she felt lousy. Often people interrupted her afternoon naps by banging on the front door of her house, even though there were emphatic instructions on the door: DO NOT DISTURB. "Boy, they just walk right through that door, as if they never even see the note!" she would complain, and I'd commiserate. Now she was at my door.

"I tell you to do things and you let them slide," she said in an aggrieved tone.

"I'm sorry."

"Get a notebook," she huffed. "Write things down."

"I'm sorry," I said again.

Marion folded her arms across her chest. "You haven't been diligent. I told you the laundry room needed to be mopped, the prayer room is a mess, and I'm tired of reminding you!" Her voice rose. "I told you the pantry needed dusting. I told you …"

I had never seen Marion so agitated. I searched my mind, wondering what my true offense might be. As Steward of the Sisters, it was my responsibility to assign chores to women and ensure they got done in a timely manner.

"Look, I appointed you to this job because I thought you could handle the responsibility," she said. "Lately you're more trouble than you're worth. Are you going to do it?"

"Do what?" I said stupidly.

"Get a notebook!"

"I will, Marion. I'm sorry." I pressed my palms together and fought the impulse to bow my head.

"Fine." Her voice was clipped. She moaned and put her hand over her mouth.

"Are you OK?" I said, reaching out to steady her.

Marion looked up at me. With furious dignity, she adjusted her scarf. "I'm fine."

"I'll tell Henry to pick up a notebook for me in town, OK?"

Marion wasn't finished. "Just what is your problem? Honestly, I don't understand how you can be so forgetful. Ed said he had to wake you up last week to make breakfast because you'd forgotten to assign anyone to it. If this job is too much for you, just say so."

"It's not. It's just—"

Marion waved that away. Then she looked around my room suspiciously. The curtains were drawn against the foggy sky. My coleus, which had expired last week due to benign neglect, testified to my slothfulness. Its demise seemed to invigorate Marion. She reminded me of those times when my mother went on a tear and suddenly decided my room needed to be turned upside down and scoured just because she couldn't find her sunglasses. (They were usually on top of her head.) "This room is a shit storm!" my mother would say as I lay in bed pretending to be absorbed in Hermann Hesse. "Clean it up this instant."

"What have you been doing up here, anyway?" Marion said. She sniffed, as if she could smell the dust buffalos gathering under my bed in a billowing herd.

"I've been"—I glanced at the Betty Crocker cookbook on the floor—"planning what kind of cake to make for Francie's wedding."

"You're making the cake?" Marion said.

"I am." What is wrong with you? Who shit in your Easter basket?

"You're making the cake? Francie asked me to make her cake."

"She asked me, too, Marion," I said. "I've already decided on a carrot cake with cream cheese frosting. See, here's the recipe." I fumbled for the cookbook and leafed through the pages. My fingers shook.

"You don't say," Marion said. She bit the inside of her cheek.

"Yes."

"Well, I'm certainly not going to stand here and argue with you about a cake!"

"Good. I think that's a good idea."

"You're way out of line, miss," she said, bristling with authority.

I looked at Marion. You're an elder's wife? You're supposed to be my role model? I don't think so.

I was tired of trying to be like Marion, who had just pulled up the drawbridge of our friendship and left me outside the castle, on the other side of the moat. I was tired of being nice. Why were we arguing? It was all so exhausting.

Suddenly I was channeling my mother. "You act like you're the fucking Queen of Sheba," I heard myself say.

"Thank you, Jesus," Marion murmured, shaking her head.

"Quick, let me get a switch so you can beat me." I looked at my watch.

"Unbelievable!" she croaked.

From an island in the middle of the Pacific, I said: "Golly, it's time for your nap." I shut the door. Locked it from the inside.

"You're in deep trouble," Marion yelled through the door, jiggling the handle.

That night, Ed reprimanded me for my rudeness. I'd upset Marion. Been snotty. Had an "attitude." Marion's husband told Ed that he was worried about her. She'd been "taking on too much." The strain was getting to her.

"You need to get right with the Lord," Ed warned. I stared at his acne scars and wondered how he'd ever managed to get married much less father a child. Melissa, his wife, fine-boned and high-strung as a little thoroughbred filly, was one of the wives who always made me feel left out of the Married Club. She puttered in the kitchen, snickering with her women friends. It was as if they were in on a private joke. I never felt more awkward or alone than in her presence. There was some essential element of friendship I was missing as a married woman, some fundamental shared experience I would never be privy to, just like my relationship with Jesus, which was supposed to be life-sustaining, but in truth left me feeling inadequate and full of doubt. The longer Ed lectured me, the stronger my sense of isolation grew.

"Ever since you and Henry got back from your honeymoon, it's like you're a different person or something. You're all wrapped up in yourself.

Don't you know how hard Marion works around here? She and Ray are *pouring out their lives* for you and you don't even notice. You're self-centered, sister. Get. Your. Heart. Right."

I did not make Francie's wedding cake. I did get a notebook. And whenever Marion talked to me about projects and errands to attend to around the ranch, I snapped to attention and diligently took notes.

"WHY IS IT THE OLDER WE GET IN THE LORD, THE MORE MISERABLE we get?" Caleb preached at the Veteran's Hall the Sunday after my blowup with Marion. He grasped the lectern and looked out at all of us. A lock of thick black hair fell over his forehead. He looked broken, sad – and young. An elder, he had authority over my life. In the world, he would've only been a college student. What was bothering him? "We get excitement in the thing ahead of us," he said. "When we get it, the excitement subsides. Is praise 'old hat' to you? What is causing your excitement? We should be looking for a quality of experience that won't fit into the same old box of Christianity."

A FEW DAYS LATER, HENRY AND I WENT JOGGING ON THE BEACH. The night before, we'd had another fight. I'd told him he was on a power trip; he'd told me to obey him. I accused him of hiding behind scriptures and putting me down so he'd appear strong. He told me that was utter nonsense.

"All I want is for you to be honest with me," I'd said.

"I *am* honest with you."

"I just want you to share your heart with me, what's really going on in your life."

"I *do* share."

"But you don't. Not really."

Ed, who heard us arguing, stopped by our room. We told him what was going on. For a long moment he was silent. Then, turning to me, he said: "You've got some hang-ups from the world, coming from the Bay Area culture where everything has to be real and profound and 'deep.'" Henry listened to Ed like he was some kind of oracle. Ed went on. "That's a real trip and you need to get over it."

Walking down to the beach for our jog, Ed's words weighed heavily on me; I didn't know how to repair things between us. I felt like the Problem Child and yet strangely detached too. How much lower could I sink? In contrast to my mood, the ocean was calm and green, the warm sun beaming down on us. Sandpipers zipped across the wet sand. I didn't know where to turn.

"Do you love me?" I asked, stopping at the water's edge. "Can you forgive me for all the wrong I've done to you?"

"You know I love you," Henry said. "I don't need to tell you that all the time. Please don't be so emotional."

Something broke inside of me. It was like a glacier calving – a big icy chunk just razoring off and plunging into the freezing water.

"Up yours," I said. I kicked the sand. My breath came in raggedy gasps. "I'm trying to apologize and you're being all self-righteous."

"Tough."

"Yes, it is tough."

"See," Henry said. "Now this is exactly what I'm talking about."

"I hate you!"

"Love, hate, what's the difference?" he scoffed. "You're all over the map. Wait five minutes and you'll feel differently." And then he started running down the beach in that odd way of his, flailing elbows, bouncing hair, energetic knees. I just watched him go.

In a red heat, I threw my things together: toothbrush, a few clothes, diary, Bible. I didn't say goodbye to anybody, just got behind the wheel of the VW and eased out of the driveway. Driving down Hookton Road toward Highway 101, passing that green wet landscape of blackberry bushes and farmhouses I knew so well, I barely saw it. My mind raced. The land dropped and curved and swelled. I had no money and no place to go, but I would go anyway. I would head south – where my parents' home had once been. Did I have a specific destination? It didn't matter. How would I pay for gas? I only had a quarter of a tank. I fought with myself.

"Where do you think you're going," the sensible part of me said.

"I'm leaving."

"You will do no such thing. Turn around immediately."

"What for?"

"You have no choice."

"Says who?"

"Me."

"You're nobody!"

I pulled off the highway in Fortuna and sat for awhile in the car. Right about now I was supposed to be leading the sisters' work meeting. Henry was probably somewhere in Eureka, trying to convince merchants to take out ads in the *Tri-City Advertiser*. My parents were in Europe, my sister, in college. I checked my wallet. I had fifty-nine cents. That would barely cover a cup of coffee. I started the engine, and headed back to the ranch. I would leave. Soon. Just not today.

Two weeks later, Henry and I sat in the living room of Ray and Marion's duplex, hinting at the Problem. Face burning, I stared at the soiled carpet, praying for the Lord to strike Henry mute. The blossom-shaped stain on the carpet looked like a peony… or was it Richard Nixon's face, with puffy chipmunk cheeks and shifty eyes?

Four months of marriage, and already ours was messed up. Ray crossed his long legs and cleared his throat. Henry said we were here because he thought we should talk to someone. He was going through "trials" at work, having troubles in his spiritual walk, and, come to think of it, he and I weren't getting along so well, either. I couldn't bring myself to look at Marion. She sat perched on the couch next to Ray, her eyebrows knitted with phony concern. Inside she must be gloating. Yes, the carpet stain definitely looked like Nixon. Nervous rat eyes.

"And another thing," Henry said, laughing nervously. "Is there such a thing as –"

I tried to silence Henry with one meaningful wifely glance.

"Is there such a thing as what?" Ray prompted.

Holy mother of pearl.

"Well," Henry moaned. He buried his head in his hands. "This is hard to talk about."

"It's OK," Marion soothed, catching my eye.

Here it comes, I thought. Bend over.

"Do you think, that is, is it possible that there's such a thing as, well, having too much sex?"

Marion didn't blink. "Is this a problem?" she said with a straight face.

"I just sometimes think it's unspiritual to have sex."

"Sweetheart," Ray told Marion, "get me my Bible."

He flipped through the gilt pages and turned to the Book of Hebrews. "'Marriage should be honored by all, and the marriage bed kept pure, for God will judge the adulterer and the immoral,'" Ray read.

"So how does that apply to us?" Henry said.

"Once you're married, anything goes," Ray said. "Your marriage bed is pure, as long as you're faithful to your vows. Don't worry about how much sex you're having."

I stared at my crossed thighs. I was going on a diet. This time I would do it. Water and carrots until my skin turned orange.

"It's just that sometimes I'm not in the mood for it as much as she is," Henry said, gesturing toward me. How could he betray me like this? How could he sit there and spill our secrets? I had been trying to hold onto a little piece of my dignity, but now I could see I wouldn't be spared. I was in for total humiliation.

Marion sighed deeply and nodded. To her credit, she didn't laugh.

Me, I wanted to bray like a donkey, paw the ground, feign a seizure, moon them all. Ed's words were prophetic ten times over: I was in deep trouble. Past shame, I was now a spiritual leper. I will never live this down, I thought. I will die staring at this pitiful rug. Roll me up like a burrito and carry me out.

Ray cleared his throat. "The important thing is to be right with the Lord."

"Absolutely," Marion echoed.

"Look, you guys," Henry said, "I thought marriage was going to be easy, but it's …"

"A lot of work," Marion put in. "Trust us, we know."

Nixon's face grew a five o'clock shadow.

"*Sometimes*," Marion said slowly, "people get confused between sex and love. *Sometimes* they think sex will fill a deeper need, the need for God."

Sometimes people should mind their own business.

"You know, this reminds me a lot of when Ray and I first got married," Marion said. "We went through a lot of trials. I was really insecure about his love for me and I would push him and test him to where it would really hurt him until he would say, 'Hey! Stop it! I love you. What are we doing?'"

Henry squeezed my hand. I couldn't look at him.

Marion stared at me. "Does this sound like you?" she said softly.

Pigs in a Blanket

IT WAS CLEAR WE NEEDED TO WORK ON "THE MARRIAGE." "It" was in trouble. That's how the relationship seemed to me – a colicky pronoun that required attention. When Bob and Tamara, a young couple who attended church services at Deliverance Temple but didn't live communally, said they needed a housesitter for ten days, the elders chose Henry and me for the job. The house in Eureka was a modest rancher, nothing fancy, but it seemed palatial to me. A washer and dryer. Fully stocked deep freeze. Big color TV. Stereo. Coffee-maker. Sunken bathtub. Inside the avocado refrigerator, cold cuts and cheeses competed for shelf space with tubs of Cool Whip, Pillsbury Poppin' Fresh Biscuits, and aerosol Cheez-Whiz. The pantry was the stuff of an Aunt Clarissa food fantasy: Betty Crocker cake mixes, jars of maraschino cherries, canisters of Pringles, boxes of Lipton's French Onion Soup mix. Whistling at the bounty, I declared the house a lentil-free zone. To earn our keep, all Henry and I had to do was water the plants, collect the mail, and feed Sammy, Bob and Tamara's noisy Siamese.

"The Lord has given you this time," Marion counseled before I left. "Use it wisely." I planned to. It was with the highest of expectations that I began each day in the suburbs, planning to fast, spend time in His Word, Seek His Face. Instead I got sucked into *General Hospital*, snooped in the medicine cabinets, and experimented with Tamara's makeup, applying Maybelline eyeliner before her GE Lighted Makeup Mirror.

"Make yourselves at home," Tamara had told us, and so I had. I borrowed her earrings, her electric curlers, and helped myself to her perfume. I wore her lingerie too, while Henry was at work. Lounging around the house in a pair of satin mules, a red silk peignoir, and plum eye shadow that made me look like I'd been mugged, I guzzled Tang and did my nails. We'd been instructed to sleep in the guest bedroom down the hall, but during the day I often stretched out on their waterbed, casually thumbing through the stack of women's magazines Tamara kept on top of her night table. Lying against their hot pink Marimekko cotton pillowcases, I smelled traces of Tamara's signature scent, Tabu. I liberated her favorite shampoo, dulled her Lady Schick razor, and made a dent in her stash of Calgon bath oil beads hidden in the linen closet. The only thing I didn't borrow was Tamara's toothbrush. Sammy – off his diet of dried cat food – grew plump and glossy on canned tuna and cold cuts.

The house was only a few blocks from downtown, but I seldom left it during the day. Mostly I watched TV – and cooked. With Clarissa-like determination, I made Jell-O pudding cakes and assembled nightly platters of hors d'œuvres. I delighted in arranging pimento bologna slices and little canapés lathered with ham and cheese spreads. It wasn't exactly the kind of cocktail-hour fare my grandmother and Bob would've served up on their Sedona patio, but offering Henry those snacks made me feel, well, like the lady of the house.

Tamara's energy in the house grew fainter with each languorous day. Around four in the afternoon, I got up, ran the vacuum, and stood in front of the fridge, trying to decide what to make for dinner. Sammy, now trained to come running every time the fridge door opened, crouched at my ankles expectantly, butting his head against my legs.

To Henry, house-sitting was a happy windfall, an unexpected blessing, a short-term fluke. But to me, after the grim wilderness of the ranch, it was like reaching the Promised Land. And wasn't I one of God's chosen people? I asked myself as I made miniature pizzas out of English muffins and tomato sauce. Didn't I deserve a little milk and honey? Henry would come home from work, slip on a pair of jeans, and relax in Bob's La-Z-Boy, idly flipping through the pages of the *Eureka Times-Standard* like Robert Young in *Father Knows Best*.

"What did you do today?" he'd ask, a glass of ginger ale in his hand.

"Oh, nothing much," I'd reply, glancing at my lacquered nails.

"Really? Nothing at all?" Hiding behind the newspaper like a TV dad.

"Well, I prayed some."

"And?" Henry put down the paper.

"Read the Bible."

"Really?" (Disbelieving.) "Which part?"

"Oh, all of it."

"*You read the entire Bible?*"

"Just kidding."

"Hah."

The first days at Bob and Tamara's, Henry treated me gently – as if I were a mental patient in a mountainside sanitarium. I was being careful with him too. I suspected he liked the idea of a wife more than he really liked the one he had. But after a while we just reverted to our natural selves. My goofing off while he toiled in town trying to peddle ads to skeptical merchants irritated him. House-sitting in the suburbs wasn't his idea of fun, although he knew I needed a break. We were too far from the hubbub of the ranch. He was anxious to get back. He wanted to be in the swing of things, spiritually speaking.

"You know, that makeup looks pretty weird," he said one evening.

"It does?" Had my Corn Silk Foundation cracked?

"Yes, like you walked into a door or something."

"Shall I wash it off?"

"It's up to you."

The oven timer dinged.

"Dinner's ready," I said a few minutes later holding a quiche Lorraine aloft in my mitted hands. "Shall we eat by candlelight?"

SPRAWLED OUT IN A BEAN BAG CHAIR IN THE LIVING ROOM, I often thought about what it would be like to live permanently in a house like this. What would we do with our lives? What would Henry do? What would I do? Become a mother? Hide behind babies and diapers? I could go to college – except I'd barely graduated high school. Everything came with a price. Bob and Tamara's kitchen appliances weren't free – hard work paid for them. I could work too. But doing what? I had no marketable skills. The only thing I liked to do was write, but Aunt Clarissa had been a lie and the Bargain Lady a spaced-out failure.

I SUSPECT HENRY WAS JUST AS UNMOORED AS I WAS, ONLY HE didn't know it yet. I must've scared him, mirroring back his own sense of removal. One day I'd been radiant with virtue as I'd made peanut butter sandwiches in the ranch kitchen in my baggy corduroy jumper; the next I was whipping up Pigs in a Blanket, posing like a stripper named Midnight. The borrowed nighties, the teetery high heels, the perfume that shielded me from real life like a chartreuse parasol – he hadn't bargained for any of this. Greeting him at the door with Cleopatra eyeliner, no wonder he blanched. I was a parody of a partner.

THE DAY BEFORE WE LEAVE, I VACUUM THE HOUSE, DUST THE stereo, wash Tamara's clothes, strip the sheets on the waterbed, clean out the lint trap, replace the missing bath oil beads. I wipe down the cobalt blue glass canisters of sugar and flour. I fold Tamara's freshly laundered aprons and put them back in the drawer where I found them. The clock above the stove ticks steadily, the second hand creeping forward, one minute pulsing into another. Only days ago I had wandered through this house, opening drawers, flipping on light switches, turning on the TV, pirouetting in Tamara's slippers. Now, in my wool lumberjack socks, I scour the sink with Comet. The floor gleams. Sammy's back on dry food. Is it too late to try on another set of clothes? The clock ticks, saying: Soon, soon.

More or Less?

BEFORE I'D GOTTEN MARRIED, I'D WORKED FOR THE MINISTRY'S fledgling newspaper, *The Gospel Paper*. My biggest piece was "God's Call for Single Sisters." Single sisters, I wrote, had a special role to play in the Body of Christ. They were the Lord's handmaidens, women who could devote themselves wholly unto Him. Their call was to be supportive – literally. Using the analogy of a house, I wrote that Christian men were the roof and married women the floor, but single sisters – ah, they were the pillars that kept the building upright. Or something like that. I began writing the piece before I'd gotten engaged to Henry, and after it was published, I enjoyed a *frisson* of short-lived celebrity. Pious women who had ignored me before would tell me how much the story meant to them. It was as if overnight I'd become a spokeswoman for all those unattached women struggling to feel good about themselves. When I told them that I, too, was headed for matrimony, some acted as if I'd sold out.

A few months later, my husband by my side, I found myself sitting in Sister Winifred's living room on a wet spring night. Winnie, who was elderly, lived by herself in Eureka and attended services at Deliverance Temple. She was a regular contributor to *The Gospel Paper*, and for the past year or so, the ministry's aspiring writers had been meeting regularly at her house to talk about upcoming stories and critique one another's work. In the upcoming issue, Henry was going to share his "testimony" – how he met the Lord in the rugged mountains of Oaxaca, Mexico. I had helped put his words in a narrative form, just as I had helped other people parlay their experiences into stories. I'd written Norm's account of his meeting Jesus after he and his wife, Maureen, came to the ranch in an old van. The account wasn't exactly *The Confessions of St. Augustine* but it did have a certain zing to it as Norm described problems he'd had in the past with the sins of the flesh, being tempted with thoughts of other women. Norm was what Elvis would call "a hunka hunka burnin' love" – a good-looking charmer with a lazy smile and bedroom eyes. Now he and Maureen were right with the Lord, sanctified saints in the family of God. On this night, as Henry and I sat in Winnie's living room, I felt proud of the job I'd done with Henry's story. It was a shapely piece: succinct and elegant, profound and true. Every time I read it, I was moved by my handiwork. I was proud of my writing ability, having long ago claimed Psalm 45:1 as my personal motto:

My heart is stirred by a noble theme
as I recite my verses for the king:
my tongue is the pen of a skillful writer.

Yet sitting in Winnie's house that night, I was discomfited by some nameless burden. I always felt anxious at Winnie's. Humped and slow-moving, Winnie was known in the ministry as a "prayer warrior." She said she had a calling for intercessory prayer. Hobbled by flesh, old age, and infirmities, I imagined how Winnie must look to Jesus when she went to Him in prayer. In the spirit, I envisioned her fierce and fleet, not old and enormous, but a radiant woman dappled in light as she claimed the promises of God. I secretly speculated that she had X-ray vision. Sometimes when she looked at me, I thought she could see straight into my soul. Her shifting nature – lightning-quickness in the spirit, physical pain – left me with a profound sense of cognitive dissonance. Old lady or oracle?

Her house, a little bungalow, embodied that elusive quality. A musty, earthy odor clung to her walls and permeated the furniture. It smelled as if something rootlike and peppery had simmered for days on some forgotten hotplate. What was that smell? I couldn't place it, although it stirred up scent images of mushy tubers and homemade herbal remedies. Once, browsing through her kitchen, I noticed the counter was cluttered with little vials of powder and strange-looking vegetables.

As Henry read his testimony aloud, I rubbed my sweating palms on my skirt. Winnie sat in her rocking chair, draped in a long skirt and a heavy shawl. Her eyes were hooded. "'As I prayed in the mountains of Oaxaca with my Mexican brothers, I wondered if Jesus really could be the Messiah,'" Henry read. There was a charming quaver in his voice. "'All my years of wandering, all my doubts, all my pride and all my sins, fell away as I knelt in the dirt and …'"

Winnie lifted a hand. "That's very nice," she told him perfunctorily, then turned to me. "Tell me, is this, ah, narrative written word for word as Henry dictated it to you or was it –" she hesitated here, trying to be delicate – "more of a collaboration?"

"Well," I began, glancing over at Henry. "He told me how he met the Lord in Mexico, and I wrote it down."

"In his words?" said Winnie, her man-in-the-moon face blossoming in the growing, fungal dark. Her cheeks glowed like mushrooms in the basement. Knobby, blue-veined hands grasped her cane.

"More or less."

"Ah," Winnie said. She flicked on a goose-necked lamp. Faint light splashed into the corners of the room. Now the furniture's fuzzy contours became definite and sharp-edged. "More or less."

"Why?"

"Because this is *your* story, dear, *your* voice," Winnie said. She twirled the handle of her cane a little between her palms. "Your words. It sounds like you. It is you. More or less."

I glanced at Henry. He raised his eyebrows helplessly.

Winnie murmured something. A sad musical sound fluttered up from her throat – it sounded like doves calling to each other at dusk. *Hoo-hoo-hoo! Hoo-hoo-hoo! Who are you? Who are you?* I'm his wife, that's who, I thought.

"Look, he asked for my help," I sputtered.

"Yes, dear," Winnie said. "And why was that?"

Because he'd asked for help and I wanted him to need me. Because he was too lazy to tell the story in his own words. Because I was the writer, the family scribe. Because I was happy to sit at his feet and take down his words, for as long as he would have me. Because it's none of your business who tells the stories in this family. But it was Winnie's business.

"Hey," Henry said, then laughed a little, as if laughter could banish unpleasantness. "All she did was write down my words and put them in story form. It's all true."

"There's truth and then there's truth, dear heart," said Winnie. Her words drifted up like puffs of smoke, like that elusive smell in her house stoked by a hidden source.

She pressed her lips together and sighed. "It's just this doesn't sound… real. You know, there are some stories that you have to tell yourself. It's not always the skill in which a story is told, but the authenticity of the speaker." I knew what she was really getting at. She thought I was smothering Henry, overpowering him. I need to back off, let him have the spotlight. I was too loud, I talked too much, I was a show-off. I needed to be less so that Henry could be more.

"Oh shoot," Winnie said. "Now I've made you cry." She pulled a Kleenex from her sweater sleeve. I balled it up in my hand.

"Hey, I'm fine," I blurted, sobbing now.

"Oh, mercy!" Winnie said, clucking her tongue. "Such tears!"

"I love you," Henry said. "It's OK." I loved him.

He shifted in his seat. "But you know, Winnie's got a point. I should've written this myself, praise God." I stared at him.

Winnie pulled herself up from her chair and shuffled into the kitchen. "Let's have a cup of tea, shall we?" she sang. I heard her rattling the spoons and opening jars. The kettle screamed. Winnie appeared in the doorway with a tray, the whorl of her body framed in the light like a giant snail.

JIM DURKIN HAD BEEN PRAYING WITH HIS HAND-PICKED ELDERS about sending an outreach group to New York. Evangelical teams had already been sent to Europe, Vancouver, and Alaska. Now it was time to establish a Gospel Outreach beachhead in the godless Big Apple. In a matter of months, a team of disciples would be "raised up" and sent there. Henry and I prayed about going to New York. Was it God's will for us? The elders believed we were called to be sent out. Our place on the New York team seemed to be a revealed truth, and frankly, I was happy to confirm that wisdom. I was restless, I wanted to go anywhere, though I knew better than to express that feeling in such a carnal way. I'd been on a new self-improvement kick. I wasn't going to write any of Henry's stories anymore, and I wasn't going to suggest to anyone that I knew the mind of God. That was my husband's job. Me, I was going to keep my head down and my mouth shut.

As if the Lord were testing me, Henry was picked to go on a special tree-planting expedition near Lebanon, Oregon. Tree planting was one of the biggest sources of revenue; the cash raised was used for outreach teams. Typically, a crew of a dozen men from the Lighthouse Ranch and surrounding ministries were sent to Oregon to work for large lumber corporations. The work – often on very steep mountainsides – was grueling. I'd heard stories of grown men breaking down in the mountains, slugging it out with other men on the crew, or leaving in the middle of the night. It was, one chastened sunburned brother reported when he returned, "a real soul purge."

I wasn't invited. Only a handful of single sisters, unencumbered with children, would go along to handle the cooking, laundry, and shopping. I was jealous and mad, but mostly, I was scared. What if Henry left and realized how great it was being without me? What if he realized he didn't love me after all? I was inconsolable. What made matters worse was that Henry didn't seem to mind at all. Satan must've been happy. He was playing with my head. I wasn't good enough to go on the trip. I was too fat, too loud, too undesirable, too everything. Jesus was punishing me.

"Are you excited about the trip?" I asked Henry before we drifted off to sleep. "Are you glad you're going? Are you going to miss me?"

"Of course," Henry replied, sphinxlike. "Absolutely."

A week before the crew was scheduled to leave, I went into pretrip grieving, missing my husband, even as he snored by my side in his underwear, larger than life. I pouted. I fumed. I plotted. Nothing worked. Finally, I played my last card: prayer.

On the Sunday before the crew was scheduled to leave, we gathered in Deliverance Temple, dressed in our best Lighthouse Ranch finery—dowdy jumpers, Indian print skirts, overalls and flannel shirts. I was stoic as we sang:

Our Lord, you know, I have no friend like you!
If heaven's not my home, then Lord, what shall I do?
The angels beckoned me from heaven's golden shore
And I don't feel at home in this world anymore!

That song made me mad. *I don't feel at home in this world anymore.* Yeah, right. *I have no friend like you!* Thanks, Jesus, for breaking my heart. Henry's leaving me and nobody gives a fried fig. I looked around the church. There was Leo, his brown hair growing thick and wild out of his head like crabgrass, stroking his guitar like a lover. Rose stood next to him, lifting her strong clear voice up in praise. Ella clutched her Bible to her chest like the good child she was, and Gretchen, who could use a shave, sawed away on her violin with all her hairy might. Brother Leroy the Holy Terror lifted his hands in supplication, arched his back like he was about to do a handspring, and cried, "*Abba!*"

I looked around the room as if I were seeing these people for the first time. This was the living, breathing body of Christ: holy, dumpy, brave, and broken. I kept singing. I had no place else to go. God's anointing was upon us.

In Romans 8:26, Paul writes: "In the same way, the Spirit helps us with our weakness. We do not know what we ought to pray for, but the Spirit himself intercedes for us with groans that words cannot express." The verse reminded of me a woman in labor, except her travail was of the spirit, not the body. In church that morning in Eureka, my pain was internal. My faith was weak. I was a fraud. And while I could fool some of my brothers and sisters, I couldn't fool God. Familiar hymns gave way to impromptu worship. Some people shouted, others spoke in tongues. There was clapping, stomping, crying. "Let me but touch the hem of your garment, Lord!" Ella called out, lifting her hands. Dacie seemed to have a hot line to the Holy Spirit. I watched her closely. A slight smile played across her pale, unlined face. She had the kindest, steadiest eyes I'd ever seen, and I'd never heard her utter an unkind word about anybody. Yet she filled me with inexplicable dread because I never knew what God might say through her.

A pregnant hush fell across the congregation. My palms began to sweat. And then Dacie – just as I'd known she would – began speaking in tongues. This was usually a precursor to a prophecy. She twitched and shook, as if she'd deliberately stuck a fork in the toaster. What kind of voltage was she feeling? And then Dacie began to speak in English.

"Henry!" Dacie boomed. We jumped in our seats. I grabbed his hand and lowered my head.

"I am testing you, yea, I am trying you, refining you in the fire of my love," Dacie prophesied. "Know that I love you, that I will never leave you, and that ..." Dacie fell silent for a long moment. I held my breath.

"...you will emerge from this test purged," she continued. A baby began wailing. "Your wife is ..." Another long pause. Henry squeezed my hand. *Please, God*, I prayed, *don't let her say it.*

"Your wife is your heart," Dacie said. "She is your sounding board. Trust her. Confide in her for she is wise. Love her as you would love yourself. For I have called you two together to do a mighty work." Pause. "Thus sayeth the Lord." I know she said these words because I wrote them down and now, many years later, I sometimes read them and wonder if they were true. At the time I wanted so much for them to be. Perhaps Dacie's words of us doing a "mighty work" stirred the elders, because at the end of the service, when the tree-planting team was called forward for an anointing, my name was called too. So it was that I got to head to Oregon with Henry.

Sneeze

IN THE DENSE WOODS OF OREGON, WE SOOTHED AND SERVED the men. Tree planting seemed to tap into their most primal hungers. After a day spent shoving baby trees into the ground and hoping they'd grow, the men returned to camp, reeking of sweat, tree sap, the very gism of life. Groaning dramatically, they unlaced their heavy boots, unpeeled thick white socks, and stared at their bent toes in wonderment, as if those pale digits were artifacts unearthed in some remote archaeological dig. There was an ecstatic weariness in the men's voices, now that the day was behind them, and beneath it, this unspoken refrain: *Woman, I worked harder today than you'll ever toil in your whole life.*

I didn't begrudge them lording it over us. I had a healthy respect for labor. Back in Eureka, I'd been in charge of the big Sunday meal we served at the Veterans' Hall between the morning and afternoon church services. Bettina, a hawk-nosed German woman with an elegant bearing, watched me with admiration as I juggled heads of lettuce, set the table, opened gallon-sized cans of pineapple. In her customary ankle-length skirts and wool shawls, Bettina looked like she stepped from the pages of a Grimms' folktale.

"I see your heart and so does the Lordt," she'd say, nodding with approval as I hefted trays of eggplant Parmesan into the oven. Later she gave me an apron she'd made out of navy blue velveteen. Across the bodice she'd embroidered these words:

To do what is right and just is more acceptable to the Lord than sacrifice (Proverbs 21:3).

"You haff the heart of a servant," Bettina said with genuine approval.

The tree-planting camp was set up around a complex of small cabins and a central dining hall, where we congregated for meals, worship, and Bible study. Henry and I were given a one-room cabin at the edge of camp. Dark, cramped, and dusty, it was as far as you could get from Bob and Tamara's spacious, appliance-filled rancher, but I loved it because it gave us more privacy than we had at the ranch. Over our bed was a picture of a bearded Jesus strolling across the Sea of Galilee. The Lord looked relaxed and happy in his sandals and wheat-colored robe, as if he were the manager of a winning baseball team instead of the Son of God.

Ever since Dacie had prophesied that I was Henry's sounding board, a wise woman, and a patient one at that, I'd vowed to live up to her words. Winnie's too. I would be less, rather than more. In fact, I had a whole list of don'ts: don't talk too much, don't think too much, don't interrupt, don't nag, don't nap, don't read ungodly books, don't gossip, don't indulge in idle speculation. Instead, be meek, quiet, industrious, and subservient. Adopting these characteristics would be as easy as suppressing a sneeze, but Lord willing, I would choose to be a good woman.

The tree-planting crew took off before dawn, leaving the camp to the women. We cooked, whipping up gargantuan meat loaves for dinner: shaping mounds of hamburger, onions, and bread crumbs into steaming hillocks of protein. We baked whole wheat bread, stirred up vast vats of honey granola, peeled piles of potatoes. In our headscarves and long skirts, we could've passed for Amish farm wives overseeing the fall canning. There were holes in the day though, small, hand-sized pockets of free time. One afternoon I hiked to an isolated lake a few miles away. Stripping down to my bra and underwear, I tiptoed in. Each step stirred up muddy water, but farther out, it was clearer, as if it had been poured through a tea strainer. Spreading out my arms like Jesus on the cross, I floated, and the sun percolated through the water; through damp lashes I watched cumulus clouds piling up against the sky. As I grew more buoyant, the scab of false spirituality began to loosen. Gazing at the underside of the sky, I backstroked farther toward the center of the lake. I had spent two years seeking the Lord, but now I realized that the harder I tried to find Him, the more elusive He became. (Don't think too much.)

As Christians, we were supposed to draw a line between ourselves and "them" – the unsaved. Those who didn't know Jesus were "in the world," as if the world could be neatly separated like an orange. I didn't have a burden for sinners. (Don't indulge in idle speculation.) I never had. In fact, I'd felt apologetic toward the people I'd witnessed to, embarrassed as I told them God could save them if they trusted in Jesus. They didn't believe in the Good News – it was a trip I laid on them – and sometimes I had trouble swallowing it myself. Still, I had tried to be good, spiritual, worthy. (Be meek.)

It seemed like I spent most of my Christian walk either experiencing trials and wondering how to get out of them, anticipating future trials, or feeling utterly condemned for not living up to self-imposed spiritual standards. In fact, sometimes it seemed like I made up problems just so I wouldn't have to receive God's love. I couldn't forgive myself. Old arguments, raised voices, tears and denunciations, me running through the halls of the married quarters like the family madwoman released from the basement for ten frantic minutes of calisthenics. Henry's aviator glasses flying off his shocked face when I slapped him. A red imprint on the smooth cheek of a kind man. God, I have nothing to offer you but myself, sunburned, porous, wrinkled.

Silver clouds bled across the sun. Cattails shook. My hair did a little dance in the water. I felt the wind coming across the lake. It was cool. The past was going, washed away. Dacie's prophecy, mere words. The cypress trees on the ranch bluff, a web of roots. The milk cows in their stalls, ceded to bone meal. Suspended in water, I shuddered beneath the yellow-blue sun. In the shining afternoon, I felt emptied out and full. One day there would be an end to the Lighthouse Ranch, I thought, but there is no end to God.

DINNER WAS THE HOUR OF FELLOWSHIP. BEFORE THE MEAL, WE prayed and sang together like students at a high school football pep rally:

> *Hallelujah, I'm walking with the king!*
> *Praise his Holy name!*
> *Walking with the King!*

Were we really pumped up with the Spirit? Happy? Fervent? Were we that blessed? We were dizzy, though whether from exhaustion or ecstasy, it was hard to say. How much shouting could ease our fears of mere mortality? Standing together in a circle with our arms oppressively wrapped around each other like drunken octopi, calling on God, well, I wanted to weep.

A few nights after swimming in the lake, I was on dinner duty. As I served up salad and lasagna, Roy held his empty glass aloft. He shook it. Impatiently. It was a summons. Ice cubes rattled in the glass.

Tinkle, tinkle.

"Sister," Roy called in a bullying tone. I caught my breath.

Roy had shown up at the ranch a few months after I did, a surfer jock from La Jolla with a backpack full of shorts and loud Hawaiian shirts. A lunk of a hunk with curly black hair and a skier's compact build, he'd been a flirt in the world, one of those people whose good looks had opened doors for him. He moved with an athlete's natural, well-oiled ease, accustomed to accomplishment. He seemed to have one eye on the waves and the other on those pretty single sisters who seemed willing to drop everything to patch a brother's jeans or wash a pillowcase of greasy Pendletons. In time Roy was transformed into a SMOG, a humorless, scripture-quoting, get-thee-behind-me-Satan kind of brother. It happened even to the nicest ones. Flip-flops and cut-offs were replaced with creased Levis and flannel shirts fussily buttoned at the neck like some sixty-five-year-old retiree. This man who had loved women now eschewed them. And he seemed to have memorized every scripture about how women were the "weaker vessels," little lambs of the Lord who should remain silent in church while the men held forth.

He made my teeth itch. His passion for righteousness and moral rectitude disguised a tremendous will for getting his own way. On this trip, just as surely as Eve ate from the Tree of Knowledge, something was eating Roy.

Tinkle, tinkle.

"Hey, you!"

Time stops. The glass rattles. Roy's a betting man playing craps in Las Vegas, wagering that he can make me run. Something in his gesture reveals the way Roy perceives women, or at least me.

Tinkle, tinkle.

Pour the man his water already. Give it to him, quick, so he'll shut up.

But I'm busy suddenly. There's bread to pass, praise God, salt shakers to fetch, plates to clear. I'm humming.

Roy leans back in his chair. "Yoo hoo!" he shouts, holding up his glass, glaring.

"What?" I call over the din of clinking silverware and loud talk.

He shakes his glass at me once more. "Water. Over here. On the double."

"Pardon?" I'm Helen Keller; I can't see him.

"Give me some water!" He makes choking noises, miming that he's dying of thirst, hands squeezed around his throat. "Over," croaks, "here!"

"Just a sec," I call over my shoulder, taking my time to fill another round of half-full water glasses. Lady Virtue, ministering to the saints.

Roy whispers something to the man sitting next to him. He shakes his head, smirks. Muffled laughter. I scan the dining room, looking for Henry. He's deep in conversation with another brother.

"Hop to it," Roy snaps.

"Hang on, please."

"Hurry up."

"Yas, master." (Be meek!)

"Now."

Roy stands up. His chair falls over backwards. He's striding over to me and he's gripping his glass.

"I said I'd be there in a minute, Roy," I say, suppressing an unvoiced expletive.

"Just give it to me."

"I'm coming! Hold your weenie already!" (Where did that come from?)

Roy's mouth drops open. Before my disbelieving eyes, he lunges for the pitcher.

We grapple over it, bending and sidestepping, gawky flamingos pursuing the same minnow. Water sloshes onto the floor.

"Look, you're spilling it, you klutz!"

"Too bad."

"Sit down, Roy."

Roy squints at me. "What did you say?"

"You heard me," I say, and add under my breath, "shithead."

Roy stares. "Just what is your problem?"

"Stop sneering."

"All I want is a glass of water!"

"You mean, all I want is a glass of water, please. Isn't that what you mean?"

"What's gotten into you?"

"What a child you are, Roy!"

Henry is still talking, gesturing earnestly with a slice of French bread.

"May I please have some water?" Roy says in a mocking tone. With balletic grace, he gets down on one knee and holds his glass aloft. I can smell his sweat and the coconut oil of his hair conditioner. I gaze down at the hair curled at the nape of his neck. Streaks of condensation run down the sides of the pitcher. Slowly my wrist bends. Water, frosty and clear, rolls up one side. Everything is happening in slo-mo. I want to aim for Roy's head instead of his proffered glass. I want to baptize him in ice cubes. I don't, but in the few seconds it takes for the liquid to tumble from my vessel into his, something more than water passes between us – unquenchable contempt. Roy takes a little drink, smacks his lips, wipes his mouth with the back of his hand. "Now," he says, "was that so hard?"

THAT NIGHT IN OUR CABIN, I REMINDED MYSELF OF MARABEL Morgan's top ten rules to please men. "Don't tell him what's bothering you," she'd counseled in her marital guide *The Total Woman*. "Then, don't remind him." Yes, Marabel, but you're not stuck in the woods.

"Why did you let Roy treat me like that?" I fumed to Henry. "Why didn't you step in?"

Henry could barely keep his eyes open. He sighed. "Forget about it. Let the Lord deal with him."

"I can't believe you're not upset about this."

"My feet are killing me," Henry mumbled, rubbing his temples. "And I've got to get up tomorrow and do it all over again."

"He acted like I was a waitress or something."

"What?"

"Roy. He's a jerk."

"That's your soul talking."

"He's rude. He's –"

"Enough now," Henry said, holding up his hand. "Calm down."

"You calm down!"

Henry's face was wind-burned. His eyelids looked sandblasted, pitted with little red pinpricks. He opened one eye. "Sweetie, you're the one who begged and begged to come on this trip. You knew it would be a lot of work, you knew people would be going through trials, but you insisted on coming."

"So what are you saying?"

"Maybe you just should've stayed home."

"You're just like him!" I said. "You're just like all of them!"

"Them? Oh, please."

"Why aren't you on my side?"

"Quit being so dramatic; there are no sides."

"You don't love me," I whispered.

"I love you," he repeated dully, turning over on his side. "Lord, I'm so tired. Let's talk tomorrow."

I turned off the light. It was ten o'clock on a summer's night in the woods of Oregon. I could hear the crickets chirping and the moths circling around the lights. And farther down the hill, in the dining hall, the saints singing of the saints.

St. Marks Place

COMMUTING FROM MY JOB IN MANHATTAN, PEOPLE NERVOUSLY eyed the large wooden cross I wore around my neck. I was an archetype to them, not a person, just like the Amish with barns and buggies were archetypes to me. It is hard to see the heart of the genuine person underneath if they're wearing a uniform. When I gave a pregnant woman with swollen ankles my seat on the subway, she plopped down without a word of acknowledgment. Motherhood was sacrosanct – a life-giving, affirming act. At least that's the way we viewed it in the ministry.

"When's your baby due?" I asked.

"Another month," she said, staring fixedly at a point over my left shoulder.

"Motherhood. Wow, what a high calling."

"Oh, don't hand me that shit."

I had been married eleven months and just turned twenty-one when Henry and I left for New York and settled into the tall brownstone on St. Marks Place in Brooklyn. We lived communally with a handful of other Christians, including Bettina, the wealthy older German woman who'd been so enamored of my work ethic. My friend Jessie, who'd come to the ranch shortly after I had, also lived in the house, as well as a few single brothers and another family. Jessie was a former biker chick turned child of God, as down to earth as a meadow mushroom. She had a blue star tattooed on the back of one hand, and her skin bore a few faint acne scars, but she was beautiful to me in a wind-tousled cowgirl way. She had a laconic way of moving and talking; she never broke a sweat.

Gerald and Sue, the elders in charge, lived in the basement with their little girl, Delia. Sue and Delia seemed to originate from some mythic race of blue-eyed white people. They were so pale, they looked like they grew up in caves. It was as if they'd been dipped in a vat of Clorox and hung on the line to dry on some windy, hot Nebraska morning. Sue was lithe and fine-boned, with appraising blue eyes and diamond-hard calves chiseled from alabaster. Her husband was *al dente* spaghetti – long and loose. There was a wooliness about this string bean; he favored corduroy trousers and Shetland sweaters, and he always seemed to have a cold. Years later, I would identify him as a certain "type": the preoccupied English professor who can't find his grade book and is always late for class.

I was the only married woman in the house with a regular outside job where I punched a time clock. Having a job, I'd argued, would allow me to be a strong Christian witness. Gerald consented, and with the help of an employment agency, I found a job in Manhattan as a file clerk on the Avenue of the Americas. This was my first real job since I'd arrived at the Lighthouse Ranch three years earlier. I wouldn't get to keep my salary – seventy-five dollars a week – but I wanted the experience being in the world.

In that upright house, squeezed between other brownstones on the narrow street, we found our places. We seemed to be squirreled away in various compartments, like presents behind the paper doors of an Advent calendar, just waiting to be opened. There was a dorm for single men on the third floor, and a room for single women on the second floor. Henry and I lived on the second floor too, in a room with cream-colored walls that looked out onto the street. At night when we tried to sleep, we could hear the people next door laughing and partying.

If only I could stop being the person I was in California. This was a chance to start fresh. Before arriving in Brooklyn, I'd fantasized about reinventing myself. Henry and I would save souls for Christ, and our marriage would be blessed. I imagined us striding through crowded Central Park, eyes blazing with holy love. I envisioned us preaching, healing, and baptizing new Christians in Bethesda Fountain. In a cotton pinafore, I'd hand new converts thick terry cloth towels as they clambered out of the water with streaming hair and puckered skin. "Thanks be to God, you're new in Christ!" I'd say, and Henry would look over at me and smile.

But New York wasn't a welcoming place. It was grimy. I felt sorry for the trees and wondered how they survived in all that tumult and pollution and traffic. They grew out of the cracked, dirty sidewalks, stoic witnesses to the uproar around them. In the winter, their skeletal arms quivered with the passing cars. There was trash in the streets, and, after the snow melted, little land mines of dog shit on the sidewalks you had to hopscotch around. People weren't anxious to know you in New York. They didn't look you in the eye or say "excuse me" if they bumped into you, they just kept brusquely walking. In Eureka, some of the people in town knew who we were because of our big blue school bus, Zion, and because of the way we talked and dressed. For the most part, they were tolerant of us. Sure, we were Jesus freaks but we were *their* Jesus freaks, homespun hippies who lived out on windy Table Bluff. We were as threatening as granola.

I wasn't privy to the ministry's financial statements, but it was clear that we needed to be self-sufficient. Henry got a job as a driver with a medical supply company in Manhattan. He hated everything about the job: the boat-sized van he had to steer through the streets filled with som-

nambulistic pedestrians; the eternal gridlock; and Mo, his boss, who be-
rated him for being too slow. Delivering bed pans, blood pressure mon-
itors, and oxygen canisters to geriatric customers didn't square with his
idea of himself as a Mighty Man of God.

At the money order company where I worked, I kept track of the orders
the salesmen peddled to mom and pop grocery stores in the boroughs.
Artie, my boss, a thickset man who combed his greasy hair back like a
middle-aged, thick-waisted James Dean, didn't know what to make of
me. I didn't go out for drinks with the rest of the crew after work or eat
the pastries he brought in every morning. My reluctance to join in irritated him, but I couldn't forget who I was. Little Arminda, one of the clerks,
had a withered leg and a heart-shaped face the color of crème brûlée. She
favored bright-colored frocks with ties and ribbons. Eileen, the reception-
ist, wore tight jumpsuits and stiletto heels. Her bright green eye shadow
shimmered under the harsh fluorescent lighting. Eileen was a thrilling
potty mouth. "It's goddamn freezing in here," she would say, snapping
her gum and rubbing her bare, goose-pimpled arms as she sat at her desk.
"Brrr, I went to the bathroom and nearly froze. I thought I was gonna stick
to the seat." Sotto voce, she'd add: "I swear to god, I thought I was shitting
icicles." Office manager Mary Ann, broad in the beam and maternal, lived
on Staten Island with her husband, a cop who worked check fraud. She
rode the ferry home to her husband every night, collected S & H Green
Stamps, had a wallet full of charge cards. On Monday mornings, she talked
about her weekend. It was a sitcom suburban life: barbecue with other
cops and their wives, pinochle with the in-laws, Sunday Mass, and an
on-going, not-very-funny game of hide the charge card bills. Sometimes
she called Bob "the detective" because of his vigilance about her spending
habits. How could I tell her I never cashed my own paycheck, had never
established a line of credit, and didn't own a TV? How could I say my
"family" didn't buy lottery tickets, subscribe to the *New York Post*, or keep
a frosty keg of Old Milwaukee on tap in the basement, next to the pool
table? Mary Ann and I, we weren't even on the same planet. With my
hairy legs, my Bible, my wooden cross, and my makeshift "good" clothes
purchased from thrift stores, I was simply "that way" to her. She was

gentle with me the way that people are gentle with the handicapped.

Her pity barely registered with me, so great was my sense of psychic dislocation. New York, after the rural isolation of the ranch, was disorienting. Standing in line for a coffee to go from Horn & Hardart, I would suddenly recall the big, black-handed clock on the beige wall in the ranch dining hall, its robotic jerk as it moved from second to second, tallying the time as Caleb preached and paced before us. Time had been gentler at the ranch, with a wake-up gong sounding through the morning fog instead of police sirens, boom boxes, and car alarms. In California, we'd sailed forth to meet the world on our terms, urging it to conform to godliness, but in New York, the world came to us with a hard-on: junkies nodding out on nearby stoops and street people rifling through the trash, seeking redemption through aluminum cans.

The drama of people's lives played out on the streets. I saw couples in New York holding hands, hugging, kissing ruthlessly, tasting each other. They were everywhere – in bus shelters, coffee shops, laundromats, and museums – flaunting their happiness. Seeing them made me watchful, wistful, and uneasy. Robust love was everywhere, even in the Bible, but it was lacking in my own life. In the Song of Songs 7:11–12, I read:

> Come, my lover, let us go to the countryside,
> let us spend the night in the villages.
> Let us go early to the vineyards
> to see if the vines have budded,
> if their blossoms have opened,
> and if the pomegranates are in bloom –
> there I will give you my love.

On the subway a man sitting across from me held a bouquet of daisies. It trembled in his hands. His long tapered fingers curled around the crackly green tissue paper. What was going through his mind? Was he nervous or scared? His face bore the faraway expression of an awake dreamer. I looked closer and saw he'd nicked his face shaving. I tried to see the world through his eyes. Was he going to the countryside or would he spend the night in the villages?

In my village – St. Marks Place – another world awaited behind the wrought-iron fence flanking our brownstone. It was a close domestic world where toiling men greeted aproned women at the end of the day. I wiped off the day in Manhattan as easily as I wiped my feet on the front mat and stepped into the vestibule.

Sue was pregnant and tired and looked even paler than usual. The blue veins shone through her skin. I didn't know what was really going on – if she was angry or frightened or bored with her life. It was not her place as an elder's wife to share those feelings with someone like me a sister who wore her heart on her sleeve and whose unhappiness was plainly evident to all. There was some kind of tension between her and Gerald, a long-standing grievance or argument, but it rarely spilled out into the open. They may have been going through the same pressures and doubts we all did. Lack of money, time, privacy – take your pick. Perhaps they felt the need to appear invincible.

The things that had troubled me at the ranch – the lack of boundaries, the legalistic spirit – were amplified in New York, where everybody's motives and aspirations, frustrations and achievements, were exposed in sharp relief. A personality conflict with someone wasn't just a generic trial designed to sand the sharp edges off one's soul; here, it was a serious contretemps that required airing and quick resolution. Two opposing forces – idealism and egotism – lay at the center of our communal experience. Sometimes it was hard to tell them apart.

I spent my free time at the Brooklyn Central Library, a massive Beaux-Arts building on Grand Army Plaza a few blocks from the house. I took particular comfort from this inscription on its Indiana limestone exterior:

The spirit and the senses
so easily grow dead to the
impressions of the beautiful and
perfect that one ought every
day to hear a little song, read
a good poem, see a fine picture
and, if it were possible,
to speak a few reasonable words.

That's what I craved – a few reasonable words. At Sunday services, held in a hall above some stores in the Bay Ridge neighborhood, we stomped our feet and called on Jesus to direct our paths, bless our lives, heal our shitty pasts.

Slightly stoop-shouldered, Gerald stands before us, preaching. The arms of his jacket are a little short. "In the beginning, God spoke all things into existence," Gerald says, his handkerchief balled up in one hand. "He said, 'Let there be light and there was light.' He confessed something and it came to be. We're not saved by our faith but by His faith. His faith is what enables us to go on." He pauses a moment. I count to ten. Sitting in that stuffy hall on a metal folding chair, I know I'm a leaden fake. "Let's just soak in the presence of the Lord," Gerald says. "Do you feel the calming presence of the Holy Spirit? Do you feel it moving among us? Rays of love, rays of light. Praise you, Lord!"

I don't know where I am. What year is it? What day? It is 1975, a Sunday in February in Brooklyn, where the tape of my life plays continuously in an endless loop. I am lost. I can't find my way. People around me are speaking in tongues. Dogs howling at the moon, crones keening, an eternal siren. Do I feel the calming presence of the Holy Spirit, the rays of love, the rays of light? I do not. What I feel is a knot of misery in my stomach, the pregnant sense of doom, the struggle to appear normal.

People around me start groaning and twitching, hollering and chanting. It's all wrong, there's no air, it's impossible to tell if I'm imploding or scattering. I can't stop looking at Sue, who is so yellow-white she looks like she's melting into a pat of human butter. Her arms are spread out and I can see the sun shining behind her head. "Sing, everybody, sing," Gerald says. My thighs are slick with sweat. My fingers shake. I tuck them under my armpits and I sing … *Hallelujah … I'm walking with the King! … Praise His holy name!*

Kung Fu Fighting

HENRY QUIT HIS DELIVERY JOB IN THE SPRING AND STARTED working with some of the brothers in a new vinyl repair business. He roamed around New York with his little toolbox of paints and brushes, trying to drum up business at used-car lots. He could repair torn car seats by melting plastic with a hot metal wand and touching up the surface with matching paint. The idea was to melt, blend, become one.

"It's seamless work," he said proudly one night after work. I was oddly moved by his sense of accomplishment. "There's an art to it."

"Oh, honey," I said, "it sounds hard."

"The car lots along Flatbush Avenue are the worst. Those guys, always trying to wrangle a discount. Sheesh!"

"Fair is fair," I said. "Stand your ground."

"Yeah, I'm getting pretty good at it. And God's using me, I think."

"Lucky you."

The Lord wasn't using me, or if He was, I didn't know it. I wore my cross. I rode the subway to work with my Bible and my sack lunch. I pressed my lips together when smutty Eileen told her jokes, and I didn't say anything when Artie pursued Arminda. At night, we read the Bible, prayed, sang. Lying in bed, rock music from the stereo next door ricocheted off our headboard, scored by a pounding bass line that got under my skin. I knew the scriptures by heart about self-denial, dying to the flesh, staying the course. "Watch and pray so that you will not fall into temptation," Jesus said. "The spirit is willing, but the flesh is weak." It was hard to sustain an ongoing sense of purpose, keep the vision. So many times we'd talked about the high cost of discipleship, and being gung-ho for Jesus, instead of lukewarm followers who opted for a more comfortable path. Years later I would recognize our spiritual pride and self-congratulation for what it was – a game of religious one-upmanship. Although we stressed a personal relationship with Jesus, we didn't trust one another when our private experiences led us to different interpretations of God's Word. Faith was lockstep. You were either in or out – there was no rapprochement or neutral territory.

I RARELY SPOKE TO MY SISTER, WHO WAS BUSY IN SAN FRANCISCO, studying to become a nurse. Her phone call one cold spring evening caught me off-guard.

"How are you?" she sang.

"I'm good, really, ah, blessed," I stammered. "Henry's got a new job. He's working in vinyl repair."

"Vinyl repair?" Mary echoed. There was a long pause. "You're kidding."

"I'm serious." The line crackled.

"*Vinyl* repair? Oh, my god, vinyl repair!" From three thousand miles away, her mirth was palpable.

"What's so funny about that? Vinyl rips. You repair it. It's a decent living."

Muffled chortling. It sounded like she was smothering herself with a pillow. "It's just a little bizarre, don't you think?"

"I don't think it's bizarre at all," I said coldly, but I understood her perfectly. She was alluding to *The Graduate*, the 1967 movie starring Dustin Hoffman as an apathetic college grad. At his graduation party, an old family friend sidles up to Benjamin Braddock to give him a word of advice about employment and investment opportunities: "I just want to say one word to you, just one word – plastics."

"Mary, it's a good job."

"I'm sure it is," Mary burbled.

"It's better than working at a department store approving credit cards," I said.

"Whatever you say," she said, a smug tone in her voice. "So how does one repair vinyl?"

"Well, he uses a hot wand and a – "

"Wait. Ohmigod. A hot … wand? Oh, that's too much!" She was off again. "So tell me, what do you do for a living? 'Oh, I'm in vinyl repair.'"

"Ha, ha," I said.

"D'Arce, don't get huffy."

"I'm not getting huffy. I'm just glad you think my life is so funny."

"I'm just teasing! Lighten up, for Christ's sake!"

"Fine. Listen, I've got to go."

"Wait. How are you?"

"We're blessed."

"Now you're supposed to ask me how I am. It's called making conversation. What's the matter with you anyway? Jesus!"

"How are you?"

"Well, I'm working my buns off studying. Do you ever think about coming back to California? You can always stay with me, you know. Remember that. I love you, sweetie. Is everything OK? Do you need anything?"

"Mary, I'm fine. I love you too. I've got to go. Thanks for calling."

"OK," she said. "Say hi to Henry" – she was laughing – "and that wand of his!"

The line went dead. I stared at the phone in my hand. What was so funny about vinyl repair? I rolled the words around in my mouth. Vinyl repair. Plastic restoration. Vinyl: The world's most versatile plastic. Vinyl-re-pair, vi-nyl-re-pair, vi-nyl-re-pair. Oh, Lord, mend my plastic life. As I repeated the words, they lost their context. After a few more tries, I couldn't say "vinyl repair" with a straight face.

"PUT ON THE FULL ARMOR OF GOD SO THAT YOU CAN TAKE YOUR stand against the devil's schemes," the apostle Paul warned. Our battle, he wrote, was not against people of flesh and blood but against the forces of evil. As if taking a cue from Satan himself, the disco hit song "Kung Fu Fighting" began playing next door. The walls buzzed. I tried to concentrate on Paul's letter to the Ephesians: "Stand firm then, with the belt of truth buckled around your waist, with the breastplate of righteousness in place, and with your feet fitted with the readiness that comes from the gospel of peace." Amen, I thought, and then somebody next door really cranked it up and Carl Douglas's voice came bouncing through the bricks, complete with karate chop grunts:

> Oh-oh-oh-oh, oh-oh-oh-oh, oh-oh-oh-oh, oh-oh-oh-oh!
> Everybody was Kung Fu fighting (ugh!)
> Those kicks were fast as lightning.
> In fact it was a little bit frightening
> But they fought with expert timing.

A car screeched outside and somebody leaned on the horn. I closed my Bible and parted the billowing curtains to check on the Blisstons, the family that lived across the street. I liked watching their comings and goings, even though I'd never met them. All I knew was they were a young couple with a little boy. I had concocted an elaborate fantasy about them – I named the preppy-looking man in the topsiders and khaki trousers John and gave him a job as a freelance writer for *National Geographic*. Claire, an earth mother with flaming red hair, worked as a nurse at Planned Parenthood, dispensing birth control pills and advice about V D. Little Trevor went to a Montessori preschool near Saint Augustine's on Sixth Avenue, where he was encouraged to express himself through finger painting and music. I imagined their house full of small and beautiful things: a sculpted bonsai tree, a dried sea horse, a glass paperweight containing a robin's blue egg. Maybe John really wrote violent porn for a living; maybe Claire was sloshed on gin and staggering into walls in her Dr. Scholl's toe-grip sandals by noon; the truth about their lives was less important than my fantasy. If they could be happy in the world, outside of the shadow of the ministry, perhaps there was hope for Henry and me too. Every outward sign pointed to a peaceful existence: three-speed bicycle chained to the wrought-iron fence in front of the apartment; Christmas lights that were still up in February; plastic Playskool toys scattered at the bottom of the stoop. I sent the Blisstons to a cabin in the Adirondacks for weekend getaways, made them vote a straight Democratic ticket, and penciled them in for Friday night bowling. They were hoping for a second child, I decided, and they were having a lot of fun trying. Sometimes, gazing into their living room window very late at night, I caught sight of their TV flickering in the dark and wondered what was keeping them up so late. Then a deflated feeling would wash over me; perhaps they were just ordinary after all, just as troubled as the rest of us.

I knocked on Jessie's door down the hall.

"You feel like getting out of here for a while?" I said, leaning against the doorjamb.

She set her book down and ran a hand through her hair. "What do you have in mind?"

I hesitated. Finally I said: "Is it a sin to drink a beer? I am really craving a beer. And I don't even like beer very much. It just sounds good to me right now."

"How long has it been since you've had one?"

"Honestly? Years."

"Oh, that sounds so good!" she drawled, rolling her eyes. "Let's go do our laundry and see what happens next." We went down to the Laundromat on Third Avenue. I rammed quarters into the machine. My mind was on that drink.

"Do you think Gerald will know?" I said.

"Why should he? And besides, we're not doing anything wrong."

An hour later, we lugged bags of clean clothes to the Chinese restaurant and slunk into a torn ox-blood vinyl booth. A candle sputtered.

"You should tell Henry to come here," said Jessie, pointing to a tear in the vinyl seat.

"Two Heinekens," I told a waitress with silver bangles on her wrist. I waited for something to happen, like maybe a siren to go off or somebody in a bloodied apron to pull me into the kitchen for questioning: *You want what? Are you absolutely sure you should?* The waitress came back a minute later carrying a tray with bottles and glasses. Jessie and I looked at each other as she poured, not saying a word as the bangles tinkled and the foam rose higher in the glasses. I closed my eyes, put the glass to my mouth, and swallowed. Thank you, Lord.

"I could sit here forever," I said. "Is beer mentioned in the Bible?"

"Wine is, I know that."

"Jesus drank wine. What's it say in Psalms? It 'gladdens the heart of man.' I'm getting glad, Jess." I drained my glass.

"Me too. Should we have another?"

I closed my eyes. "I'm praying about it."

"And?"

"I'm feeling warm all over," I said.

"Um, shall I take this as a sign?"

"Maybe I just have to pee."

"I think it's OK with the Lord," she said.

She smiled at me and began laughing. And then I started laughing too, so hard tears came to my eyes.

We took another route back to the house, laughing and singing and dragging our laundry bags, which had become quite heavy. In front of the house, we bumped into Gerald, who was unloading groceries from his car. "What are you girls up to?" he asked.

"Laundry," Jessie said virtuously, hoisting up her bag with a grunt. "Why do you ask?"

Gerald grinned. "You're both smirking."

Several years later, I would meet Gerald and Sue in a San Francisco bar and drink more margaritas than I should. In the eternal twilight of the bar, we'd argue about the Lord and I'd storm out in my Frye boots and knit dress, wiping the running mascara off my face with a cocktail napkin. But on this brisk winter evening in Brooklyn I'm a long way from drunk and a longer way from San Francisco. The cold tangerine sun is setting through the trees that line St. Marks Place. Gerald is carrying in the groceries, and I stop to give him a hand.

Grounded

"I HAD A DREAM ABOUT YOU," SISTER ROXANNE TOLD ME ONE Sunday evening after we put away the folding chairs in the upstairs loft where we met for church. Tall, brassy, and confident, Roxy believed she had the gift of prophecy. God spoke to her in her dreams, she asserted, and who knows, maybe He did. She put a hand on my shoulder and looked me in the eye. Involuntarily, I took a step back. Roxy had an astonishing bosom. Like Jayne Mansfield, her cup runneth over. Whenever I was around her, I found my eyes involuntarily drawn to her bust line. Her breasts seemed like cannons. When she pointed them at me, I wanted to duck. It felt like a full-frontal assault. *Ka-bloey!*

"Yes?" I said with a sinking heart, shifting my feet.

"I dreamed you were sitting on the toilet in the bathroom," she said, "*and the door was open.*" She blew her nose.

"How droll," I said.

"This is a sign from the Lord. It means you haven't shut the door on the world yet."

"I'll have to think about that one."

She sneezed. "This is a sign from God!"

"Maybe the dream is about *you*, Rox. Maybe it's about you needing privacy." Or modesty.

Roxanne shook her head. "This dream is about you," she insisted.

"Well, thanks for telling me." Our eyes met. I looked down at my shoes.

"All I'm asking is for you to search your heart," she said. "This is a word from the Lord."

Search your heart. A sign from God. A word from the Lord. How come God only spoke to me through his earthly emissaries?

"What is it that you really want?" Rox said in a confiding tone. She put her arm around me. "What's in your heart?"

"I don't know," I said, and thought: If I knew, Roxanne, you'd be the last person I'd tell. But I did know. When we'd stayed at Bob and Tamara's, my 1000-watt fantasies about being married to Henry had been tied up with Irish linens and fancy cutlery, clipping recipes and browsing for the perfect china pattern in a department store staffed by solicitous clerks who knew my name. Now my wish had narrowed to this modest candle of yearning: to leave the ministry.

BETTINA NO LONGER APPROVED OF ME. I WAS AN AFFRONT TO her work ethic. After living together with me for a few months, she was wise to the fact that I wasn't the same conscientious little handmaiden who had labored in the Veterans' Hall kitchen. When it came to cleaning, I had adopted my mother's slogan: Fuck Housework. Life was short; it was more edifying to read a book or take a bath than get down on your knees with a toothbrush, combing under the radiator for crumbs.

Bettina didn't believe in shortcuts, had no truck for shoddy handiwork of any kind. She had an eye for quality: boar-bristle hairbrushes, tortoiseshell combs, linen sheets, French press coffee. She was not the kind of person you'd see at Wal-Mart buying white cotton underpants or a bag of Cheeze Doodles.

One day as I ironed seam tape onto a ripped blouse in the sisters' dorm, she sat on her bed in a high-necked white cotton nightgown, reading her Bible. Every now and then she looked up through her bifocals and sighed.

"That is not the way to fix a blouse!"

"This is fine," I said, continuing my work.

"No, it's not!" she said, shaking her head. "You mend a blouse with little tiny stitches. Neat ones, *ja*? Like so … "

"Trust me, I know what I'm doing."

"It should be perfect," Bettina warned.

"Don't worry about it."

"For shame!"

I glanced up, surprised by her growing agitation. A feeling of warmth stole over me. For the first time in days, I felt calm and powerful. I began to hum. *La, la, la.*

"We should be faithful in little things," Bettina fumed. "And in big things. In everything. God sees it all."

"It's a blouse, Bets," I said. *La, la, la.* "A ratty old blouse I bought second-hand." *La.*

"Ach!" Bettina said. The mattress coils creaked as she got out of bed. "You've changed. You used to like to verk. Now I see maybe I was wrong, *ja*?"

"*Ja*," I mimicked, "I don't like to verk."

Bettina smiled bitterly. If she'd been my mother she would've told me where to get off. Instead, she started pulling the pins from her hair. Thick iron-gray hair fell about her shoulders. With quick yanks, she ran her brush through her hair. Seeing my reflection in the mirror, she frowned. Her eyes narrowed.

"I used to think you had a gentle spirit, a meek spirit."

"Oh, please."

"You never wanted to serve the body of Christ? Never?"

"Bettina—"

The telephone rang. I heard somebody running to get it.

"It's between you and the Lordt," Bettina said with a wave of her hand. "Unplug the iron when you're done and put it away."

A STRANGE THING WAS STARTING TO HAPPEN TO ME WHEN I rode the subway. As the cars raced underground through the dark tunnels and bounced on the tracks, I heard a child sobbing. It wasn't something audible; I heard it in my mind, although sometimes the weeping was so loud that I glanced around uneasily. I closed my eyes and tried to soothe the child, but she wouldn't quit sobbing.

My parents had moved from California to Munich the year before with my younger brothers. My mother sounded ecstatic in her letters, enjoying the European culture and new financial security with my father's military job. In New York, I thought of her often; her spirit seemed linked with mine. I missed her feistiness and sense of fun. Her presence was powerful in my life; in her absence, I drew closer, eager for what she had to teach me. My mother has an emphatic way of talking, especially when she's mad or feels things strongly. Her internalized voice – impatient, irritated – spoke to me in New York: "Listen kiddo, you don't have to put up with any of this shit. Remember that." I kept it in mind.

AT DINNER, JESSIE LADLED CHILI INTO HER BOWL AND SHOOK on the Tabasco sauce. "So how was your day?" she said, looking at me. "How's your job?"

"It's OK," I said, "although I think Artie, my boss, is in love with Arminda." "In love" was the PG-13 version. Artie pawed her whenever he could. It wasn't sweet to watch. But questions about my job and the people I worked with required careful, edited answers. Arminda was Puerto Rican, wore a special orthopedic shoe and lacy dresses that reminded me of doilies on a velvet divan. She was like a sturdy little doll in a plastic box: if you touched her, she batted her lashes and squealed. At the office, she seemed overwhelmed by Artie's single-minded ardor. She danced away from him, skipping a little as she limped around the desks and chairs. Artie followed, his tie askew. "Artie," Arminda would say in a shaky voice. "I know you're kidding, but I've got work to do. Please. Artie! Please!"

Sue clucked her tongue at my story of the office love affair and poured Delia another glass of milk. The little girl looked back at me over the rim of her glass with her enormous pale blue eyes.

"Isn't he married?" Jessie said.

"I think so."

Bettina leaned back in her chair and watched me. "We should pray for him. He needs the Lordt."

"We should pray for Arminda," I said. "She needs a new job."

"Boy," Jessie said, grimacing. "It sounds awful."

"I guess," I said, unconvinced.

Gerald looked at me. His eyes were flat. My story about Artie disturbed him. In a few minutes, I would discover why.

We sat in the living room on the Scandinavian teak wood sofa. "Name one person who's met the Lord through your job," Gerald challenged me. Involuntarily, I glanced out the window at the Blisstons'. It didn't look like anybody was home.

"Oh, come on," I said. "I haven't been there very long! Give me a chance!"

"Look," he said gently. "I think it's better if you stay here with us."

I looked at my hands. "I disagree."

"Henry thinks you'd be happier here."

"What does he know about anything?"

Gerald ignored that. "Henry and I have been praying for you. You seem so–"

"I'm not quitting, Gerald." My voice broke. "Sorry. No can do."

"We've already prayed about it."

"Well, I haven't."

"Don't get upset."

"Please, Gerald," I said, like the dumb bunny that I was. I heard echoes of Arminda pleading with Artie. Gerald nodded sympathetically. I could tell he felt sorry for me. I could also tell it was a done deal.

"Taking the subway is expensive," he said. "It adds up, you know. We're barely breaking even. Frankly, it's cheaper if you stay home and help out around here." When I argued that the job had been a chance to be a witness for the Lord, Gerald countered he'd seen scant evidence of that. Where were the souls? Where was the fruit? Branches that weren't productive got pruned. End of story.

"We've prayed about it already and feel it's God's will for you to stay home," Gerald repeated.

"You guys sure are busy these days," I said bitterly.

"Boy," said Gerald, drawing away from me. "I'm sensing a lot of anger and bitterness from you. You need to get right with the Lord."

I gave notice the following week. Quitting was easier than I thought. Artie and Mary Ann, Arminda, Eileen the potty mouth, none of them seemed sad or surprised that I was leaving.

"Moving on, are you?" Mary Ann asked, putting her arm around me. "Well, it's been a slice."

"It's my husband," I said, adding, "he needs me." Why was I lying?

Arminda nodded.

"He has cancer," I babbled. "Cancer of the mouth."

Arminda looked stricken. "Oh, cancer is terrible! I'll pray to the Blessed Virgin for him."

"We'll miss you, kiddo," Mary Ann said kindly. "We'll think of you." I knew that wasn't true. They weren't going to miss me, and if they thought of me at all, it probably would be in the shape of a joke.

IN THE MINISTRY, IF YOU WERE SICK, OR SUFFERING FROM depression, anxiety, or some mental problem, you were thought to be under demonic attack. This was a scary thought. What was natural and what was supernatural? My blood ran cold at the thought that some satanic spirit – like some all-knowing puppeteer – could peer down inside my head, know all my weaknesses in an instant, and try to jerk my strings.

One Friday night on St. Marks Place, our Bible study turned into an impromptu worship session. I dreaded nights like this. People cried, confessed their sins, spoke in tongues, and prophesied. The singing and clamoring, the noise, the clapping and crying, all of it just unhinged me. I was sure even the Blisstons could hear us. I retreated into the smallest room in my soul and pleaded with Jesus to deliver me from this hell. Later, I wrote in my diary: *"This evening during worship Gerald was sitting next to me! He put his hands on me as I was pretending to pray in tongues. He started praying fervently. I was afraid he was going to rebuke me in the spirit. I just wanted to get away."*

I lay low, cleaned the house, cooked, shopped. One morning I saw Claire Blisston at the grocery store, pushing her cart through the produce section. Up close, she wasn't as young as I'd imagined her. I'd pegged her for twenty-five but I could see now she was closer to thirty. I also realized she colored her hair and could probably stand to lose about twenty pounds. When she bent over to bag some peaches, the raggedy hem of her slip showed. I wanted to say, *Hi, how was your vacation in the Adirondacks? How's Trevor?* But I was afraid she'd look at me coldly and say, *Do I know you? Have we met?* And I would have to answer, *No, we haven't.*

A change was coming. I could sense it the way animals can sense a coming storm. There was something in the air, negative ions, charged particles, shifting barometric pressure, colliding fronts. Maybe it would blow the roof off my world. All I could do was brace myself and wait.

I thought constantly about leaving. It was a scab I couldn't stop picking, one that I never let heal. Once I put my mind to it and really began thinking in earnest about how much better life could be for Henry and me, I became obsessed. My mother was right. It was time to go. I was tired of trying to be good.

I reached for Henry's hand in the dark. I knew he was awake. I thought I could hear the blood pounding in his veins.

"Henry?"

"What?"

"Do you love me?"

He was quiet for a few seconds. Then he said, "Of course."

"Remember when we were in Mexico and we ate at that café in El Golfo? Remember the shrimp, how good it was?"

"Sure."

"I'd like to go back there sometime."

"So would I. I'd like to go a lot of places."

"Why don't we, then?"

Henry sighed. "God wants us here. Let's not fight about this, OK?"

That night I dreamt I was having a baby. I was in an igloo with my grandmother Mary in the Antarctic and there was a fierce blizzard outside. It felt like I had been in labor for days. Jagged icicles stabbed me between my legs. I was trying to push the infant through the birth canal, but my cervix wouldn't open wide enough. My grandmother squeezed my hands until they turned white. She said push, push, you've got to push, and as I pushed I could smell all my grandmother's scents mingling together – Halo shampoo, Evening in Paris perfume, Early Times bourbon, mint. I can't, I told her. Yes, you can, she said, push, damn it, and the baby's head crowned like a small blood-covered bowler. The body slid out of me like a little seal pup and my grandmother caught it in her jeweled hands. She wiped the baby off with a turquoise towel and handed it to me. I looked down and saw that it was a baby girl. Her eyes were shut. She had her balled-up fist in her mouth, and she was kicking hard, and she was beautiful.

Middle C

THE FACE FRAMED IN THE DOOR WAS TAN, THE IRISH POTATO nose bigger than before, the silver eyebrows bushy as a Scottish terrier's. My father's blue eyes were the color of sharp inquiry. I hadn't seen him in more than a year. His visit was no small gesture. He had flown from his home in Munich, Germany, to Washington, D.C., on military business and then taken another plane to see me.

We walked in the Brooklyn Botanic Gardens. Spring, seventy-five degrees, petals everywhere. The cherry trees were in bloom. Little explosions of pink confetti spiraled in the breeze. We talked about nothing important. It was a kind of dance. I wiped my sweaty hands on my Madras skirt, accepted a lemonade from him, stepped into the cool shade under sighing trees. Slant of sunlight on the grass. Spray of a fountain. The world was cool and green and wet. Dad, I ached to say, I need to tell you something. My husband doesn't like me, I hate myself, and Jesus never rose from the dead. Instead we strolled in courtly silence, watching the tourists and clutching our bottles of lemonade.

When I was an adolescent, my father used to sit next to me on the piano bench while I hammered out dispirited Bach sonatinas. My mother would hum along. "That's pretty, honey," she would call out. "Sounds good!" And then I would blow it on the trills. I hear it now – fingers on the keys – the way my breath quickened because the sixteenth notes were just a few bars away, and I knew I wasn't going to be able to make those lightning quick strokes; I was going to muff it, just like I always did and always would no matter how much I practiced. It cost twenty dollars for a one-hour music lesson, and I didn't have much talent. My father was the one with natural musical abilities. He could play by ear. He played Cole Porter's "Begin the Beguine" mostly on the black keys. He'd lean back his head, savor the melody, and let it rip.

I could only bear my father's closeness at the piano for so long. Then I had to get up and walk away. He was just too much, all noise and feeling, hammering, singing, sometimes even dancing. He was a fountain of expression. The proximity to that much shameless joy made me want to back away. He'd get up and steeple his hands together over his head like a Balinese dancer, swaying along with imaginary palm trees while an unseen orchestra played down by the shore under the stars. There was a waggle in his hips. For such a short stocky guy, my father was amazingly light on his feet.

Now we walked past stone lions and hot dog vendors. Nodding tulips genuflected before us. My father, whom I believed to be a certified genius, spoke five languages, including Russian and Chinese. He could build boats, read rivers, crack codes. He knew the root meanings of words. Once when I was fifteen and had been caught after sneaking out for a midnight joyride with friends, my parents threatened to send me to a psychiatrist. "You're psychologically fucking me over," I told them. My dad looked stunned at my use of that four-letter word. He paused.

"Do you know what that word means?"

"Yeah." I glowered at him.

"It comes from a Germanic root. Some etymologists say its original meaning was 'to plow the ground.'"

Now he said, "How's it going, Cool-in-the-Face?"

"I'm great." A graceless lie. The petals blew. One landed on my blouse. I picked it off. "I'm just really happy."

"Well, honey, that's terrific." My father affected a hearty manner. Who knew what he was really thinking? "How's Henry? What kind of job does he have these days?" He tapped a Camel out of the pack.

"For a while he was working as a deliveryman for a medical supply company."

"Ah, yes, bedpans and oxygen – the stuff of life! When you gotta go, you gotta go."

"Now he's working doing vinyl repair with the other brothers."

"Does he like it?"

"It's OK," I said, anxious to change the subject. "How's mom? How are the boys?"

"Your mother is absolutely grand." Again, that forced hearty tone. "She's a peach. I tell you she's in her element over there in Germany. She's learning German, goes to the opera, and takes the train to Italy every couple of months. She sends you her love."

"And the boys?"

My dad ran a hand across his silvery crew cut. "They're staying out of trouble, I guess."

"You mean you hope!"

"So what are you doing with yourself these days?"

I shrugged. "Cooking. Cleaning. There's a lot to do."

"The Lord's work!" my dad said, laughing. The click of his lighter. Long inhale. I didn't have the heart to witness to him again. Two years earlier, when Forrest had asked him if he knew the Lord, he said he did. He said he also knew Buddha, Yahweh, and Gerard Manley Hopkins. We watched two little kids playing in the fountain. They were pouring water on each other with plastic cups.

"Honey, I can't stay long," my father said. "I just wanted to drop by and see how you're doing."

"How *am* I doing?"

"You tell me." He put his arm around me. Bees droned. I felt little again, so small my feet couldn't reach the piano pedals. I remembered my father sitting next to me on the piano bench, showing me the white keys and the black keys, showing me middle C, the piano's continental divide between high and low.

"I'm blessed, dad."

"Are you? You seem sort of, I don't know, sad. Are you sad, sweetheart?"

Years later my father would tell me how scared I seemed to him that spring day in Brooklyn, how I seemed both vulnerable and wooden. "I wanted to gather you up in my arms and just hold you," he would tell me.

I told my father again I was happy.

He nodded, lit another cigarette. I didn't want my father to leave, but there was nothing I could do or say to induce him to stay. And I couldn't invite him back to the house for an extended visit. It was hard to imagine him sitting around the dining room table with all the Praise-the-Lording saints. If they witnessed to him, he'd witness back, quoting poetry or a Tibetan riddle, maybe his favorite invocation at mealtimes: *Hail Mary, full of grace/two potatoes had a race.*

"Dad," I said, leaning against him.

"What is it?"

"I'm glad you came."

The Blood Store

"YOU CAN MAKE A DIFFERENCE!" A SIGN IN THE PLASMA CLINIC said. "Give something back to others!" When I invited Jesus into my heart in 1972 I would not have guessed that three years later I would be sitting in a seedy building with darkened windows waiting to give a pint of my plasma. It just didn't figure into my idea of myself. How did a healthy, married woman turn into someone who would sell life-sustaining bodily fluids for cash? But that's who I'd become: someone who would bleed for money; money I needed to make my break. I planned to drive the VW to Montreal and live with Felix, Henry's brother. He had seemed sympathetic to my plight. I hadn't exactly confided in him how unhappy I was, but I sensed he knew and cared. Of course, moving in with Felix would mean moving in with Ma, since he was staying at her place, but I wasn't going to worry about social niceties right now. The plan was fuzzy but I was sure it would take shape, say, by the time I'd crossed the border.

The plasma center was depressing: bright orange plastic bucket chairs, scuffed linoleum floor, and a lineup of donors who looked like they spent their free time and spare money at off-track betting outlets or massage parlors. The mood in the waiting room was oppressive. Dressed in a long-sleeved blue blouse and skirt that reached my ankles, I squirmed in my chair.

A middle-aged woman in a white uniform bustled into the room and called my name. She wore her glasses on a filigree chain and had a faint moustache.

In the examining room, she pricked my finger to test if my protein level was acceptable. "Dear," she said, holding up a Dixie cup and pointing to the bathroom. "Would you mind?"

A few minutes later, she said, "Sweetheart, have you ever received money or drugs for performing sex?"

"No."

"Have you ever had any sexually transmitted diseases?"

"No."

"Have you ever had hepatitis?"

"No."

She poked around, trying to find the vein. The needle was huge. Puncturing my skin a third time, she found the radial vein. My blood curled up through the tubing and into a plastic bag. Watching it shoot out in warm spurts, I felt my throat burn, as if I'd run a long ways.

"Now just make yourself comfortable," she said, patting my arm. "Can I get you a magazine? *Good Housekeeping? Reader's Digest?*"

I shook my head. My blood was surprising in its vigor. I marveled at the color – not bright red like I'd expected, but the slow, lazy deep red of garnets. A song we sang in church hammered in time with my heartbeat: "There is *pow*-er! *Pow*-er! Wonderworking power! In the blood of the Lamb!" I ran my tongue across my teeth. There was a coppery taste in my mouth, a tinfoil lozenge of shame that I couldn't swallow.

The Bible is full of blood talk: blood of bulls and men, blood that whitens, blood that purchases and redeems, blood that cries out from the thirsty earth and bears witness to the truth. Innocent blood, binding blood, drinking blood. All-knowing blood, claiming and naming blood. Blood that betrays, blood that forgives. The prophet Isaiah wrote:

> *"Come now, let us reason together," says the Lord.*
> *"Though your sins are like scarlet,*
> *they shall be white as snow;*

> though they be red as crimson,
> they shall be like wool."

The bag was filling up. I studied the signs on the wall. "The clock is ticking for trauma and transplant patients!" My blood shot into the bag. *Pow-er! Pow-er!* "Help a trauma victim!" *Pow-er!* "Save a life!" I can't even save my own life, I thought, closing my eyes. Behind thin eyelids, the fluorescent lights pulsed pink. My skin tingled. It occurred to me that my soul might be leaving my body, the way it did sometimes at night in dreams when I soared and dipped over stormy waters, frightened that I would crash into foaming whitecaps, marveling that I somehow stayed aloft. Dread and wonder, wonder and dread – how narrow the space between the two. I would wake up with a sharp ache in my chest, and realize with growing relief that I was still earthbound. Life. In the blood. Jesus says that the man who loves his life will lose it, while the one who hates his life in this world will keep it forever in the next. I loved this world and I never wanted to leave it, not even for Jesus. Sitting in the plasma center, I prayed to the only God I knew by name. All I could say was "I'm sorry" and even that sounded lame.

They ran my blood through a separating machine and took out the plasma, the straw-colored part of the blood in which red and white blood cells and platelets are suspended like tiny jewels. A few minutes later, when the blood was injected back into my body, I was chilled to my core. The blood was cold. It felt like a Slurpee churning through my veins. I thought of it racing back to the chambers of my heart, where it would be warmed and embraced. I knew it would recirculate through my body, but I felt changed. You've come to the end of yourself. You can't sink any lower, I thought as the cashier handed me two tens. Bank on it.

IT IS LATE SATURDAY AFTERNOON, OUR DAY OFF. HENRY AND I are in our room. He sits on a chair, practicing his guitar, and I'm stretched out on our unmade bed, reading *A Separate Peace*. Or trying to. Dirty clothes are piled by the window. There's a knock at the door. With a sigh, I slide my book under the pillow and look at Henry. "Just a minute," Henry calls. Gerald. He looms in the doorway, holding a large enamel basin filled with water. Sue stands behind him in the dimly lit hallway, a towel over her shoulder.

"I hope we're not bothering you," Gerald says.

Henry stands at the door, his hand on the knob. A few seconds tick by.

"Can we come in?" Gerald says.

"Of course," Henry says, stepping aside. Gerald sets the bowl down on Henry's chair and fingers his mustache. A little water sloshes onto the gray corduroy cushion and leaves a wet spot. Gerald takes in the mess in our room: dirty coffee cups on the windowsill, a fistful of coins and a box of Tampax on the nightstand.

Henry scoots next to me on the bed. The mattress groans. "So what's up, you guys?" he says.

Sue's eyes are gigantic, brimming solemn blue. She glances at Gerald and clears her throat. "We'd like to wash your feet," she says.

"You're kidding," Henry says. I look out the window. The Blisstons' station wagon is parked at the curb.

"I'm, I'm touched," Henry says, a little flustered.

In ancient Israel, washing someone's feet was a menial task normally performed by a slave. But in the Gospel of John, during the Last Supper, Jesus tenderly washed his disciples' feet. It was a sublime example of servitude and humility. When I read the scene as described by John, Jesus seemed at his most vulnerable. He had gotten up from the table, taken off his outer garments, and wrapped a towel around his waist. Imagining God with a towel around his waist always made Him human, life-size. I couldn't read that passage without imagining his slender body, counting his ribs, seeing the hair under his arms, discerning the tan line on the back of his neck. John wrote that Jesus poured water into a basin and began to wash the feet of his followers. All of his love for his disciples came out of the tips of his fingers.

When it was Simon Peter's turn, the disciple, puzzled that Jesus would perform this lowly act, said, "No, you shall never wash my feet."

"Unless I wash you, you have no part with me," Jesus said.

"Then, Lord, not just my feet but my hands and my head as well!" Peter replied with characteristic gusto. That same evening, Judas would betray

Jesus by delivering him to the chief priests and Pharisees. And three times Peter would deny knowing his Lord.

In Gospel Outreach, foot washing was a rare ritual. It was about humble service and was only done by people in authority. For instance, an elder might wash the feet of someone under his authority, but it was a one-way street. The highest washed the lowest; a subordinate never washed the feet of an elder.

The idea of having Gerald and Sue wash my feet this afternoon makes me uneasy. What are their motivations? I've been marked as a troublemaker and a "trial," a woman who obviously doesn't grasp the principle of wifely submission. In the past few months I've become more estranged from the people I live with, especially Gerald and Sue. Sometimes I wonder if I've been possessed by some unclean spirit, some spiritual entity, some thing that lies sleeping in my chest, only to awaken during worship services, where it wants to hurl insults, scream profanities. I am lost – to the brethren, to Henry, and mostly to myself. I don't know where I am anymore.

An uncomfortable silence fills the room, ballooning around us like an opened parachute in the wind.

"I hope you don't mind," Sue says. I stare at her.

"Of course not," Henry says, spreading his palms.

"Do you want some coffee?" I say, getting up. "I can make some in a minute. We've got Sanka, I think."

"No coffee," Sue says.

"It's no trouble."

"No coffee," she says again, and gives Gerald a meaningful look.

I sit back down on the bed. Sue kneels at our feet, and looks up at us. I edge away from her.

"You've been in our hearts," Gerald says, kneeling next to his wife. He takes Sue's hand. "We love you." Sue nods earnestly. "We *want* to do this."

But I don't want you to, I reply wordlessly. They are so oddly matched: the pale, silent woman, the fussy man in the Shetland sweater. Gerald starts unwrapping the bar of Dial that has magically appeared in his hands. Who are you, really? I wonder, watching them both. You people who have so much power over us, what's it like to be you? I don't know you at all. I glance at my husband, the man I've been wed to for sixteen months and add silently: You either. There are so many things about you I don't understand. We live our lives largely underwater, submerged even from ourselves. Henry's lashes are thick with unshed tears.

He's changed. When I first met him, he'd been the guy who picked oranges on the *kibbutz*, the one who knew all the folk dances and card tricks, the one who spoke French and impersonated Elvis. That lighthearted soul had been replaced by a haggard man who bit his nails, fretted about money, and was constantly taking his spiritual temperature.

Henry rolls up his trouser legs, slips off his Hush Puppies, peels off his socks. Neatly, he rolls them up together in a ball, just like he does every night before climbing into bed. The down on his slender ankles catches the light. Slowly, he dips his feet into the basin and this naked gesture makes me think of Jesus in a towel. Henry's feet splash softly, sloppily, puppies playing in a milk pail. Gerald places his hands on Henry's feet and closes his eyes in prayer. I catch my breath and shiver as he soaps my husband's toes. Over and over, the bar slides across the tops of my husband's slick, white, nearly hairless feet.

"Dear Jesus, thank you for your servant Henry," Gerald says. "We want to lift him up to You, oh Lord. Bless him."

A tear slides down the side of Henry's nose. He takes his glasses off and wipes his eyes with the back of his hand. Sue makes a soft little mewling sound that reminds me of a very contented cat: "BlesshimLord, blesshimLord, blesshimLord." The thing in my chest wakes up and yawns; chilled blood runs through my veins, headed straight for my heart.

"*Corba robba, haya ta-meshi,*" Gerald prays in tongues.

I pray too: *Spare me.*

Gerald pats Henry's feet dry and rubs them with Nivea moisturizer. Sue leaves the room to get fresh water and a clean towel.

Gerald looks up at me. I tuck my legs up beneath me. Is there any way to refuse? Dear Jesus, I pray. No way! Oh sweet sweet Lord. Sue comes back and kneels down. The air feels thick and stale.

I would rather stand up in the front of the church.

And confess all my secret sins.

Than allow my feet to be washed.

What is the problem? You take off your shoes and put your feet in a bowl of water, where they're washed like coffee mugs.

No. Absolutely not.

Sue raises an eyebrow and smiles. Lamplight glows on her high serious forehead.

"Look," I sputter, "I'm very moved, I really appreciate this, I mean, I understand the symbolism, I'm touched, deeply moved, but I – "

"Shh," Gerald says, putting a finger to his lips. "Don't worry."

"Like I said, I appreciate the gesture and all but I'd really rather not."

"Take your socks off," Sue says.

"I'm OK. Really." *Rully.* Cheerily: "Thanks though!"

"We know you're OK," Gerald says. "You're more than OK."

"Come on, honey," Henry says, nudging me in the ribs. "It's a blessing."

"Maybe some other time."

"We want to do this," Gerald repeats.

I take my socks off and fight the urge to sniff them. What is wrong with me? I place my feet squarely on the carpet, noting the long wiry black hairs sprouting from my big toes like seal's whiskers.

"Here," Gerald says softly, as if I'm just a little slow, "let's place our feet in the basin, shall we?"

We lift our feet. We slip them in the basin. We grit our teeth. Sue bends over and splashes water over them; something about her gesture reminds me of a raccoon washing an apple. For the millionth time, I stare in wonderment at her wiring – all the blue veins under her skin twisting like grapevines. Gerald prays: "Dear Lord, bless this woman and let her know how much You love her."

Gerald's shaggy hair brushes over his frayed shirt collar. "Let her know how much we love her and cherish her."

Sue's fingers reach between my toes. Ping! Ping! Water swirls in the basin. I try to call up Jesus, the Jesus inside me, but instead I find a glass of cold beer and vinyl-repair paints and a book hidden under my pillow. There's Roxy's prophecy and Bettina's disapproval and "Kung Fu Fighting" but Jesus is clearly not within this vessel.

The splashing continues and I remember how, long ago, water was my friend, as elemental as air. In Florida, when I was twelve, we lived on a canal. In those days, swimming was my mode of transportation. I swam to friends' houses, to the store for potato chips and soda, I even swam home in the dark, towing a little dinghy behind me. I was fearless. There were small sharks and barracudas in the water, and snakes, and other dangerous things that I couldn't see, but I never worried about what lived beneath the surface. I was healthy, unafraid, and unselfconscious. A decade later, sitting in my bedroom in New York, as a woman washes my feet, I am caught up in a riptide of shame and fear.

Sue lifts my feet from the basin. Water streams down my arches. I shrink at the sight of her, the way she purses her mouth as she reaches for the towel and dries between my toes with such concentration, as if she's diapering her infant son. Is this just another task for her or does she really care about me? It doesn't matter.

With a sinking heart, I see my future: days in the airless brownstone making dinner, raising children in the basement, hot afternoons spent folding diapers in the Laundromat. A life of rules and rituals, estranged from hope. I stare at Sue's white hair and think: You will never touch me again, I will not allow it, even if I'm damned.

There is nowhere to go, nothing to say but the prayer of the broken, right here, right now:

I can't stand this, Lord, I really can't. A year and a half ago, I stood in Deliverance Temple with Henry and suppressed the urge to scream and I stand before you now. You called me by name and now I call on You by name. I beseech You to help me, hear me, heal me. Most of all, free me. No more prophecies or blood selling or speaking in tongues or laying on of hands. No more foot washing or fears of demonic oppression. I don't want any part of it or the people who claim to know Your will. In the name of Jesus, I beg You: Give me back my life. Amen.

Epilogue: A Thin Space

I LIVED. I THRIVED. I GRABBED MY LIFE AND RAN WITH IT. Henry and I left the ministry and moved to Montreal a few unhappy months after the foot washing. We split up a year or so later, and I moved to Northern California. What lay ahead were real-world dramas: finding an apartment, reconnecting with parents, applying to college. Sister Roxy's prophecy proved correct: I hadn't shut the door on the world, which turned out to be a more complicated, difficult place to live than I'd imagined. And more wonderful too. Revelation wasn't just the last book in the Bible, it was my life. Everything was new: good friends outside the ministry, bylines in the college paper, an artist boyfriend, a pet dog. I was making up for lost time, growing up at last.

Sometimes, driving my 1959 VW Beetle home from an evening class at the College of Marin, I would glance nervously in the rearview mirror, half expecting to see a terrible face staring back at me. It was the face of my accusers, it was me, it was guilt. I was twenty-five, twenty-six, twenty-seven years old, waiting for the bottom to fall out of my life. Once, at a Safeway in San Rafael, I spied some of the men I'd known at the ranch. They were stocking up on cold cuts and bread, food they would probably eat in the car on their drive north. I hurried to another corner of the store and hid, watching them nervously as they paid for their groceries and left.

I returned to the ranch twelve years after I'd first arrived as a teenage hitchhiker. I was working for the *Long Beach Press-Telegram*, and my assignment was to write a three-part series about the ranch, interviewing the people who had left the ministry and those who had joined it. Between these bookends of the past and the present, I would frame the story. That was the excuse for returning. But despite what my laminated press pass said, I wasn't an objective reporter trying to get the "news." The news at the ranch was the Good News, now and forever more, and although the cast of characters there had changed, the mission was still the same: evangelize to the world. What was the point of returning to this crucible where my identity had been forged? I hoped to answer the seemingly unanswerable questions of who I had been and who I had become.

My return to the ranch was a bittersweet homecoming. In the kitchen a woman I'd never met asked me point blank if I was still a Christian. "What happened between you and your husband?" she also asked.

My heart pounded. I was prepared for these questions, but a blue flame of anger blossomed in my chest nonetheless.

"I'm not currently involved in a church," I replied, trying to keep my voice steady. "Henry and I are divorced now."

"And Jesus?" the woman persisted, thrusting her chin at me. There was a smudge of flour on her apron. "Do you still believe in Him?"

"I'm not sure."

"How can you live with yourself?" the woman said. "You're breaking Jesus' heart." Her index finger stabbed the air. "Write this down in your notebook. Write down that you've turned your back on God." My hands shook as I wrote her words down in a furious blur.

Driving back to Southern California, I thought about something one woman at the ranch had said. "The difference between living at the ranch and being out in the world is that in the world you avoid confrontations ... you try as much as you can to make life really easy and comfortable," she told me. "Living here you're stretched to deal with different people and different situations."

I thought she had it all wrong. It was the world that was filled with confrontation and difficulties, where you constantly had to make compromises, weigh right and wrong, take responsibility for your own actions. When I had lived at the ranch, I allowed other people to make some of life's most important decisions for me. I handed my power over to others and I didn't think twice about it. It was so easy to do. It let me off the hook, absolved me of moral responsibility, kept me in perpetual adolescence, relying on authority figures to bail me out. The ranch offered simple, one-dimensional answers to complicated dilemmas.

I went back to the newspaper, wrote the story, moved on to the next one. I never stopped thinking about the ranch. It is the story of my life, of wondering and wandering, finding a home and leaving it, wondering and wandering anew.

SIX YEARS AGO I STARTED WRITING THIS BOOK, WHICH BLOSSOMED from what I believed would be a straightforward memoir about a misguided teenager into a deeper conversation with myself, with the ghosts of the past, and yes, with Jesus Christ. This is not the soft-focus Jesus of my dreams, the heavenly hottie I fantasized about at the Lighthouse Ranch when I was a moony toddler in the Lord, but the Jesus of the Bible, the Jesus who stubbornly refuses to let me go, the one who asserts, "I have called you by name."

It's been thirty years since the night when I sat at the edge of the steep bluff of the Lighthouse Ranch and a pug-nosed, guitar-strumming sister told me Jesus loved me. How far I have wandered from that night. Today, as I write these words, an arctic storm sweeps down from the Northern Rockies. Snowflakes swirl through the misshapen Ponderosa pines in my backyard; wind rattles the windowsills, and then changes direction, skidding like a drunk on a wobbly skateboard. I listen for the voice of God in the soughing trees, for the still, small voice of the Holy Spirit, but honestly, most of the time all I can hear is the wind, a sound that makes me rejoice at being alive and warm and safe.

I still seek the "thin space" some mystics claim exists in certain places, where the gulf between God and us isn't so wide. One thin space is the Chartres Cathedral in France, with its inlaid black marble labyrinth – a path symbolizing the Christian's pilgrimage to Jerusalem, following in the footsteps of Jesus. I haven't been to Chartres but I sometimes walk a canvas replica of its labyrinth at the First Congregational Church in downtown Colorado Springs. In my socks, I make the same twisting walk toward the center of the maze – a flower with six petals, the symbolic points of illumination. As I retrace the steps of Middle Ages supplicants, I keep thinking: I'm going in the wrong direction. I'm on the wrong path. I've made a wrong turn in this metaphor of life's journey. But I keep walking, tracing this mystical path, and the prayer is always the same: God, who are you? Reveal yourself to me. I wind toward the center, and then head back toward the circumference, and at some point, almost without warning, the center appears. Sometimes when I bump into people who are coming in the opposite direction, negotiation and compromise are called for. It's the physical turning, turning, that clears the mind: I'm in and I'm out and I keep on walking through time and space, exactly where I'm supposed to be, hoping, believing I'll reach the center. Once when I was walking the labyrinth, there were just two other people on the path, a harried-looking young woman in a corduroy maternity smock and an elderly woman clutching a gray rain bonnet.

I'm in the middle stage between those two women now, just as I am between the past and the future, navigating my life. Closing my eyes, I feel disoriented as I give myself over to purposeful meandering. As I step along the path in the candle-lit room, I hear soft footsteps, and wonder who scuffles behind me. I glance and see a thin-shouldered woman with silver hair and a quizzical smile. With her cardigan sweater and wire-rimmed glasses, she reminds me of Aunt Clarissa, who once glowed like a star in my dark sky, lighting the way for the others. As I walk, I reflect on another alter ego, the Bargain Lady. With her notebook, she skulked along the sidewalks of Eureka, making a weekly pilgrimage dictated by deadlines and local sales. Her path was circuitous, but meaningful nonetheless, affording stops at the public library. Behind Aunt Clarissa and the Bargain Lady, I hear the rustling cotton of the Little Flower of Frankfurt, a girl in a sheet who wanted to be a nun until she lost herself in the black sheen of Elvis's black pompadour, a perfect wave that never crested. And coming toward me in the opposite direction strides a teenager carrying a backpack. She scowls as she puzzles over the riddle of her life, and the mother who blocks her path. Where is she going? Does she know yet that the way in is the way out? Years ago she wept by the side of a freeway after a truck driver pronounced her ruint because she wasn't a virgin, because something inside her had been broken. I feel the presence of these women brush against me, on journeys of their own. And I tell myself: It's all right. There's room for all of us. We're exactly where we should be. Follow the steps in the flickering dark. Walk, breathe, turn. Tremble like a sputtering flame. Reach the center, find yourself: whole, intact, and purified.

Titles available from Hawthorne Books

AT YOUR LOCAL BOOKSELLER OR FROM OUR WEBSITE: *hawthornebooks.com*

Saving Stanley: The Brickman Stories
BY SCOTT NADELSON

This debut collection of interrelated short stories are graceful, vivid narratives that bring into sudden focus the spirit and the stubborn resilience of the Brickmans, a Jewish family of four living in suburban New Jersey. The central character, Daniel Brickman, forges obstinately through his own plots and desires as he struggles to balance his sense of identity with his longing to gain acceptance from his family and peers. This fierce collection provides an unblinking examination of family life and the human instinct for attachment.

SCOTT NADELSON PLAYFULLY INTRODUCES *us to a fascinating family of characters with sharp and entertaining psychological observations in gracefully beautiful language, reminiscent of young Updike. I wish I could write such sentences. There is a lot of eros and humor here – a perfectly enjoyable book.* —JOSIP NOVAKOVICH
author of *Salvation and Other Disasters*

So Late, So Soon
BY D'ARCY FALLON

This memoir offers an irreverent, fly-on-the-wall view of the Lighthouse Ranch, the Christian commune D'Arcy Fallon called home for three years in the mid-1970s. At eighteen years old, when life's questions overwhelmed her and reconciling her family past with her future seemed impossible, she accidentally came upon the Ranch during a hitchhike gone awry. Perched on a windswept bluff in Loleta, a dozen miles from anywhere in Northern California, this community of lost and found twenty-somethings lured her in with promises of abounding love, spiritual serenity, and a hardy, pioneer existence. What she didn't count on was the fog.

I FOUND FALLON'S STORY *fascinating, as will anyone who has ever wondered about the role women play in fundamental religious sects. What would draw an otherwise independent woman to a life of menial labor and subservience? Fallon's answer is this story, both an inside look at 70s commune life and a funny, irreverent, poignant coming of age.* —JUDY BLUNT
author of *Breaking Clean*

HAWTHORNE BOOKS & LITERARY ARTS :: Portland, Oregon

God Clobbers Us All
BY POE BALLANTINE

Set against the dilapidated halls of a San Diego rest home in the 1970s, God Clobbers Us All is the shimmering, hysterical, and melancholy story of eighteen-year-old surfer-boy orderly Edgar Donahoe's struggles with friendship, death, and an ill-advised affair with the wife of a maladjusted war veteran. All of Edgar's problems become mundane, however, when he and his lesbian Blackfoot nurse's aide best friend, Pat Fillmore, become responsible for the disappearance of their fellow worker after an LSD party gone awry. God Clobbers Us All is guaranteed to satisfy longtime Ballantine fans as well as convert those lucky enough to be discovering his work for the first time.

Things I Like About America
BY POE BALLANTINE

These risky, personal essays are populated with odd jobs, eccentric characters, boarding houses, buses, and beer. Ballantine takes us along on his Greyhound journey through small-town America, exploring what it means to be human. Written with piercing intimacy and self-effacing humor, Ballantine's writings provide entertainment, social commentary, and completely compelling slices of life.

IN HIS SEARCH *for the real America, Poe Ballantine reminds me of the legendary musk deer, who wanders from valley to valley and hilltop to hilltop searching for the source of the intoxicating musk fragrance that actually comes from him. Along the way, he writes some of the best prose I've ever read.* —SY SAFRANSKY
Editor, *The Sun*

September 11:
West Coast Writers Approach Ground Zero
EDITED BY JEFF MEYERS

The myriad repercussions and varied and often contradictory responses to the acts of terrorism perpetuated on September 11, 2001 have inspired thirty-four West Coast writers to come together in their attempts to make meaning from chaos. By virtue of history and geography, the West Coast has developed a community different from that of the East, but ultimately shared experiences bridge the distinctions in provocative and heartening ways. Jeff Meyers anthologizes the voices of American writers as history unfolds and the country braces, mourns, and rebuilds.

CONTRIBUTORS INCLUDE: *Diana Abu-Jaber, T. C. Boyle, Michael Byers, Tom Clark, Joshua Clover, Peter Coyote, John Daniel, Harlan Ellison, Lawrence Ferlinghetti, Amy Gerstler, Lawrence Grobel, Ehud Havazelet, Ken Kesey, Maxine Hong Kingston, Stacey Levine, Tom Spanbauer, Primus St. John, Sallie Tisdale, Alice Walker, and many others.*

HAWTHORNE BOOKS & LITERARY ARTS :: *Portland, Oregon*

A Walkabout Home

BY STEPHANIE ROSE BIRD

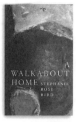

The American mystical practice of Hoodoo seeped into Stephanie Rose Bird's consciousness before she even knew its name. During her childhood, she took long walks amidst the lush green landscape of Southern New Jersey – a landscape bounded by the wetlands, the Pine Barrens, the Atlantic Ocean, and a rich tradition of folklore. The power of this walking – of these human foot tracks – has been the subject of many incantations, chants, and songs. The folkloric tradition pays careful attention to the cleansing of pathways, especially the pathway home. Steeped in these worlds, *A Walkabout Home* tells the story of an African American writer and artist raised in the Pine Barrens of New Jersey who has traveled the globe in search of art and home.

In the end, Bird is not one to shy away from the harder questions in life. On nearly every page her words here seem to ask, indirectly and in just so many words: Who am I? Why am I as I am? What has formed me? *But because of Bird's travel across cultures and continents, the book's ultimate subject is the way these questions provide a connection between people. A Walkabout Home is an eloquent bridge across the span of human experience.*

—MICHAEL FALLON
Annuals Editor, Llewellyn Publications

Dastgah: Diary of a Headtrip

BY MARK MORDUE

From India to Paris, Iran to New York, Australian award-winning journalist Mark Mordue chronicles his year long world trip with his girlfriend, Lisa Nicol. Mordue explores countries most Americans never see as well as issues of world citizenship in the 21st century.

I just took a trip around the world in one go, first zigzagging my way through this incredible book, and finally, almost feverishly, making sure I hadn't missed out on a chapter along the way. I'm not sure what I'd call it now: A road movie of the mind, a diary, a love story, a new version of the subterranean homesick and wanderlust blues – anyway, it's a great ride. Paul Bowles and Kerouac are in the back, and Mark Mordue has taken over the wheel of that pickup truck from Bruce Chatwin, who's dozing in the passenger seat. —WIM WENDERS
Director of *Paris, Texas; Wings of Desire;*
and *The Buena Vista Social Club*

www.hawthornebooks.com